T0365672

Four Years

of

Dolce Vita

Four Years

of

A Memoir of Love, Art, and
Self-Discovery in 1970s Rome

A MEMOIR BY

ZAIN BABA

Copyright © 2024 Zain Baba.

All rights reserved. No part of this book may be used or reproduced by any means, graphic, electronic, or mechanical, including photocopying, recording, taping or by any information storage retrieval system without the written permission of the author except in the case of brief quotations embodied in critical articles and reviews.

This book is a work of non-fiction. Unless otherwise noted, the author and the publisher make no explicit guarantees as to the accuracy of the information contained in this book and in some cases, names of people and places have been altered to protect their privacy.

Archway Publishing books may be ordered through booksellers or by contacting:

Archway Publishing
1663 Liberty Drive
Bloomington, IN 47403
www.archwaypublishing.com
844-669-3957

Because of the dynamic nature of the Internet, any web addresses or links contained in this book may have changed since publication and may no longer be valid. The views expressed in this work are solely those of the author and do not necessarily reflect the views of the publisher, and the publisher hereby disclaims any responsibility for them.

Any people depicted in stock imagery provided by Getty Images are models, and such images are being used for illustrative purposes only. Certain stock imagery © Getty Images.

ISBN: 978-1-6657-6922-8 (sc)
ISBN: 978-1-6657-6923-5 (e)

Library of Congress Control Number: 2024924898

Print information available on the last page.

Archway Publishing rev. date: 01/06/2025

All names appearing in this memoir have been changed to mask identities, except a few key characters, including Michael and Barbara of the American College and my loving host Lucille. At least ten per cent of the contents of the memoir, including some descriptions, are of a fictious nature that embellishes certain events, but the characters are real. Dates of events have been checked for accuracy to the best of my knowledge.

To my dear friend Zana, who left this world years ago.

To wander is to discover not just distant lands, but the uncharted corners of the self, where fleeting moments become lasting memories.

CONTENTS

Section 4: The Year 1980: A Taste of the Good Life

Section 5: The Culture Trail 1981

Section 6: A Dream Comes True: Fall 1982

Section 7: 1982–1983: Farewell Dolce Vita

PROLOGUE

There are moments in life when the past resurfaces not as a distant memory but as a vivid, pulsating experience—alive with the sights, sounds, and sensations of a time long gone. For me, that time is the late 1970s, and the place is Europe. It was an era of unhurried afternoons, of meandering conversations in cafe-lined piazzas, of discovering art and culture in ways I could never have imagined growing up in a world thousands of miles apart. The Europe I found was still basking in the afterglow of *la dolce vita*, its cities breathing history and modernity in equal measure. I was young, curious, and full of longing for something greater than the familiar comforts of home. Little did I know that this journey would shape me in ways I could neither foresee nor fully understand at the time.

At the heart of this story lies Rome—the eternal city and my gateway to a world far larger than the one I had known. I arrived as a dreamer but ended up as a college student, eager to immerse myself in a foreign culture but unaware of how much this place would come to define me. In Rome, the remnants of antiquity stood shoulder to shoulder with the vibrancy of modern life, and as I walked its ancient streets, I felt a palpable connection to the history that had shaped it. Yet it was more than just the grandeur of the city that captured my heart; it was the people I met, the friendships forged across cultures, and the brief yet unforgettable romantic encounters that wove themselves into the fabric of my time there.

As I journeyed across Italy, from the Greek ruins of Sicily to the Renaissance marvels of Florence, and to the quiet beauty of Lake Garda,

I felt the world opening up to me. Study tours blurred the lines between learning and living, and each new city brought its own revelations. The landscape of Italy, in all its diversity, mirrored the complexity of my inner world: vast, evolving, and, at times, contradictory. But there was also freedom—an intoxicating sense of possibility that came from being away from the expectations of family, of society, of the life I had always known.

Yet Italy was only part of the story. The summer I spent in Paris and Normandy was like stepping into a dream—one in which every moment was tinged with a kind of romantic melancholy. Paris was more than just a city; it was a world unto itself, with its own rhythm and soul, drawing me deeper into its embrace with every passing day.

In the years that followed, the memories of my time in Europe would return to me, not in a nostalgic haze, but with a clarity that demanded to be captured and shared. This memoir is the story of those years—four years of discovery, of growth, and of a kind of joy that comes only when you are fully alive to the world around you.

It is, quite simply, my *dolce vita*.

Zain Baba
London, September 2024

Section One

ZAIN IN WONDERLAND: 17 TO 25 MAY, 1979

Landing in Europe or America was a long-cherished dream of Zain, and when he arrives in Rome in mid-May 1979, he sees Italy as a sort of wonderland. But unlike the average dreamer from South Asia, Zain is ambitious. His journey doesn't stop here, and there are more journeys yet to be realized. Within a time of one week, he sets his goals and embarks on a mission. This section describes his mission and the challenges he faces while enjoying his first European visit.

1

ALL ROADS LEAD
TO ROME

It was on a beautiful evening in mid-May, just before dusk, that our Alitalia flight from Jeddah touched down at Fiumicino Airport in Rome. Not many of the formalities were noticed in passport control, and passengers swiftly passed through the gate to the exit. On the way out, there was nothing unusual other than waiting for the luggage to arrive late. Being a first-time visitor to Italy, I felt that the air was full of anxiety and excitement. I was aptly dressed in an American-made chequered blazer. At the exit, my curiosity drew my attention to a couple of men arguing with vigorous hand gestures, which made me somewhat nervous at first, but I later saw them sharing cigarettes and exchanging friendly talk as if they were eternal friends.

After changing some dollars to lira at the Bureau de Exchange, I found my way to a bus stop outside the exit lobby. With a bit of struggle, I managed to find the right coach, which showed a sign reading 'Statione Termini'. Another passenger explained that Termini was the main railway station in Rome. I don't quite remember how much I paid in lira for the coach ride, but I think it was equivalent to a dollar or two in 1979. The coach arrived at the terminal station at approximately 8.00 p.m. after cruising for fifty minutes. The man seated next to me on the coach was an Italian in his fifties, and we had a brief chat. Massimo was an expatriate engineer who had travelled from Jeddah and spoke English. He told me that he visited home every other month, just with hand luggage. He helped me understand how chaotic Italian cities were and how to protect myself from petty criminals. After arriving in Rome, with his help, I was able to find a budget bed and breakfast, which the Italians called a *pensione*.

The main train station in Rome was congested with travellers and strollers. Massimo was kind enough to show me in the vicinity, and with a great degree of patience, he helped me find a pensione. We negotiated a very good rate for a week, which came to approximately two US dollars per night. Massimo bade me goodbye after I checked in but exchanged his contact details while saying, 'Feel free to contact me if you ever needed anything.' My room was neither posh nor cosy, but my bed was clean and comfortable for a few nights. The location seemed safe and convenient enough to get around the city centre. Over the course of a few days, I was able to scan the surrounding environment. I met a few back-packers at the hotel who were amusing and interested in getting to know me. They were mainly young and enthusiastic tourists visiting Rome on a shoestring budget. However, only a few were long-staying economic migrants. Chatting with them gave me positive feelings towards the city. Most of these migrants did not have a valid visa, and they overstayed and survived for months, and some for years, while pursuing low-paid menial jobs that an Italian would not consider doing.

My knowledge of Italian or Roman history, as well as places of in-terest, was less than average but seemed much better than that of most of the visitors I met in Rome. Obviously, young tourists from North America and the Continent or Britain showed that they had a good grasp of the Roman history and heritage. In a few days, by mingling with these visitors at the pensione, my interest in Roman as well as Italian history and heritage grew. I became fond of Italian culture, although it seemed to vary from region to region.

Almost three days had already passed since my Roman sojourn, and I thought it was time to begin searching for a suitable American or British university or college. The idea of pursuing higher studies that had been ingrained in my brain for a long time prompted me to undertake my current European journey. Not being able to pursue my university education because of a number of unavoidable causes, and with my long-cherished ambition to go abroad for education, I was determined to pursue my undergraduate studies in America or Europe. Of course, the dream was to reach America, the land of opportunity. I must have spent hours researching US universities, and I even had a few offers in the early 1970s to study in the US.

Lack of funding for studies abroad remains the main problem for many aspiring youths from developing countries. The time I spent in Saudi Arabia as an expatriate, where I collected a small savings over two years, provided funds to pursue this dream. In this regard, I also carried pages of the *International Herald Tribune* with detailed information on the US and British institutions in Europe, including Rome. Therefore, I decided to conduct groundwork to identify a suitable degree-granting institution in Rome.

The next day, in the morning, before searching for or contacting a few colleges, I thought of getting a quick bite. Although I was familiar with some popular Italian dishes because of my exposure to dining at the continental dining hall in an Aramco residence camp in Dhahran, it was not my idea to indulge in fine food during a fact-finding tour. Street foods, such as pizza and lasagne, were ubiquitous and relatively inexpensive. You might call them 'Italian fast food', although Italians seemed rather allergic to the term 'fast food'. Minutes later, with a slice of pizza in my hand, along with a can of cola to help digest the food, I sat on the bed to browse the pages of the *Herald Tribune*. John Cabot College and American College of Rome stood out, as they both offered accredited degree courses in business and economics. Since the afternoon had just started and we had a few good summer hours left before Roman working hours came to a close, I embarked on a city tour looking for John Cabot College, which I remember was located near the Piazza della Repubblica. I did call them, and I made an appointment to see the admission tutor.

As I arrived at the college, I noticed that it was a bit hectic at the lobby, just like a street market. It seemed that the students flocked to the help desk at the end of the class. I managed my way to the reception desk and met with the admission tutor, who was expecting my visit. The meeting was brief and took only thirty minutes to complete. As a mature student with a high level of motivation, I did not have any problems getting admission to the degree course with advanced standing because of my prior education and experience. However, the financing options remained a key issue. When I asked him whether I would qualify for any bursary or financial aid, his reply was 'I am not sure.' The admission tutor said that he wouldn't count on it and that the dean of studies had the final word. When I asked whether I could see him, the answer was 'After two weeks.' I didn't bother to make an appointment, as my plan was to leave for Paris in a few days.

As I stepped out, it was six in the evening, but the sunset seemed another two and a half hours away. Although I was disappointed by not being able to see someone in the upper hierarchy of John Cabot, I didn't lose my confidence. I decided to stroll around the piazza. I sat on a bench in the garden and looked over a map. Surprisingly, I found the American College of Rome close to where I was. I did have an appointment to see the dean of the college in the morning at ten, and to make it easier, I decided to walk and identify the site location. It was Via Piemonte, number twenty-six. Having sighted the century-old neoclassical Romanesque building with a massive wooden door that allowed even cars to pass through the forecourt, I took a turn and returned to the hotel. It was almost eight thirty, but the sun still showered us with formidable light and heat.

Back in my pensione after thirty minutes of leisurely walking, I went straight to the shower room. During my shower, I contemplated my scheduled meeting with the dean of American College. As I came out of the shower, the landlord of the pensione was generous enough to offer a cup of espresso that I could not refuse. She was keen to know whether I would be interested in eating out at her cousin's trattoria, a small family-run restaurant. Her English was better than my Italian, which I picked up during my three-day sojourn in Rome. Another guest at the hotel, Mark, overheard our conversation and asked me whether he could join if I decided to dine. Mark was a visitor from a small town near

Pittsburgh, Pennsylvania. Having graduated with a major in Roman and Greek history, he wanted to spend time exploring Rome.

I thought, for a change, it would be an experience to try out this eatery, which was located a few blocks away on the same street. Before I called Mark to join me, I wanted to prepare for the interview with the dean the following morning; I knew I needed to have all my supporting documents ready to convince the dean that I was serious, and some sort of financial support would be essential to pursue my studies if I were given a chance to join the college. After a while, we left the hotel for dinner around 8.00 p.m., just before sunset, and on the way, we started to chat. Mark was a bit curious to find out about me, and he wanted to know what I was doing in Rome. I didn't want to delve much, but I briefly said that I was on my way to Paris and I should leave Rome soon. He was on a monthlong trip to Europe and said that he wanted to go to Greece and Turkey to learn more about ancient Greek history as well.

The trattoria looked like a small, lively eatery with local diners who knew each other very well. It only had a handful of tables and was almost full, with a few remaining seats. There was no menu on site but a slate on the wall showing what we were to be served. We had to sit and eat whatever the chef served us, and the meal would come with a pasta dish as the *primo*, a meat or fish dish as the second dish, and a side dish or salad as the third dish. Of course, it should be accompanied by a glass of house wine along with a basket of bread served on the table.

We were first served a plate of *fettucine al-vongole*, a type of flat spaghetti in tomato-based sauce with clams simmered in olive oil. The pasta had been cooked to the right texture—as an Italian would call it, *al-dente*—and the sauce was delicious with a garlic and fresh basil flavour. The next plate was a slice of chicken breast braised in butter and porcini mushrooms with cream sauce and a slightly peppery flavour. This was accompanied by a bowl of chef salad. Overall, this was a beautiful experience and delicious meal for a pittance. It was about half past ten in the night when we returned to the hotel, and Mark seemed a bit tipsy with a few glasses of wine. Hoping to get up early in the morning, I went to bed straight away.

2

AN OFFER OF
A LIFETIME

In the morning, after an espresso doppio at the cafe next door to wake me up and a warm shower afterwards to freshen me up, I was ready to meet the dean of the American College. I was in Via Piemonte before ten, on time for the meeting, and I was led to the reception desk on the fourth floor. A young woman at the reception desk introduced herself as Susan and said that the dean was waiting for me, and she took me up another floor at the mezzanine. The dean shook my hand and said, 'Meet Michael Milanese, the dean of the college.' I introduced myself to the dean as Zain Baba with confidence. I was rather surprised to see the welcoming reception I received as we sat on the sofa opposite his desk. I was given a brief introduction, and he showed me around the college as if I were a newly appointed staff member. I had not realized that I was speaking to the dean himself the other day when I called to make an appointment. From our brief conversation on the phone, I was able to explain my ambitions, skills, and background in detail. This must have made Michael see me from a different perspective rather than just a student seeking admission to a course. In fact, he had other motives that I later came to realize.

Michael briefed me about the three different degree courses on offer at the college and recommended me the BS in Economics and

Liberal Studies based on my background. With my advanced standing, he thought I should be able to complete the degree in five semesters, including a summer school. It sounded all well so far, but when I asked about the tuition fees, which came to fifteen hundred dollars a semester, he said, 'Yeah, we can talk about it in a minute.' Michael was a very tactful person, and as an American of Italian descent, he was not far from being an Italian in his nature and approach to people. I liked him, and I thought that there was chemistry between us.

When addressing the issues of my finances and tuition fees, the dean showed interest in appointing me as college staff to supervise student services. This included attending to the welfare of some exchange students from the USA. I was honest and sincere about my situation and finances, and I stressed that I would need bursary and financial assistance to pursue my studies. Michael pointed out that I would be entitled to a reasonable remuneration by working twenty to twenty-five hours a week and that my tuition fees would be waived. As this was a small institution with roughly 100 to 150 students in total, my workload would not be difficult. However, he could not confirm the offer until early September. I did accept the offer and exchanged my contact details in France, as my friend expected me to arrive in Paris the next week.

After we finished our meeting, as I came down the stairs, I was able to meet and chat with a group of exchange students from San Antonio, Texas. They were typical Americans with southern accents, exchanging their recent experience of visiting Vatican City, which has been an autonomous entity in Italy since 1929. The highlight of their visit was the Sistine Chapel and the ceiling painting of frescoes by Michelangelo. This was painted between 1508 and 1512, during the High Renaissance. These frescos, known as 'first judgement frescos', depict God's creation of Eve, the first woman. The Texan students were chatty, but they had to bid goodbye, as they were required to get back to college for a brief summary discussion and prepare to visit the Roman Forum and the Colosseum in the afternoon.

Now the time was almost one o'clock, and down the street next to the college, I was able to see a cafe for a quick panini. Although it was my third day in Rome that I was not able to visit any places of interest, my meeting with exchange students triggered an intense desire to visit some of these places. Therefore, I decided to visit Vatican City before returning to the hotel. I received help in locating the correct tram stop from the bar attendant at the cafe. Fortunately, it was not far from the cafe I visited. A brief look at my diary reminded me that I had dinner appointments with Massimo to seven thirty in the evening. This meant that I had to return to the hotel by six so that I could wash and get ready. The tram service in Rome was better than expected, but it moved at a snail's pace. I arrived at a destination where the tram was terminated at 2.30 p.m. Within a couple of minutes of walking, I could see the massive wall and gate that led to the vast compound surrounded by Corinthian columns in which the legendary St Peter's Basilica stood.

The first thing I did when I entered the piazza was to buy a few picture postcards and post them to greet my parents and friends. When chatting with long-staying guests on the pensione, I was told that the Italian postal service was one of the world's worst. 'A postcard takes a year to deliver,' one guy sarcastically said. I was told to go to the Vatican and post my mail. The Vatican, as an independent entity with its own jurisdiction, was founded as a city-state in February 1929 after the signing of the Lateran Pacts between Italy and the Holy See.

The late spring temperature was less intense, but the piazza and basilica were packed with tourists even in May. I managed to clear my way to the basilica and got a glimpse of the frescoes on the Sistine Chapel ceiling. It was not my intention to visit the Vatican Museum or spend another hour, as I had to return to the pensione because of the dinner appointment. I decided to take the tram back to the city, as it passed through the Termini station, and my pensione was not even a five-minute walk from the station.

My third night in Rome was approaching fast, and it was six in the evening when I arrived at the pensione. As expected from an engineer, I was ready to join Massimo at seven, who was punctual. I was pleased to see him again, and we greeted each other with a hug. He brought cherries from his garden tree, which I left aside to eat. Massimo brought

his Fiat Cinquecento, which had a reputation as a city car because of its
size and manoeuvrability.

We left the hotel just before 8.00 p.m. As we passed through the city,
he showed me a few places of interest to the visitors. While crossing the
Tiber River, he said that we were heading towards an old part of the city
called Trastevere, where the restaurant was located, not far from the old
Jewish ghetto on the other side of the river. Trastevere remained an old
working-class neighbourhood with medieval houses, streets paved with
cobblestones, and narrow alleyways. The name 'Trastevere' means 'beyond the Tiber' in Latin, and it has remained a colourful and lively part
of the city since Roman times. Locals and tourists flocked to Trastevere
to enjoy authentic Roman meals. Fortunately, Massimo found a place
on the street to park his car.

We went to an osteria, and I cannot remember the name, but I was
told that this establishment had been in business since the 1930s. I was
able to see pictures of a few distinguished personalities who had patron-
ized the restaurant in the past. As we entered the main lobby, we received
a warm welcome and a drink as an aperitivo when seated at the bar. The
restaurant had a cosy atmosphere, with mild jazz music playing in the
background. In less than ten minutes, we were shown by the waiter to
take a seat at a table that was meant for two guests. He brought us the
menu and left saying 'Vengo subito,' meaning 'I will come soon [to take
orders].'

Massimo and I browsed the menu and identified the items we
wanted to order. Of course, it was in Italian, and Massimo explained to
me in detail about the items in the menu, and as expected, I had to pick
one starter under 'antipasti', a pasta dish as primo, and a main dish as
secondo. If necessary, I could pick a side dish as a contorno. In the end,
we both chose one of the popular Roman antipasti, *Carciofi al' Giudia*,
for our starter, and I picked *Polpette di Baccala* for my main dish, while
Massimo took a popular Roman dish called *Saltimbocca Ala Romana*. We
ordered some of the salads. Massimo also ordered a bottle of white wine,
Orvieto, to go with the meal. It is a classic white wine that is produced
on the outskirts of Rome.

Our starter, Carciofi al' Giudia, was a traditional Roman artichoke dish derived from Jewish culinary tradition, as was the name 'Giudia', meaning 'Juda-Jewish'. This special starter consisted of stuffed artichoke petals with freshly chopped parsley and garlic, along with stems cooked in olive oil in covered pots. It was served cold and exuded a tongue-twitching, liquorice flavour on the first bite. It was indeed delicious, and I loved it. A sip of white wine seemed to be an ideal partner for every artichoke bite. Massimo told me that it was one of his favourite antipasti.

My primary dish was fish cutlets of cod in a tomato sauce, served with roasted potatoes and roasted chicory with a dash of crushed garlic and red pepper in virgin olive oil. The stuffing consisted of olives, pine nuts, breadcrumbs, and deliciously flavoured seasoning. Saltimbocca, ordered by Massimo, is a popular Roman dish. It consists of pan-fried veal that is flattened and wrapped with prosciutto and a sage leaf, cooked in lemon juice and Marsala wine. When in Rome, we were supposed to do as Romans did, which meant taking it easy, and there was no need to rush. The entire dinner took more than two hours, and both customers were satisfied and happy. However, dinner was not complete without a dessert or espresso. We decided to take a portion of tiramisu along with a cup of coffee. Massimo wanted it to be a *café corretto*—in other words, corrected coffee, with a dash of grappa or Italian brandy. Indeed, it was wonderful to be a guest and enjoy such a nice dining experience while on a shoestring budget.

At ten-thirty, Massimo took me to the hotel and was a careful driver, unlike the average Italian man. He was conscious of his alcohol consumption and looked perfectly all right to safely drive home. I expressed my sincere thanks and bade goodbye with an 'Arrivederci'. Before heading to bed, I was working on my forthcoming trip to Paris, which would take place within the next couple of days. My priority for the following day was, therefore, to enquire and arrange to travel by overnight train from Rome to Paris.

At nine thirty the next morning, soon after a coffee and cornetto at the cafe next door, I ran to the Termini rail station. It was Tuesday, 22

May. Before reaching the information desk, I called my friend Zana in
Paris to discuss his availability to receive me at the Gare de Lyon Station
in Paris. I had already discovered an overnight train from Rome to Paris,
and the necessary formalities. Now I wanted to confirm this and book
for the twenty-fourth evening from the Termini station in Rome. I
managed to get through to my friend, and he was adamant that I leave
the next day. He said that he would be free for the entire week until
the next Monday. This sounded very good, and I immediately headed
to the ticket counter rather than the information desk. The woman at
the counter was polite and was fluent in English. She explained that
I should buy a ticket first and then pay for the bed separately. When
asked whether I needed to book the bed, she told me she could do the
reservation and ticket all at once, but she wanted to see my passport that
I had in handbag with me. She also warned me that I should arrive at
least thirty minutes before the train departed. The train ticket to Paris
cost me something like thirty or forty dollars US, and I was relieved to
see that all set and done.

3

BELLA ROMA: A TOURIST GAZE

It was almost midday, and I returned to the pensione so that I could safely put aside my tickets and travel documents before attempting to explore a few places of interest in Rome. Among the many visitor attractions that Rome had to offer, the most famous was the Colosseum, which was the first skyscraper in the ancient world. In addition, the Roman Forum appeared to shadow the minds of visitors as they stood just next to the Colosseum. Any visitor would be tempted to take a photo in the background of these attractions, and I might not be an exception. To my surprise, the Colosseum and the Forum were not far from the hotel. I was told that it would take just fifteen minutes to reach when walking leisurely. At two in the afternoon, I started walking towards the Colosseum. The weather in late May was almost similar to that of early summer; the heat was not intense, but the humidity was slightly high. From my first sight of the Colosseum, I could see tourists climbing all over the ruined walls of the massive structure. I could also hear tourists in groups listening to what their tour guides had to say. The Colosseum reminded me of the famous landmark structure of Rome I had seen in the brochures. Nobody would ever see publicity material of Rome without the Colosseum in it. This oval structure was the largest ancient amphitheatre built in the centre of the city. Its construction started in the year 72 CE and was completed in ten years.

The Colosseum was built by Emperor Vespasian and his sons using mainly Jewish slaves brought from Jerusalem after the Roman-Jewish war. Over the years, it has become a centre for entertainment, with a capacity of up to eighty thousand spectators. It is believed that hundreds of thousands of slaves, convicts, prisoners, and gladiators could have died in the Colosseum over a period of three to four hundred years. I was able to see the area and try to climb a few steps. I also listened to an American tour guide explaining the history of how this building was used in the past after it ceased to function as an amphitheatre. The last place for me to see on the agenda was the Roman Forum. All tourists who visited the Colosseum also visited the Roman Forum, which one could not miss. We could have spent the entire day learning the history of Rome by exploring the world's largest archaeological site, the Roman Forum, situated between Capitoline Hill and Palatine Hill. It was in Palatine that Romulus founded the city approximately five hundred years before the Christian era. The Roman Forum was once the societal hub of Rome and included several public buildings, temples, and monuments. It also functioned as a marketplace but later served as a place for conducting public affairs and events.

I was told that I should not miss the Roman sunset in the shadow of the Colosseum, but it seemed a bit early, still at six in the evening. I had another two and a half hours to kill, and I decided to take a walk towards Piazza Venezia, where I could spot the famous Wedding Cake, or the national monument of Victor Emmanuel II, who was the first king of unified Italy. There was nothing that we could see here but a massive white building that looked like a wedding cake. Walking away from the monument after clicking a few pictures, I crossed the main street and entered the road that led to the famous Spanish Steps. Even in May, the piazza and steps were packed with tourists. I did not think of any visitors to Rome leaving without visiting them. I sat on the Steps for ten to fifteen minutes to relax, facing the piazza. Here I could see a fully packed narrow street called Via Condotti, where one could find famous shops showing off the most expensive branded designer wear. I said to myself that I should finish all my sightseeing this evening so that I could sleep a bit more tonight and relax the next day at the pensione before taking the night train in the evening.

However, I was aware that I had to vacate the room before two o'clock in the afternoon. With this in mind, I started to take a stroll along Via Condotti and passed through meandering alleyways to end up in one of the attractions that I wanted to see before leaving Rome, Fontana di Trevi. The Trevi Fountain was designed by Nicola Salvi and completed by Giuseppe Pannini in the eighteenth century. Tourists flocked to the fountain to throw coins over their left shoulders, hoping to return to Rome. It was my turn now, and I threw a coin like everyone else. Overall, it was a very pleasant experience, and I wanted to try the famous Italian gelato from a nearby ice-cream parlour and enjoy the evening.

After a while, before returning to the Colosseum to see the sunset at eight thirty, I was craving a coffee, but I opted for a can of cola instead as I was pressed for time. Ultimately, I managed to reach the site just before sunset. There were several sunset gazers around Piazza di Colosseo, appreciating the beautiful view of the massive structure. Among the crowd, I heard someone saying that there were other places in Rome where sunset could be much better. I understand that one of these places is Piazza Navona. After appreciating the Roman sunset, I began walking home at 9.00 p.m. I grabbed a slice of pizza from a stall on my way back to the hotel. I did not bother preparing the luggage for tomorrow's journey but went to bed after a quick wash. Fortunately, I did not have to get up early in the morning, as my train was scheduled to leave around seven o'clock in the evening.

The next morning, I woke up at ten o'clock and managed to finish the morning rituals before I started packing my luggage. I wasn't planning to carry several pieces of luggage, but just one suitcase and hand luggage. In fact, I had to get rid of some items which I had carried when I came from Jeddah. At noon, I was set up and was relieved. I was excited as much as nervous. The landlord felt that I would return. When asked why she thought I would return, she said that it was a hunch. In the meantime, I pulled my purse to settle any remaining payments and tendered a fiver in US dollars. She did not hesitate to take it but suggested that I should have a plate of spaghetti, which she was cooking for lunch. After accepting the offer, I asked if I could leave the room after 4.00 p.m. instead of one o'clock, and the answer was positive, as she did not have any room reservations at night.

Mark invited me for an espresso at the cafe next door before I was ready to leave and exchanged his home address in the US. When returned, I bade arrivederci to the landlord, and at about 5.00 p.m., I left the pensione towards the rail station, which was only five minutes away. Mark accompanied me to the station and even walked inside with me while having a conversation about the night train to Paris. We were told that my train, Palatino Express, would arrive at the platform within one hour. Since the resumption of the Rome–Paris train service in the early 1950s, Rome Express, with sleeper wagons, had been operated by French and Italian national rail companies. However, in the late1960s, the name was changed to Palatino Express. From the seventies, the Palatino Express has been operated by a European consortium and marketed as a Trans-Euro Night, or TEN, service.

As the train pulled into the platform, we were allowed to enter, and Mark was still with me. More than one hour was left for the train to depart. It was easy to find my sleeper coach, and once I settled in my compartment, Mark bade me goodbye. Within fifteen minutes, my compartment was full of six occupants, but only one passenger (a middle-aged man) could speak English. As the Palatino Express pulled out of the station slowly around seven-thirty, I said to myself, 'Arrivederci a Roma.' I was told that the train would pass through Genova, Turin, and Modane to cross the border soon after midnight and reach Dijon in France by ten in the morning. As scheduled, the Palatino Express would arrive at the Paris Gare de Lyon station midday.

As the train meandered through the valleys, leaving the urban landscape behind, I admired the beauty and serenity that nature had to offer, while the majestic sun was touching the bases of the rolling hills. After sunset, everyone in my compartment was ready to retire after eating whatever they had brought with them. I even had a panini and banana in my hand luggage, which I ate. I bought a cup of coffee from a trolley to complete my dinners. By ten thirty, everyone was in bed. We were told by the conductor that the border police could wake us up if they found it necessary.

Section Two

LA BELLE FRANCE: JUNE TO SEPTEMBER 1979

Zain is in Paris with his hometown friend who invited and persuaded him to take this trip to Europe. Zain hopes Zana will rescue him when in trouble. Zain doesn't know Zana has already arranged a summer job in Normandy. In addition to his summer job as a chef for a Parisian family, Zain also can enjoy a good summer holiday in Deauville. This section describes Zain's summer job experience and taste of Parisian good life as a guest of Zana and his fiancée Julie, along with a brief romantic interlude with Julie's friend.

4

BIENVENU EN FRANCE

When I woke up at about ten in the morning, I saw that all the other passengers in my compartment were up before me, and one passenger had already gotten off at the previous stop. Sunlight hit my face from the window, as the blinds had already been raised. Fortunately, while the train crossed the border, I did not get a wake-up call from the French border police in the middle of the night, and overall, I should say that I had enjoyed quiet and restful sleep. Quickly after the morning rituals, I craved a cup of espresso and a croissant, and so I headed to the buffet car, where I could sit and enjoy the view of the French countryside. Stretches of beautiful, lush green plains and vineyards would make us feel that we should pause for a while and appreciate what the French countryside had to offer.

As the train was pulled along, we headed north through the Burgundy Region of France. Contrary to what I had seen when the train passed through rural Italy, the French rural landscape seemed to be different. There were no red-roofed villas in the hilltop villages, but distinct villages were scattered within the acres of the vineyards. Within minutes, the train arrived in the city, which I reckoned Dijon. One passenger told me that we should arrive in Paris within two hours from here. It was like a dream coming true, as I was soon to land in Paris. Back home, I had attended French classes for a few months at Alliance Frances, but I hardly remembered anything. Although I was a bit anxious, Zana was my hope who would definitely help me.

Finally, as expected, the Palatino Express arrived in Paris just before midday. As we passed through the urban jungle with glimpses of cathedrals and tower blocks, the train slowly slid like a snake and headed to the Gare de Lyon station. Voilà! I was finally in Paris, the City of Light. Most travellers appeared tired and exhausted after overnight travel, and it took a while to get off the train and pass through the platform with several pieces of luggage. I managed to plough through with my single piece of luggage and reached the platform gate to be greeted by Zana and Julie. We shared large hugs and embraces a few times. Julie said, 'Bienvenu a Paris,' with kisses on both sides of my cheeks, as the Parisians do.

I had known Zana, a family friend, for over ten years since my high school years, and it had been three years since we met back home during his last visit home. He had been living in Paris for six years since arriving in France with his elder brother on a business trip. His brother frequently visited Paris to attend exhibitions and trade shows as a trader of precious stones. Zana grew up under the guardianship of his elder brother after his parents passed away when he was a child. I didn't quite understand why someone like Zana would decide to remain in Paris working as a housekeeper when he could enjoy a comfortable lifestyle back home. He seemed to be an independent-minded and self-reliant person who loved Paris. He spoke fluent French, and his Portuguese girlfriend seemed like godsent company.

While chatting about his friends back home, we leisurely walked to the underground station, or Metro. Zana and Julie had their *Carte Orange*, or travel cards, and a *carnet de billet*, or pack of ten tickets, for me. I was told that the Paris Metro, one of the largest underground train networks in the world, had a rail track of nearly 200 km long with around three hundred stations. It was also one of the oldest networks, first opened for service in 1900. The Paris Metro was also the first to use the term 'metro' for metropolitan trains, which was derived from the name of the company that operated it. It was reckoned that it had approximately fifteen lines running north to south and east to west, and almost half of the network ran underground. In the Metro network, Gare de Lyon stood in the eleventh district, or arrondissement, of Paris, north of the Seine River. We took a train that ran from east to west towards the famous monument Arc de Triomphe. It was the yellow line towards La Défence, but Zana warned about the forthcoming train change. We got off at Franklin D. Roosevelt and changed to a yellowish-green line which ran south to Pont de Servres. In minutes, we arrived at our destination, Rue de La Pompe, in the sixteenth arrondissement, one of the exclusive districts in Paris where the embassies were located. The famous Place du Trocadéro, overlooking the Eiffel Tower, stood just around the corner and only five to ten minutes away.

Affluent homeowners in Paris, particularly in posh areas, often have a room on the uppermost floor of the building reserved for nannies and housekeepers. Madame Lamark, for whom Zana worked as a housekeeper, attended to her husband's laundry and pressing clothes and gave him a self-contained bedsit on the top floor. The houses in Rue de La Pompe were expensive multi-storied apartment houses with concierge services, most likely neoclassical buildings. As we reached the foyer after the concierge opened the door, Zana introduced me to the concierge as his cousin, and we greeted each other with a 'Bonjour, monsieur.'

Fortunately, the building was equipped with a lift so that the fifth floor could easily be reached. Since Julie had her own studio elsewhere, Zana could accommodate me conveniently at his bedsit, but we had to use a common toilet and bathroom outside the room. It was still spring weather in Paris, and at two-thirty in the afternoon, Zana planned to go for Moroccan lunch. I took a quick wash to prepare, although I did not have much time to relax after the overnight travel. When I was ready, it was already three in the afternoon, and we all headed to the Metro station. Zana told us that we were going to take the green line 1 north to get to the Avenue des Champs-Élysées, the famous avenue in Paris where the presidential palace is located. We got off Franklin D. Roosevelt

at Champs-Élysées and walked along the famous avenue before turning onto a small street leading to an alleyway where the restaurant was
situated.

The Moroccan restaurant was an ordinary eatery with a handful of
tables, targeting takeaway customers from tourist hotspots. By the time
we managed to obtain a table, it was almost 5.00 p.m. I had a portion
of the saffron rice cooked with a slightly spiced lamb. It was served with
vegetables, such as okra, that were prepared in a tomato sauce with a
wonderful flavour. I enjoyed the food, as it had been a long time since I
had eaten rice. The saffron rice and well-cooked lamb laced with cumin
had a wonderful flavour; they were delicious. Zana told me that he and
Julie dined at this place at least once a month. The restaurant also served
the traditional couscous, which is a North African specialty.

After the meal, we found the way out along the alleyway that led to
Avenue de les Champs-Élysées. It was a bit of a walk, and we decided to
spend some time strolling along a mile-long street, window-shopping.
Being a Friday evening, the streets were rather crowded. I could spot a
variety of people from all over the world, and it all looked rather colourful. Some were just taking leisure walks, and I thought they were mainly
Parisian. Others were foreign visitors addicted to shopping during their
brief sojourns in Paris. Although the traffic was horrendous, the two
streets along the grand avenue allowed the strollers and shoppers to move
around freely.

As we walked down the avenue towards the presidential palace, or Le
Palais de l'Elysée, we bumped into a couple of Julie's friends. The male
friend, Alfonso, was from Portugal, and Elena was from Brazil. They
invited us to coffee, and we all agreed. A cafe near the avenue seemed less
crowded, and we sat outside the premises, overlooking Grande Avenue.
Alfonso said that the cafe served very good ice cream, but as a coffee
addict, I decided to stick to an espresso. When the coffee came, I realized
that the French version of the espresso was a bit diluted and served in a
full cup, unlike the Italian espresso. Overall, it was a beautiful evening
on one of the most famous avenues in the world. This was a memorable
experience.

At eleven in the night, we were not tempted to walk further down towards Elysée Palace, as Julie had to work the next morning and therefore wanted to return home. As we all walked up towards the Arc de Triomphe, the second-most-popular landmark of Paris, Julie, and her friends split at George V station and stepped down to take the metro. Zana and I proceeded towards the Arc de Triomphe to capture the sight of it in the night along with the glittering lights of the summer street decorations. I took the opportunity to capture a few pictures in *Place Charles de Gaulle*, formally known as the Place de l'Étoile (meaning 'star square'), with one of the most famous monuments behind me. The Arc de Triomphe de l'Étoile was built in the early eighteen hundreds to commemorate Napoleon's victories.

By now I felt a bit tired, and my long overnight journey began to show its effects on my face. Zana thought that we should head home and hit the bed. Because we had to go to the next station to catch line 9, we stepped down to the station and took line 1 from George V. With a quick change at Franklin D. Roosevelt, we reached home before midnight. Zana had a mattress he had bought in expectation of my arrival, and it was, in fact, much comfortable than sleeping in his elevated bed. I must have fallen asleep in minutes as soon as I hit my bed. Zana warned me about his snoring, but I didn't hear a thing. It was, in fact, perfect sleep, and I did not get up until 11.00 a.m. As I raised the window blinds, I felt the signs of another gorgeous day ahead.

5

A TOURIST IN PARIS

Zana was quick to have a shower while I was still sleeping, and he was about to make a cup of coffee for me as I woke up. He pulled out some croissants from the cupboard, and we had coffee while making an itinerary for the day. For some reason, I felt that he wanted to take me around to visit a few famous attractions in a rush, as if I were to leave Paris soon. When I asked him why we were in such a hurry, he simply replied, 'You will come to know soon.' Then I continued browsing the tourist guidebook and saw something about 'Bateaux Mouches'. When I asked Zana what it was, he said, 'A boat ride or cruise on the river.' However, he suggested taking a river cruise a day later, as Julie would be free to join us.

Zana wondered whether I knew anything about the *Mona Lisa*. When I said, 'The painting by Leonardo da Vinci?' he nodded and asked, 'Why not then visit Louvre Museum today?' Since Julie did not like to visit museums, as they seemed boring to her, we decided to visit the Louvre. I rushed through to take a shower while Zana was preparing omelettes and French toast for late breakfast. On my return, we had breakfast and prepared for the day. It was almost one thirty in the afternoon when we stepped out. This time we walked some distance towards the Eiffel Tower and took pictures overlooking the tower before descending to the Trocadéro Garden via the steps next to the Place du Trocadéro. 'What a beautiful view of the Eiffel Tower and the garden below, with the spring's blossoms?' I exclaimed. Further down the garden, we crossed the road to reach the shores of the river Seine at the centuries-old elegant bridge Pont d'Iena. We decided not to cross the river; instead we walked to the metro station slowly to catch the line 9. By now I was used to line 9, which passed through Franklin D. Roosevelt. Zana said that we should take line 1 in order to reach the Louvre, so we changed over to line 1 and got off at Palais Royal–Musée du Louvre in less than ten minutes.

The Louvre Museum was claimed to be the most visited art museum of the world, even in the Dolce Vita period. The collection included well-known works of art, such as the *Mona Lisa* of da Vinci. The arts exhibited included objects from prehistoric periods to the twenty-first century, as well as Roman and Greek sculptures. The museum took its name from Louvre Palace, in which a huge art collection was held. The thirteenth-century palace also remained the primary residence of the French kings during the renaissance period. After Louis XIV deserted the palace and moved to Versailles, it became a place to display his collection of ancient Roman and Greek sculptures. This eventually paved the way for a new museum after the French Revolution. In the late seventies, the Louvre had tens of thousands of art objects on display, with many thousands of objects to be curated. The collection contained Roman, Greek, Egyptian, Etruscan, Near-Eastern, and even Islamic arts. It would take an art lover several days to see the entire collection of art. However, in my case, I was simply interested in seeing a few masterpieces, such as the *Mona Lisa*.

With renovation and expansion, the Louvre Palace had become a huge place, and getting around was a challenge for some. We entered the museum from the main entrance and went in the direction of the *Mona Lisa*. It took a while to arrive at the west wing and then to the State Hall, where the famous painting was exhibited. My first question was that of how Italian paintings had ended up in France. According to historical evidence, Leonardo da Vinci completed the painting in 1519, although it could have been finished in 1506, and was later acquired by King Francis I of France. It has been on permanent display at Louvre since 1797.

Mona Lisa, the iconic painting by Leonardo da Vinci, was claimed to be the most famous and most valuable painting in the world. It was not surprising to discover that the majority of Louvre visitors, like me, came to see just *Mona Lisa*. The beautiful woman with dark hair in the painting had a mysterious gaze which not only mesmerized me but also fascinated most people. Most art scholars thought that it was a portrait of an Italian noblewoman. Contrary to other paintings of this calibre, *Mona Lisa* does not attempt to show the status of a noblewoman with adornments. This made the gazers pay attention to the face as well as the eyes of the woman in the painting. I felt as if she were staring at me. Leonardo had done a fascinating job with his brushstrokes to deliver a real human-like and photogenic look. Moreover, for an ordinary admirer like me, the portrait looked like a real photograph, with the focus of the lens on the face without emphasizing much on the background—that is, the brushstrokes of a genius. After the notorious theft of the painting some one hundred years ago, attention was turned to protecting the precious work of art. In order to protect it from vandalism and humidity, the painting has been exhibited inside a glass case since the 1950s.

Having had a glimpse of a few works of art, I wanted to spend time exploring some of the Roman and Greek sculptures, as well as some Egyptian artefacts. Zana and I agreed that we should get out of the museum before the they shut the door. Unfortunately, we could not see the Egyptian wing, and we left the Louvre on time to meet Julie at Les Halles, a popular shopping district.

Châtelet-Les Halles was not far from where we were, and it was around the corner. Rue de Rivoli stands between the Louvre and Châtelet-Les Halles. The Canopée and underground Forum des Halles shopping malls were all within walking distance of the Louvre, not to mention late-night eateries. We were supposed to meet Julie at the Les Halles Metro station which was located within the compound. We were there ten minutes before seven. While we were waiting, Zana thought of the idea for the night. Of course, dinners were the first item on the agenda. Suddenly we saw Julie rushing through the square, and she spotted us waiting on the opposite side. She seemed excited to see us, and in minutes, I saw the usual Parisian greetings with kisses on both sides of the cheeks, and then we were all set to go.

I suggested that we should spend some time shopping at the Forum des Halles and grab rolls of shawarma from one of the eateries around the corner. We hadn't eaten anything for lunch. Julie and Zana agreed, and we went down to the underground shopping malls. It was quite an experience for me to see an extensive range of shops carrying a variety of branded clothes and cosmetics. I was a sort of fashion addict who slowly acquired a taste for branded clothes, including shirts and neckties. Yves St Laurent was my popular brand for shirts which I had encountered for the first time in Saudi Arabia, and I already had one with me. I also appreciated the eaux de toilette of Christian Dior. But for now, I had ditched all my desires to spend money shopping for branded clothes and other luxuries. In the meantime, Julie wanted to check out the Galerie Lafayette for her usual necessities, while Zana was looking for a takeaway food stall serving shawarma. When Julie was done with her shopping, we started looking for Zana. Within minutes, we spotted him looking at the menu board in front of a kebab shop. "Voilà, we found him," Julie said. We grabbed a table in the forecourt, and Zana ordered shawarma wraps for all. It did not take much time for us to finish our fast-food dinner, although Zana had an extra wrap to share. Holding our cola cans in hand, we started walking to the metro station. The next item on the agenda was visiting Rue St. Denis. I was not told why we were going there; the reason remained a secret. One thing Zana told me was that it was not far from here, just one train stop away.

For me, Rue St Denis, which stood between Rue Etienne Marcel and Rue de Turbigo, was a colourful street even at night. Historically, this street had enjoyed several names, including the title 'Grand Rue de Paris'. It was also referred to in Victor Hugo's novel *Les Misérables*. However, what brought us here was a different reason, which I came to know later. Among the many shops, restaurants, bars, and stores selling clothes, the street is scattered with sex shops. The neighbourhood established itself with a reputation as a notorious area for prostitution early on. It seemed that Julie brought me here to tease working girls. Flanking us on both sides of the street, women of all colours, mainly of a young age, shouted at potential customers. Julie pushed me to speak to one of them and asked me to act as if I were kind of lost and looking for a toilet. When the woman showed me by climbing some stairs, Zana immediately pulled me away. Later, we all walked along the street, teasing a few women by saying that I liked them but I had only twenty francs with me. One woman started shouting at me, and I thought she was going to punch me. Overall, we had fun, and the time was almost eleven o'clock at night. Before taking the train home, Zana asked whether I minded Julie coming with us to stay tonight. I said jokingly, 'As long as I have my mattress for myself, I don't mind.' It was just before midnight when we reached home, and it took a while before we got to bed.

It seemed that people could sleep for long hours during the summer. We slept past ten o'clock, and I was the first to get up to go for a shower. I had to wake up Zana and Julie when I returned to the room. While I was making coffee for all of us, Julie went to the washroom and quickly got down to fetch croissants. At the same time, chatting about the day's agenda, we sat in bed and sipped our coffee. Within five to ten minutes, Julie was back with a couple of French bread sticks which they passionately called baguettes and some croissants, along with a bottle of milk. The croissants were fresh and tasty, and I ate two.

As for the day's itinerary, Zana suggested that we go to the river cruise in the late afternoon. 'But we should first prepare some baguette sandwiches to take with us, along with a choice of fruits and drinks,' he said. I thought to myself that it was a wonderful idea and wondered how we could make simple classic baguette sandwiches. When I asked Zana, he pointed to the fridge and said, 'What about Yiddish pastrami and sliced Gruyère cheese?' The French preferred sliced French ham over pastrami. Madame Lamark gave Zana some pastrami which she had bought from a Jewish delicatessen. We had everything we wanted for the sandwich, and therefore everyone agreed. Julie and Zana promised to make the best baguette sandwich using the ingredients they had at home before three o'clock so that we could leave for a river cruise soon after.

It was about midday, and Zana seemed hungry, not having had a

good breakfast, and wanted to make a few eggs on the toast. Julie and I
didn't show much interest, although we agreed to join him for a quick
bite. While Julie started to prepare the ingredients for the baguette
sandwiches, Zana went on to prepare the eggs. She gathered several ingredients on the table, such as sun-dried tomatoes, gherkins, olives, sliced
Gruyère cheese, mustard, softened butter, and sliced pastrami. Making
a baguette sandwich did not seem like rocket science.

As I stood watching, Julie spread softened butter over the split baguette, and then a little Dijon mustard, before putting a layer of pastrami
on each side to be filled with sliced gherkins and tomatoes, and joining the sides together. A few pitted olives were inserted between them
to complete the process. There were several ways we could make this
sandwich, but the French would want ham and Emmenthal or Gruyère
cheese over softened butter, preferably *Beurre de Bordier*. The Italian
would use mortadella instead of ham, and a Scot would choose to do
so with smoked salmon. However, a freshly baked traditional baguette
would definitely make a difference.

Now, with the sandwiches made, we were ready to go. It was almost
five, and I felt a little bit cooler than on the previous evenings, although
the sun was still shining with a patchy cloud hovering over. Zana thought
we should all take a jumper with us in case the temperature dipped a bit.
At about five thirty in the evening, we left home and walked all the way
to the Metro to catch line 9. We got off at Iéna so that we could embark
on the boat at Pont d'Iéna, the main boarding point just near the Eiffel
Tower. Zana bought the tickets and embarked on the boat at six o'clock.

Several cruise-operating companies offered river cruises on the Seine
and Bateaux Mouches was one of them. Unlike other river cruises in
major European cities, the Parisian boat tours covered the key attractions
well, offering visitors a glimpse of all key monuments and landmark
attractions. The boats and the cruises themselves were attractions offering entertainment and fine-dining experiences for discerning tourists.
Depending on the options chosen, the cruise could last from one hour to
ninety minutes, with dining cruises in the evening taking more time on
board. Since we had decided to take a late afternoon cruise, we thought

the tour would last just over an hour. However, the cruise we boarded was said to be an evening cruise with drinks and music on board. We embarked on the boat on the other side of the river.

As we got onto the boat, we found a convenient site to sit on the right-hand side of the boat towards the front seats. Julie seemed hungry and eager to find out how good the baguette sandwiches were. Everyone grabbed a sandwich and enjoyed the evening meal with cola. Julie did remind us of a glass of chilled white wine, but she was a bit too lazy to walk a few metres to fetch a glass from the bar on the rear of the boat. The baguette sandwich was fantastic, and the pastrami tasted delicious. When I finished eating, I took out my jumper to wrap myself, as I felt cold. But Zana and Julie remained firm in their summer clothes.

The cruise started at six thirty sharp, and surprisingly, the boat was full of tourists even in May. The boat moved towards the south, in the direction of Les Invalides and the Assemblée Nationals, or the French Parliament. In our boat, we were lucky to have an art historian from the American College of Paris on board. As the boat moved on, the volume of music decreased whenever the announcer began to describe the attractions. While the boat was cruising, the announcer pointed at a series of army museums, a church, and a number of tombs, including Napoleon's. It was Les Invalides. The next attraction was the French Parliament, followed by the D'Orsay Museum. However, few tourists were keen to pay attention to these attractions. For some, the river cruise was a way to relax and enjoy the evening, appreciating the beautiful Parisian landscape. Most boat tours during the day might come with an art historian announcing the facts and figures, as well as the history behind the monuments and buildings we would see. Otherwise, light background music could be played, particularly during dinnertimes in the evening or night tours. Some preferred the night river cruises to see some of the attractions, such as the Eiffel Tower, with lights on.

The boat cruised through the narrow strip between the shores, boasting the Latin Quarter, or Le Quartier Latin, and the City Island, also known as the Île de la Cité. The quaint Latin Quarter, home of Sorbonne University, remained popular with bustling students, and there were many cafes and eateries. We could see some popular attractions, such as the Jardin des Plantes botanical gardens, the National Museum of Natural History, and the Panthéon, which houses the remains of Voltaire, Marie Curie, and Simone Veil. The Panthéon remained a famous monument in the fifth district of Paris. It was built in the mid-1700s. We could easily spot it, as it stood on top of Montagne Sainte-Geneviève in the centre of the Panthéon Square.

As the boat reached the end of Île de la Cité, the famous medieval cathedral, the Notre-Dame de Paris appeared on the left shore. This Catholic cathedral dedicated to the Virgin Mary represented one of the best examples of French Gothic architecture. Notre-Dame was built in 1163 to 1345 with the help of architects Jean-Baptiste Lassus and Pierre de Montreuil. Now that the cruise was returning in the opposite direction after the turn along the Notre-Dame Cathedral, the announcer lowered the music to tell us about Bastille Square, or Place de la Bastille, where the Bastille prison stood. The prison was destroyed during the French Revolution, which took place between 14 July 1789 and 14 July 1790.

We then passed through the world-famous Louvre, on which the art historian spent some time explaining the history of the palace and the famous works of art exhibited. I have already written elsewhere about the history of the museum of the arts as well as the famous *Mona Lisa*. On the cruise track, we saw the Tuileries Garden, or Le Jardin des Tuileries, after passing the Louvre. This large garden was established in 1564 as the garden of the Tuileries Palace by Catherine de' Medici, the queen of France, by marriage to King Henry II. In 1667, after the French Revolution, it became a public garden. Queen Catherine was a Medici-born Italian noblewoman from the famous Florentine banking family who had had a tremendous influence on French culture and arts, including French cuisine indirectly.

A few metres away, after passing the Tuileries Garden, the announcer brought our attention to the largest public square in Paris. The Place de la Concorde was a large square—one of the major public squares in the city, along with the Champs-Élysées. Obviously, we could not miss out on the Grand Palais that stood on Champs-Élysées. The Grand Palais des Champs-Élysées remained a historic structure, often functioning as an exhibition hall and museum complex. It was founded in the year 1900.

Finally, our river cruise came to its endpoint at about eight o'clock. The sun was still on the horizon, but we felt a bit chilly. We put on our jumpers, disembarked the boat, and decided to get off at Pont de l'Alma instead of returning to where we had embarked on the boat at Pont l'Iéna. We took a stroll until we reached l'Iéna Metro so that we could catch line 9 back home. At home, we had some leftovers from the baguette sandwiches, which Zana and I ate. Julie did not want anything to eat but joined for a cup of coffee with us after the wash. Overall, it was a pleasant evening, and we enjoyed it very much. We were up until midnight chatting and nibbling on whatever we could find in the pantry. When I asked Zana what plans he had for tomorrow, he said we could think about it in the morning. I then went to bed after a shower. So did everyone else. Within a matter of thirty minutes, Zana and Julie were asleep, and I could hear Zana snoring. Since it was a bit cool at night, the window was kept shut, and I felt it was a bit stuffy. Eventually, I fell asleep.

The next morning, I was rather late to wake up, perhaps because of the tiring day in the sun. When I got up, both Julie and Zana were already after their showers and ready to prepare breakfast. They had finished their espressos and offered me a cup. The coffee woke me up fully, and I had a shower while Zana and Julie cooked Yiddish sausages and egg toasts. Julie had even brought up some baguettes from the boulangerie down the road a couple of blocks away. Back in the room while chatting, we had breakfast. As Zana did not suggest any plans for the day, I said that we should visit the Eiffel Tower, the most recognizable landmark. The time was already one-thirty in the afternoon, and Zana nodded but suggested that we leave home around four o'clock.

After breakfast, Julie and I went for a walk, as I thought I could improve my French while talking to her when we were alone. Zana was doing some housekeeping, and he wanted to iron his clothes as well. Her

English was like my French, but we tried our best to communicate with each other without any help from a third party. She was impressed at how well I could converse in French. When we returned, Zana finished reading a book, and we all dressed up to go to the Champ de Mars. We walked to Place de Trocadéro and reached the grounds on which the Eiffel Tower stood by crossing the Pont l'Iéna. There were many people already in the Champ de Mars, but the queue to the tower was moderate. While we joined the queue, Zana went and bought tickets.

In July 1889, France commemorated the centennial of the French Revolution and hosted the World's Fair in Paris. France was eager to show off her achievements in the engineering field. Therefore, the construction of the Eiffel Tower, or La Tour Eiffel, in 1889 remained the centrepiece of the World's Fair. The Eiffel Tower, built on the Champ de Mars in Paris, was the world's tallest structure, measuring three hundred metres without the antenna, until the Chrysler Building was erected in 1930. Gustave Eiffel, with his construction company, built a tower with seven thousand five hundred tons of wrought iron in just over two years. The architects and designers involved were Sauvestre, Koechlin, and Nouguier.

The Eiffel Tower has received over three hundred million visitors since it was opened in 1889. In its construction, Gustave Eiffel secretly included an apartment to host important guests. In addition, the Eiffel Tower was supposed to be torn down after twenty years, but the government eventually decided to use it as a visitor attraction as well as a tower for radio antennas and wireless transmitters. Another interesting aspect of the tower was its post office on the first floor, which I unfortunately missed, where visitors could send a postcard with the postmark of the Eiffel Tower.

The Eiffel Tower also facilitated the study of meteorological changes during the early days. On the third floor of the tower, a scientific lab was dedicated to the study of aerodynamics, wind movement, and other meteorological observations. It was also believed that there was a Champagne bar at the top of the tower if anyone was brave enough to reach the top to enjoy a glass of bubbly. My vivid memory of the visit to the tower is limited to lining up in the queue and taking the lift to the third floor. Of course, the spectacular view of the city on a bright, sunny afternoon remains a memorable experience.

As we walked down home after the descent, we picked up some takeaway dinners from a Vietnamese fast-food stall at Pont de l'Alma. It was too early to return home, so we decided to sit on the riverbank and enjoy our food. It was just a takeaway consisting of either rice noodles or fried rice with spicy sauce, topped with a choice of meat or seafood. I consumed noodles and seafood. I vaguely remember all of us choosing the same meal. I didn't dare try to use chopsticks, but Zana chose to do so. I thought that the well-cooked noodles tempered with crushed garlic and ginger, along with soya sauce, resulted in a typical Cantonese flavour. The seafood consisted of clams, squid, cuttlefish, and large prawns sautéed in chilli-boosted soya sauce with lemongrass, ginger, and tamarind sauce. It was, after all, a good meal, and we wondered what was next.

Julie suggested we visit Montparnasse Tower, one of the tallest buildings in Paris, which has a rooftop restaurant and bar. When I asked Julie why I would want to visit this skyscraper, she said that I could see the panoramic view of Paris from the observatory. We agreed with Julie and proceeded to go to Avenue du Maine at Montparnasse. Le Tour Montparnasse, or the Montparnasse Tower, a 210-metre-high skyscraper located in the Montparnasse area, was constructed in 1969 and opened to the public as an observation tower in 1973. Until recently, it was the tallest office building in Europe.

As we made an exit at the Montparnasse Metro station, I could see that this impressive tall tower dominated the landscape. It was just about nine in the evening, and Zana wanted us to hurry up so that we could see the sunset from the observatory, as it was a beautiful day without any clouds hovering over in the horizon. In fact, we managed to get to the top before sunset at 9.40. The observatory on the fifty-ninth floor offered us a unique panoramic view of the city and gave me the chance to see one of the most beautiful sunsets in my life. It was worth the effort, and I thank Julie for suggesting the visit. The open space was rather crowded where everyone was trying to get a glimpse of the panoramic view and the sunset. Later, we got down to the fifty-sixth floor to browse the kiosks and cafes. This floor was an enclosed space covered by glass structures, and we could see the Parisian landscape while sipping coffee in a cafe.

There wasn't much to see in the tower, as it was occupied by offices—mainly those of the company that owned the skyscraper. Back on the ground, we took time to walk around the area for a while. The Montparnasse area was as busy as ever at night, with bustling bistros and restaurants. Montparnasse cemetery, where several prominent intellectuals, such as Jean-Paul Sartre, were buried, was another attraction for many during the daytime. A few museums in the area attracted visitors to Montparnasse during the day. This part of the city, not far from the popular Latin Quarter, remained an attraction among tourists.

Zana reminded me that Julie had to go to work in the morning and so needed to go home early. Therefore, we all headed to the Montparnasse Metro station to catch line 6, which would take us to Trocadéro. From there, Zana and I could take line 9. Julie split from us, and we proceeded to go home. At home, before we hit the bed, Zana said that we had an important meeting the following day, but he didn't elaborate much other than to saying that Madame Lamark wanted to see him with me. I wondered to myself why I had to see her, but then I considered that he had perhaps introduced me as his cousin. Who knew what was in store? Nevertheless, I asked him what time we had a meeting with Madame Lamark. 'At ten-thirty in the morning, and we should get up before nine o'clock,' he replied.

I went to bed saying, 'Bon Nuit.'

6

A MEMORABLE
SUMMER IN FRANCE

The next morning, we were up and ready even before ten o'clock. After a cup of coffee and croissant, we both arrived for the meeting at ten-thirty sharp. Madame Lamark, a charming lady in her early forties, opened the door and greeted us with a 'Bon Jour monsieur.' Zana introduced me as his cousin and briefly described my background. I figured out that she already knew much more about me than I thought she did. She spoke both French and English. Monsieur Lamark, who was seated in an armchair and reading a newspaper, got up and came to greet me, but he did not speak any English. We were seated and offered coffee while Madame Lamark enquired about my work experiences and education. She thought I could cook. I began to understand that Zana had arranged for me to do household chores for Madame Lamark during the summer in a seaside resort in Normandy. In fact, she wanted someone to help her with cooking and serving breakfast and dinners. When I said that my cooking skills were at a beginner's level and I knew nothing about French cuisine, Madame Lamark assured me by saying that was nothing to worry about and that I would soon be learning to cook French food. It was rather surprising to see what was unfolding, but at the same time I was excited. Now I had just a week or two to spend in Paris.

When I was still in Rome, I told Zana to find me a summer job until

September, hoping that I would return to Rome in September to start my studies at the American College of Rome. My thirst for a summer job matched Madame's search for a summer cook. However, Zana never told me about this secret arrangement. Since I didn't hear Madame saying anything about the benefits or rewards, I wondered whether Zana had already negotiated a deal. Later, I found out that I would be paid 1,500 francs a month with lots of leisure time and a comfortable room with my own bathroom. Over 350 US dollars a month was not bad for a summer job in 1979. My only job was to cook and serve breakfast and dinner for the family—three at most, when Monsieur Lamark was present at home. I also understood that an Irish nanny called Anna would be there to mind seven-year-old Geraldine. Anna also was to help Madame with other household chores.

Having accepted the offer, I told Zana that I had enough time to kill in Paris and insisted that we should do something different and fun today. We went to get some baguettes and saw a poster about an exciting horse race in one of the famous racecourses in Paris, Le Course Longchamp. The Longchamp racecourse was not far from where we lived, and it was just a couple of Metro stations away. Zana suggested going home and cooking one of his favourite dishes with canned mackerel to eat with baguettes, along with a good green salad. Armed with baguettes, canned fish, onions, and two types of salad leaves, we headed home.

While I was on the shower, he was ready for cooking. As I watched, he prepared the onions by finely slicing them and then cooking them in melted butter while adding chopped garlic and chilli until they became brown. When dumping in the open can of mackerel during the preparation, he added a dash of hot chilli powder, cumin powder, and a few bay leaves to provide a wonderful flavour. Before we sat down to eat, Zana rushed to the shower room, asking me to prepare the green salad and baguettes. It was hot, spicy, and a wonderful dish to go with a baguette, and the salad was a plus. With full stomachs, we were too lazy to make a move and decided to relax. Zana promised me that we would make a visit to Longchamb another day.

Over the next couple of days, I would be free to explore Paris myself, as Zana had to work. With a Carte Orange covering all zones, I was able to take advantage of the Metro network and visit Paris from east to west and north to south. I visited several parks, and one of my favourites was Jardin du Luxembourg. This twenty-five-hectare garden was established in 1612 by Queen Marie de Medici. It consisted of two sections: French and English gardens, with a forest and a pond in between. I loved this garden so much, and thus I visited it several times during my stay in Paris. Another hotspot I cherished visiting was the Latin Quarter. These places were always packed with tourists, and among them were Japanese tourists with cameras and, sometimes, tourist guidebooks in their hands.

Days passed quickly, and Zana was able to find some time in between his work schedules to be with me before my departure to Normandy. One bright Saturday morning, Zana suggested that we should go to the racecourse and headed to prepare something to eat. After lunch, I reckoned that we should take line 9 from our Metro station towards Auteuil and then a bus ride before walking to the Longchamp racetrack. The racetrack was situated along the famous Bois de Boulogne, the largest park in Paris, which bordered the sixteenth arrondissements to the right. The Longchamp was large and consisted of several tracks of varying lengths, including a challenging hill track for thoroughbreds. I was told that half of the Category A or Group One races in France had been held at this famous racetrack since it was open in April 1857. Distinguished personalities, including princes and aristocrats, had often attended racing events in Longchamp since its opening. Interestingly, even during German occupation, Longchamp hosted racing events. The nearby racetrack, Auteuil Hippodrome, which was opened sixteen years later, seemed smaller but was accessible to ordinary folks. This was primarily used for steeplechase, and an important event in the calendar included the Prix du President de la Republique, held in April. I told Zana that I wanted to see the Longchamp when the famous Prix de l'Arc de Triomphe was held in October.

When we reached racecourse, some of the races had already been held. We headed to the cheapest stand, but it had all of the basic facilities.

The punters were not essentially gamblers but ordinary folks seeking fun and entertainment. It was a day out for families with children. There were food and beverage stalls, betting counters, and toilets. For most punters, it seemed like the challenge was to pick the winning horse rather than to win any money. Zana and I felt the same and had a fantastic time, as it was the first time I had ever been to a racetrack. I realized that there was more to enjoy when visiting a racetrack and watching a horse race than gambling. To pick the winning horse, punters would check the horses' histories, pedigrees, trainers, and jockeys, as well as the betting odds shown on the board. I don't remember the name of races or horses, but I simply tended to pick them based on the odds, But I did once picked the winning horse, and a couple of times either second or third place. Zana picked the winning horse a few times, as he was keen to follow the race history as well as the jockeys. We stayed there until 7.00 p.m. and watched several races.

On the way back, we visited a supermarket and picked up some groceries, including a baguette for the next morning. We also decided to grab a takeaway pizza from a nearby pizza shop. By the time we reached home, it was nine, and we simply decided to relax with a cup of tea with milk, as we used to do back home. We all knew how to make a good cuppa, and Zana had good-quality tea from home. The pizza was already cold, and we didn't mind eating cold pizza later after taking a shower, but we enjoyed the cuppa while chatting about Zana's plan for the future, as he wanted to live in France. When he asked me about my plan, I reaffirmed that I wanted to return to Rome as soon as I heard from the dean of the American College of Rome. He wasn't happy about my plan but said that was up to me. It was just about midnight when we went to sleep after taking a shower and eating cold pizza with a glass of fruit juice.

In the morning, I didn't have to rush, as we didn't have any plans for the day. We woke up after midday and had breakfast and coffee together. He proposed the idea of visiting Montmartre, where tourists flocked during the night, seeking nocturnal entertainment, or during the day, seeking a bargain in the open market packed with amateur artists trying

to make a living by painting the caricatures of visitors. But we decided
to postpone this visit until I returned from Normandy. Another famous
attraction, the Moulin Rouge, was also located on Montmartre. In the
end, we thought we should just take a walk towards Pont l'Alma and
explore the riverbank.

As we tried to pass across the bridge, Zana spotted a betting shop
where people flocked to place bets on horse races. He had some francs
left that he had won at Longchamp and, perhaps having got the taste
of gambling earlier, wanted to try out his luck. At the betting shop, we
studied the details of the races held in Deauville that day. We used the
betting format called 'pari-mutuel', in which we picked the three winning houses from the three listed races. This was similar to betting on a
jackpot win, but the minimum bet was just one franc. Zana placed a few
bets each with either five or ten francs, using various combinations. I was
tempted to place a few bets, too, and I placed several bets using various
combinations as well, but each bet was for just one franc. Between a few
cans of cola, Zana lost all of his gains from Longchamp. We escaped
the chaos in the premises, as it was rather crowded, and took a short
walk until the results were released. As we returned after some time, we
found that most of the punters had left, and it was much easier to see
our trio results. To my surprise, I had a winning combination, but Zana
had lost all his bets. As my bet was for just one franc, the winning pot
was just 1,500 francs—about 350 US dollars. Not bad for one franc. I
was so excited, and I said, 'What about a dinner on my account tonight?'
Zana then told me that he had planned to meet Julie and her roommate
Fernanda for a dinner at a Lebanese-French restaurant near Les Halles.
Julie had already made a reservation, and we had to be at the restaurant at
eight o'clock sharp. He asked whether I could take the tab, and I agreed.

I was excited about my win, as this was equal to one month's worth
of the wage that Madame Lamark had proposed paying me for my summer job. Even Zana seemed happy that I had some money in my hands
to spend. I collected money and slowly and leisurely went to Les Halles.
The restaurant was outside the station and a few blocks away, towards
Rue St Denise, and we managed to get there on time. However, Julie

and her friend were already there, waiting for us to join. With the usual greetings, Julie introduced me to Fernanda, a good friend who shared the room with her.

As guests with seat reservations, we had priority when it came to seating arrangements, and we were shown to a corner table adjacent to a glass window. Reading the menu, I found that it was more a Lebanese restaurant than a Lebanese-French restaurant. Julie and Zana loved Lebanese mezzes or starters, which perhaps was what prompted them to choose this restaurant. I sort of liked Lebanese food, as I enjoyed the taste of Arabic-Lebanese food in Saudi Arabia. From the variety of mezzes in the menu, we ordered tabbouleh and *Mouttabal*. Tabbouleh consisted of cooked bulgur wheat mixed with finely chopped parsley and mint leaves, as well as chopped spring onions, garlic, tomatoes, and cucumber, mixed and tossed in lemon juice and olive oil. Mouttabal, a common mezze found in countries across the Middle East, consists of burnt or baked aubergine mixed with yogurt and tahini sauce. We also ordered a plate of *Taratour*, spicy prawns that were fried and drizzled with tahini sauce. The last item we ordered was veggie fritters made of grated courgette and carrots mixed with crumbled feta and eggs. It came with a basket of Lebanese bread. Julie and Fernanda were also keen to get some white wine to go with the mezzes.

As for the main dish, we chose one item which we could share: Lebanese-style roast lamb shoulder on a bed of roasted vegetables. The tender lamb shoulder was roasted slowly until the meat almost came off the bones. The roasted vegetables included thickly sliced fennel, split onion chunks, carrots, diced celery roots, and potato cubes. The lamb shoulder had been marinated overnight in a Lebanese sauce. Even the roasted vegetables were sprinkled with marinade. We all enjoyed the food very much, but we should have gone a bit light on mezzes, as we all seemed full and lost our appetites when the main dish arrived. However, time was not a limiting factor, and we managed to consume the food leisurely, but we were soon conscious of my trip to Deauville with Madame Lamark. The meal was complemented with a cup of Lebanese coffee, and as soon as the bill was paid, we moved out to return home.

On the street, Fernanda seemed a bit tipsy, and we clung together. Julie and her friend knew I was about to leave Paris, and perhaps that instigated the idea that they both spend the night with us. They proposed this by asking Zana whether they should leave us. Obviously, Zana was in favour of inviting them home. In any case, we decided to get home as early as possible, and thus made our way to the Metro after a short stroll. Back home, I understood that Fernanda was to sleep on a mattress with me, and Zana passed me a hint that she liked me. I wished that she spoke good English, but she was not as bad as I thought. She had learned English in high school. Fernanda was an attractive slim girl with a sharp brain in her late twenties. She had been living in Paris for a couple of years, with an au pair visa at first and later with a care worker resident permit. I did like her, but it was a drag not being able to converse fluently in English.

All in all, it was a memorable experience with Fernanda on my bed, and I should say that it was an exciting night, but I was able to sleep well for only a few hours. I didn't experience much disturbance from Julie and Zana. In the morning, I got up around eight thirty as the summer sunshine reflected on the mirror through the window blinds. As I entered the room after a quick shower, I could see everyone else was up, and Julie started making fun of us while Zana was making a purring sound with his lips closed. In the meantime, I began packing my luggage while breakfast was being prepared by the others, as I was going to be away, beginning the following day, for at least a couple of months. After breakfast, Fernanda bade me farewell with a hug and kiss, as she had to work in the afternoon. Zana and Julie went out, leaving me alone for the entire afternoon, which I did not mind.

On a Friday afternoon in early June, we left Paris and headed for Normandy. It was a beautiful day, and the traffic was not as bad as expected. Monsieur Lamark was himself, driving his luxury model of Citroën, while Madame Lamark tried to explain to me the nature of the French countryside. Their seven-year-old daughter, seated behind me, was asleep during a good part of the journey. As we reached Normandy, I felt and breathed the air, which was laced with methane, as is usually the case in cattle farming areas. The road was beautifully flanked with oak and birch trees. Madame Lamark explained that their country house in Tourgéville was spacious and surrounded by a large garden. She went on to say that the commune of Tourgéville, located in the Calvados district in the Normandy region, was also the home of the world-famous Deauville Racecourse, l'Hippodrome de Deauville, and that the popular beach resort town of Deauville was not far from here.

After nearly three hours of driving, we reached our destination. As Madame Lamark had described, the house was large and two-storeyed, and a hundred-metre driveway was paved with asphalt. Apple and cherry trees were scattered throughout the garden. Monsieur Lamark drove the car towards the rear and parked in the back. As we entered the house from the side door, I was shown my room upstairs. In the meantime, I helped Madame Lamark unload the contents from the car, and it seemed she had already done grocery shopping in Paris. This meant that we did not need to go out in the evening for errands. While both Monsieur and Madame began to unwind with a class of chilled white wine in the garden, I went for a shower.

Back in my room after a refreshing shower, I found myself relieved, as the room was spacious and comfortable. Even the bed and mattress were exceptionally good, much more than what I could expect as a summer domestic worker. I looked through the large window facing the garden, and I was tempted to make a brisk survey of my surroundings, so I stepped out. In addition to the apple and cherry trees that held ready-to-eat fruits ripe for plucking, there were a few birch and oak trees. One feature of the garden I liked was the designated area for growing vegetables and flower plants. I could see ripened tomatoes, sprouting leeks, and blooming flowers, such as lilies and roses. I thought Madame Lamark had tried her luck during her spring visit to the cottage to work on the plots to grow plants. Another observation that pleased me was the bicycle in the garden shed. The shed was large enough to hold a small Renault town car as well as several pieces of garden equipment, including a lawn mower.

Suddenly I heard Madame Lamark calling me to let me know that we did not have a grand dinner that night, but just a simple salad with baguettes and cheese. I prepared a dinner table with plates, cutlery, and an open bottle of white wine, while Madame gathered ingredients, such as a few varieties of salad leaves, onions, tomatoes, halved boiled eggs, marinated artichoke hearts, sliced smoked salmon, and some pastrami. She also made some French vinaigrette sauce for the salad while preparing baguettes and cheese. Voilà! Dinner was prepared in minutes. It was nine-thirty, about the time of sunset, and we all enjoyed dinner before we called it a day. Back in the kitchen, Madame showed me how the kitchen appliances worked and where the ingredients were in the pantry before making a cup of coffee for her husband. I bade her a good night and headed upstairs saying I would be ready to make breakfast by eight in the morning.

After a good night's sleep, I hoped to make a cup of coffee for myself, but I was surprised to see the Lamarks already sipping their morning coffee. I poured the leftover from the coffee jar and prepared a breakfast. However, Madame hinted that we were not going to have a big breakfast; it would consist only of some fried eggs on toast, served with some sausages she had got from Paris. Geraldine wanted cereal and bananas. I was so relieved that I began to work promptly on it. It was about ten o'clock when I finished cleaning the breakfast table, and Madame wanted me to go with her to the market to get some fresh fish for dinner before heading to the beach.

I was in the front seat of the small Renault, where madame drove herself. She wanted me to be comfortable and even introduced herself as Catherine. But I kept calling her Madame, as French customs would expect. She drove her town car and passed through Deauville to reach a commune called Trouville-sur-Mer, where fishmongers were selling fresh fish. Freshly caught cod and halibut were the specialities of the day, and we obtained a couple of kilos of both popular catches. Cleaned, skinned, and boned cod halves or fillets, as well as sliced stakes of halibut, seemed ideal for meeting the needs of a couple of dinners. At night, we decided to try the cod fillets first. In addition, from the street market, we picked a few vegetables, including asparagus and fresh herbs. On the way back,

Catherine briefed me on how to prepare *Cabillaud au beurre blanc*. Gently pan-fried cod fillets were topped with beurre blanc sauce. It was to be served with asparagus and boiled and buttered baby potatoes.

As we arrived home, Monsieur Lamark and Geraldine were eagerly waiting to go to the beach, and Catherine picked up some luncheon staff and got ready to join them, leaving me all by myself. She hinted that she would help me cook after returning home before half past eight. I thought I had plenty of time to relax and enjoy, but a thorough clean-up of the kitchen seemed necessary. I ended up spending two hours cleaning the kitchen as well as most of the appliances. When finished, I wanted to relax, but as I didn't have the habit of taking a nap during the day, I opted to check the garden. Using a quick baguette sandwich, I stepped out and sat on a bench in the garden. What a nice day it was as I gazed at a beautiful landscape in the shadow of an oak tree.

In the evening, my first day of work as a cook was not bad. With the help of Catherine, I managed to make a delicious beurre blanc sauce with butter, shallots, and peppercorns to go with thick stripes of gently fried cod fillets. The dinner was served at about ten after sunset. It was, after all, a wonderful first dinner with gently fried cod, braised asparagus, and boiled and sautéed baby potatoes. At the dinner table, while I received compliments from Monsieur Lamark, I said they should all go to Madame, who had made me a cook.

The next morning, Monsieur Lamark, who wanted me to call him Gerald, left for Paris. He travelled back and forth during the weekends until the summer break started in August. Catherine engaged herself with recreational activities or gardening most of the time, unless spending the time on the beach with Geraldine. Occasionally, the family visited their friends at dinner or at dinners hosted by the Lamark family. From time to time, I accompanied Catherine when she went grocery shopping. She would also call me to go with the family for certain events or when visiting tourist attractions around Normandy.

Every morning, as a habit, I would get up as early as seven, when all others were still in bed, to prepare breakfast, which consisted of the usual items, including eggs and sausages. At times, Catherine would ask me to make some crêpes, either with savoury or sweet sauces. She was not picky about breakfast. Geraldine loved crêpes made with chocolate sauce and sliced banana. Gerald preferred breakfast cereals instead of a heavy meal. After coffee and a croissant in the morning, I tended to skip breakfast, but I used to eat something between breakfast and lunch when I was alone. One of my favourites was potato salad made with freshly made mayonnaise blended with chopped scallion and cured anchovy. Nothing could be better than my potato salad with freshly baked baguettes. As for lunch, I was not responsible, and everyone looked after themselves.

During midweek, both Catherine and Geraldine spent a few days on the beach, and one day she took me to the village market, which was packed with hawkers and bustling with people. The market also had stalls selling day-to-day produce, as well as antiques. We shopped weekly for green groceries, meat, and poultry. I was keen to pick up some fresh herbs, such as parsley and rosemary. I could also find one of my favourite vegetables, fennel, although available only when in season. In the meantime, Catherine bought a variety of cheese, including the famous local Normandy cheeses: Camembert, Pont-l'Évêque, Livarot, and Neufchâtel. All four cheeses were AOC certified or held a protected designation of origin label, and their names stood for the villages from which they came. Although Neufchâtel was claimed to be the oldest cheese in Normandy, I loved the taste of Pont-l'Évêque. I thought this was better than Camembert. To complete the shopping list, we headed towards the fruit seller, where we could find seasonal berries and cherries.

On the way back, I was alerted to the roads and directions so that I could explore the area with a bicycle later on. In fact, the entire area was part of a commune called La Touques, where the famous Deauville Racecourse could be found. Tourgéville was not far from La Touques—just ten minutes by car. Madame even suggested that I should take a bicycle and explore the area when I found free time. When we got out of the car, Geraldine wanted to go somewhere with her mum, so I unloaded the stuff quickly. For dinner, Catherine hinted that we would make some steaks or entrecôte but did not elaborate. After they both left, I, with a handful of cherries, began to relax in the garden.

A week flew by much faster than expected, and on Friday evening Gerald returned from Paris, but with another visitor. Anna was from Ireland, and she was only nineteen years old. She came up as a nanny-cum-au pair. She was expected to mind Geraldine and help Catherine with some household chores. She was, like me, another summer worker, and a child minder who was expected to sleep in Geraldine's room. Gerald introduced me to Anna, and I didn't have any problem communicating with her, although her Irish accent was something new to me, and it took me a while to understand her. Anna spoke French much better than I did, and I found her pleasant and well-mannered.

Fortunately, I didn't have to prepare any meals for the night, as the family had been invited to dinner by one of Catherine's friends. I showed Anna what was available in the fridge, prepared a green salad, and ate some leftovers. With a good cup of coffee, we sat and had a long chat after dinner before heading to the bedrooms just before midnight. Anna was as naive as I when it came to French culture, and she wanted to improve her French language skills. She wanted to go to university when she returned to Ireland and wanted to study language and history. I didn't find anything in common with her except for her interest in travelling and other cultures. She wanted to know something about me, and I briefly explained what had brought me to Normandy. I said that I hoped to return to Rome in September. She was born and bred in a small town in the suburb of Dublin but had lived in England briefly when she was young, while her father was working in a factory in Manchester. She was not a foodie but knew how to cook a few Irish dishes.

It seemed that the Lamark family arrived home late at night, which meant that breakfast was missing the next morning. I saw Catherine take some cereal and milk upstairs with their coffee at eleven in the morning. I heard they were preparing to go to the beach, and this would include Monsieur as well as Anna, to be with Geraldine. I was also asked to join them if I wished. I nodded and said I would take the bicycle after making arrangements for the dinner. To make it easier and simpler, I suggested baking seafood pizzas for dinner, which Catherine agreed upon. While the family was leaving for the beach, I kneaded the flour with a bit of yeast and a spoonful of olive oil, and left it to rest at room temperature. Since we had only two large pizza trays, I divided the dough before covering it with cling film. I was also conscious of the available ingredients, such as canned tuna, squid, and prawns in the fridge. Before I headed to the beach, I spent some time making pizza sauce with canned crushed tomatoes and herbs, such as oregano, parsley, and thyme.

It was a fifteen-minute ride to the beach from home, and riding on the rural roads was much easier than expected. The roads were almost empty and were shadowed by trees flanking the edges. Even the bike was easy to pedal, as it had been maintained in good form by Gerald. I had a few Perrier bottles to quench my thirst, along with a banana and an apple in my bag. As a South Asian, I would not need to tan my skin but would need to protect it from radiation. Therefore, I had a sun cream tube in my bag. I didn't forget my sunglasses or my head cap. As I passed through the town and the Hippodrome de Clairefontaine, I saw Tourgéville Beach, which was situated in the south of Deauville Beach, where I could leave my bike and lie at rest on the sand at Sunset Beach. Fortunately, the sun's rays were not harsh on the day owing to hovering clouds, but rain was not in the forecast that day. I spent an hour reading a book on the beach and ventured to take a dip in the shallow waters a few yards from where I was. After some time, I pedalled along the beach towards Deauville to see whether I could spot the Lamark family, but later I realized that they were in a private beach area. The beach in Deauville is packed with parasols that sprout like mushrooms. Almost everyone there enjoyed the sunny weather, though some were lucky to be in the shadow of a parasol.

When I rode back home, it was about 7.30 p.m., and I had plenty of time to prepare for making dinner before everyone else headed home. I noticed that the pizza dough had risen well and everything else was ready and looked good. Therefore, a fresh and refreshing shower was my first priority; but for the time being, I sat on the bench and stretched myself out with a glass of chilled water in my hand to quench my thirst. For a while, I thought that my summer job in Normandy was nothing but a sort of summer holiday thanks to Zana. In fact, I missed Zana and

Julie. My brief but unforgettable experience with Fernanda popped up
in my mind.

After a long shower, I saw the Lamark family return, and everyone
rushed shower as well. The time was right for me to start preparing my
pizzas for baking. When I gathered all the ingredients for topping the
pizza base, I also found a bottle of marinated artichoke hearts and capers,
as well as some canned anchovies. I knew these would go very well with
squid, tuna, and prawns. My pizza sauce was slightly spicy and full of
flavours, but I had to add some tomato puree to make it consistent and
for texture. As Anna watched me, I prepared the dough to be laid on two
large baking trays. I wanted Anna to grate some Gruyère cheese and put
it on the pizza, over the toppings. As soon as I put them in the preheated
oven, I sat to prepare salad and vinaigrette sauce. Anna helped me lay
out the dinner table, and we were all set to go as soon as everybody was
ready for an authentic Sicilian dinner.

We sat at the table for dinner at ten thirty, and it all looked colourful, as described by Gerald and Catherine. As we sat to eat, Madame
asked whether I had been able go on the beach. When I said that I
had been looking for them everywhere, she apologized for not giving
me directions to the private beach that they had rented. In the end, it
went wonderfully, and Gerald made a comment about the pizza being a
masterpiece. Geraldine wanted me to bake the pizza every other night.
Gerald ate three slices, which surprised Catherine. Anna said that the
pizza was delicious and was one of the best pizzas she had eaten. I was
very delighted, and I thought I would most likely do pizza dinner again.
Dinner was completed by a variety of seasonal fruits on the table. As the
dust fell, the couple sat on their armchairs with glasses of their favourite
cognac, Rémy Martin, while I was tidying up the kitchen. I was craving
a cup of coffee, and I made one before I left the kitchen. Gerald was
to return to Paris in the morning, so I bade him goodnight and went
upstairs. Catherine reminded me of the need to prepare breakfast for
Gerald and suggested that an egg on toast with sausage would be fine.
It was almost midnight when I went asleep.

7

A WORKING HOLIDAY
IN NORMANDY

A few weeks had already passed since I came to Tourgéville, and I didn't realize how fast the time was passing. I wanted to speak to Zana, and Catherine said that she would ask him to call me whenever he happened to be at home, pressing clothes. In Tourgéville, I never felt as if I was doing a summer job. I felt as if I were a family member enjoying the time, whether I was making food or going out on leisure trips. I had the opportunity to visit several attractions across Normandy, including the beaches of the D-Day landings and the famous racetracks of Deauville. Most of the time, I went with Catherine and the family members. Normandy's reputation for horses, cattle and dairy farms, popular cheeses, beaches, and seafood cannot be underestimated. The most affluent Parisians had second homes in Normandy, particularly around Deauville. By fluke, I happened to be a long-staying tourist who was paid to spend time in Normandy. Since I enjoyed cooking and learning by doing it, my summer job could be labelled a summer holiday instead, as I was able to visit and gaze at several attractions that Normandy offered.

During the summer, the Lamark family hosted a few dinners, but they were all informal, as they should be during a holiday period. Nevertheless, the number of guests wouldn't exceed five or six, as Madame Lamark normally hosted only one family at a time. One summer evening, I was asked to cook a rice-based meal, and I suggested fried rice, a type of Chinese and Malaysian fusion. The fried rice would be accompanied by strips of sirloin beef sautéed with ginger and garlic, and a pinch of mustard, and then cooked slowly in bean sauce and hot chilli paste. When that was cooked, diced carrots, green peppers, and onions were added, along with soya sauce, and then all was simmered on a low-burning stove. The fried rice contained chopped omelettes made of onions and sliced mushrooms seasoned with spices. Diced spring onions or scallions were also added when the rice was blended with other ingredients, including small cooked prawns with a little butter and sesame seed oil. I also fried sausage cubes coated with satay sauce sprinkled with a dash of cayenne pepper to serve as a starter. Thick pan-fried slices of halved aubergine soaked in soya sauce and garlic were made as a side dish. We had just the Lamark family and the three guests—a couple and a teenaged daughter—sitting at the table. The dinner was to be served when the guests were ready to dine after an hour-long chat over a few glasses of wine. As soon as the host called the guests 'a-table', the food was served.

The hosts and guests seemed to have enjoyed the food, which was different from typical French cuisine. One of the guests commented that it was 'marvellous and something extraordinary'. Madame Lamark was pleased and called me '*Chef du la Maison Lamark*'. Our guests had brought with them a nice gateau, which I served them with a scoop of strawberry ice cream for dessert. Anna and I had some food afterwards while Catherine made coffee for the guests. It seemed like Gerald had a plan to return to Paris in the afternoon the next day, and I was convinced that the guests would stay chatting for much longer than expected. It was my first cooking event for invited guests, and I was sure that I would see a few more such events in the weeks to come. The next day, everyone got up late except me, but I didn't have to prepare breakfast. In the afternoon, after Gerald left to go to Paris, the rest went to town to meet a family friend over lunch. I was pleased that I could relax or do some gardening. These remained the usual activities we would perform as a ritual almost every day. Sometimes I would join them to go to the beach, or Catherine and I spent time doing some gardening. Occasionally, Catherine would take us to visit places of interest, including museums and gardens. Normandy, one of the largest provinces in France, offers a variety of attractions and several places of interest to visit. One of the nearby cities situated on the banks of the Honfleur Estuary remained popular among the French, as well as visitors from elsewhere.

One afternoon on a Saturday, Catherine suggested that we should visit Honfleur, and we all got packed up at once. Honfleur, essentially an estuary town, was the old harbour town to the north of Deauville, and we were able to reach it in less than an hour. It was a beautiful town with colourful sixteenth to eighteenth century townhouses on the banks of the Seine River where it joined the English Channel. It used to be popular among painters like Claude Monet and was the home of the native artist Eugene Boudin, which was inspired by the century-old townhouses found mainly in Vieux Bassin, or the old harbour. Looking at the picturesque streets with beautiful timber-frame houses of various colours could only make one fall in love with Honfleur. At Honfleur, we visited a few places of interest, including the maritime museum and fifteenth-century Sainte Catherine's Church, which boasted a vaulted timber structure. We also managed to get to the hilltop of Mont-Joli, where the Chapel of Notre-Dame-de-Grâce is situated. Honfleur is a city of historic significance.

At the end of the day, Madame Lamark could not resist tasting fresh oysters, for which this part of the country is famous. There were many restaurants and cafes in the old harbour area, and we stepped into one family-run eatery. At seven-thirty in the evening, it was almost the time for early dinner, and thus Madame opted for a quick and simple dinner with oysters as hors d'oeuvres. The menu for the day was a fillet of fresh sole caught in the English Channel. Gently pan-fried sole was served with blanc beurre, along with French beans and Jersey potatoes. When a plate of fresh half-shell oysters was brought with *Mignonette* sauce, I was very tempted to try them. Catherine was the first to try them, and she seemed very much pleased with the quality and taste. She explained to me that the tradition of sucking fresh oysters with mignonette sauce had remained for over a hundred years. I tried my luck at sucking fresh oysters, which was the first time I ever did so. It was okay, and I didn't have anything to complain about. Chilled Mignonette sauce made with freshly diced shallots and red wine vinegar seemed better than vinaigrette for fresh oysters.

It was a wonderful day out and a pleasant summer evening. Anna and I thanked Catherine for the trip to Honfleur, and it was a memorable experience for me. On the way back, I could see the entire area was well-lit and looked beautiful. We arrived home before ten o'clock, but the summer sun still refused to sink. For me, there was nothing I could do other than hit the bed after a good shower. In the meantime, I overheard Anna going to make a cup of coffee for Catherine. This was another day in another week, and the sojourn in Tourgéville passed faster than expected.

From time to time, as on the morning of the next day, Catherine would take Geraldine and Anna to the beach soon after breakfast and return home so she could spend time in the garden. I was, in fact, a great help to Catherine in this regard by working in the garden to clear weeds and prepare beds for planting. I even helped her mow the lawn every other week. Cooking dinners often remained simple, especially when there were no guests or when Gerald was away in Paris. However, in August, Monsieur would remain home throughout. It was in late July while tending the garden one afternoon that Catherine hinted we all should go to see a horse racing event at the Clairefontaine racetrack. I later learned that she had received four complimentary tickets for a forthcoming Wednesday event. When I showed my interest, Catherine also said that she would ask Monsieur Lamark to take all of us one day in August to see the world-famous Deauville racetrack at La Touques.

As we kept chatting while picking the tomatoes and courgettes from the garden, I said that we should find a recipe to cook these vegetables. She immediately came up with the idea of creating a traditional French stew called ratatouille. She said that we had all the necessary ingredients, including aubergine and red and yellow capsicum, to go with the courgettes and tomatoes. This classic French recipe from Provence consists of these vegetables and is cooked with garlic, basil, thyme, and red wine vinegar. I cooked ratatouille for dinner and served rice pilaf and lamb roasts. The ratatouille was delicious, and it was a wonderful dinner, as noted by Catherine and Anna.

On Wednesday, as planned, we all went to the racetrack, which was only a couple of kilometres away. It was a beautifully maintained racetrack but was smaller than the main course at La Touques. It was affectionately called the 'little Clairefontaine' when it was officially opened in 1928. Later, in the late 1930s, the course was expanded and hosted all three types of races, including hurdles and trots, along with flat racing. On the day we visited, it was an occasion for steeplechase. All races on weekdays started slightly late, but we were there on time for the first race on the card.

My experience of visiting and betting at the racetrack in Paris with Zana helped me greatly in figuring out what was going on and how we could bet on the horses. It seemed like Madame wanted to entertain herself and enjoy having a day out during an event like this. I realized how entertaining it could be for the entire family when we visited an event like a horse race. I felt there were quite a few families from Paris who were holidaying in Deauville during summer. For them, a visit to the racetrack remained a not-to-be-missed item on their holiday calendar during their sojourn. I could see that Catherine was mingling with several other like-minded visitors or punters. Even Geraldine had a nice time with children of the same age group. Interestingly, nobody seemed bothered by losing money, but winning a bet, of course, made a lot of difference. As for betting, I did not have any luck picking the winning horse, and neither did Catherine nor Anna. However, I heard that Geraldine was able to pick a horse which came third. There were plenty of good vibes and cheers, as well as food and drinks. I was with Anna, trying to pick the winning horse, but both of us were clueless about the pedigrees of the horses and the skill levels of the trainers and jockeys. We simply looked at the published odds when placing the bets on the board. In the afternoon, we watched five or six races and stayed until the last hour, when the winning horses were paraded with their riders and trainers before the prizes were given. I am not able to remember the names of the prizes and races, or the names of the winning horses or riders. Overall, this is a memorable experience. When we returned home, it was six-thirty in the evening. I understood that I had to prepare something for dinners. A quick and simple menu of hamburgers and chips came to mind. When I suggested this to Catherine, she nodded, saying 'Super.'

At night, as usual, I bade a good night and headed upstairs. It was a relief when Catherine said that she wanted to go to Paris on Friday with a friend and that she would return with her husband on Saturday. Even Geraldine was expected to travel with her. Also, she had been invited to a party the following night, so I thought I could go easy on dinner. In any case, they planned to go to the beach early in the morning. As Catherine had to go to a party, they were expected to return home in the early evening. This is exactly what happened. On the way, they even picked up takeaway food, which made my life much easier by not necessitating my spending time in the kitchen. As dusk fell, at about eight thirty, a friend of Catherine picked up her to go to the party. She was aptly dressed up and looked gorgeous, although she had turned forty just a few years prior. In any case, I knew I had to wait awake until she returned home late at night.

Meanwhile, Geraldine and Anna were busy eating their take-home meals while I went upstairs to press my clothes and tidy up my room. Within a couple of hours, I was just by myself and rushed through my dinner, hoping to sit and watch TV. There was not much programming in those days, with only a few channels, but I just wanted to see whether I could improve my French by watching TV shows. I sometimes enjoyed watching French TV. Suddenly I heard the sound of the car arriving at the gate, and I stood up to see that Catherine had arrived. Her friends had dropped off and driven away. As I opened the door for her, she almost tripped over the steps, and I had to hold her and lead her gently. Catherine was in a pleasant mood although tipsy, but she was very much conscious of what she was doing.

She thanked me and asked me to sit on a chair while sitting on the sofa. She told me that she had gone to the birthday party of a friend and started talking about her fortieth birthday a few years ago when she hosted a party in Paris. As she put her legs on the coffee table with her gown half-open, I felt that my heartbeat was fast. Even in her forties, she was attractive and had a wonderful figure. The summer temperature, even at midnight, was unbearable, and she was almost ready to strip off her clothes, causing my bodily temperature to rise because of the not-so-decent exposure of her curvature. In fact, she was unashamedly revealing her body, and I thought it was an invitation to respond. It was quite tempting, but I was confused by some unexpected scenes that had unfolded at night. I had sometimes seen her flirting with other men, such as the plumber who visited the house once, and occasionally with me, but always with mixed signals. This made it difficult for me to understand her true personality. In any case, I was very conscious of what I was doing and did not feel it was right for me to respond to her advances.

I made a cup of coffee for her, which I thought would make her feel better. In fact, she felt good and started chatting with me. She wanted me to stay in Paris with them and said that Monsieur Lamark had promised to sponsor me and get my residence permit, and as the head of a prefecture outside Paris, he seemed very powerful and influential. In fact, all immigration matters in France were handled by the regional prefecture rather than by the central government. But when I said that I really intended to go back to Rome to continue my higher education, she responded by saying sarcastically, 'Oh, you want to become a Harvard professor.' Her offer was sincere, but I could not consider doing a housekeeping job in Paris instead of pursuing my higher studies, which had prompted me to take the risk of travelling to Europe. I tried to explain my side of the story, but she treated me as an economic migrant. I didn't blame her, as thousands flocked to Europe every year to seek economic opportunities. After chatting, she felt that she wanted to go to bed, and I bade her goodnight.

In the morning, we all woke up late, and I had some omelettes for breakfast. Catherine was to leave for Paris in the late afternoon and would return on Saturday evening with Monsieur Lamark. In the evening, Anna and I wanted to ride through the countryside, and I made sure that the bikes were in good condition. Later, we spent some time in the garden after Catherine and Geraldine bade us au revoir. The air was rather humid, and an hour of garden work made us tired. We decided to take a break with an ice-cold drink on a garden bench. I wanted to know more about Ireland, and Anna managed to explain rural versus urban life in Ireland, as she'd had the experience of living in both types of places. Being a Catholic country, Ireland seemed very conservative as well as orthodox in rural areas. I said to her that life in South Asia was not much different from that in Ireland in many ways.

We had a leisurely bike ride in the evening, and how nice it was to pedal through the countryside under the shadow of oak and chestnut trees covering the road. We rode between ten and fifteen kilometres. The next morning, Anna wanted to go biking again after breakfast. We went to a town called Pont l'Évêque, where famous cheeses of the same name were produced. We visited a dairy farm and watched the cheese being produced. We were even given the opportunity to taste the cheese, and I thought it was much better than the famous Camembert cheese. In the afternoon, I spent time in the garden while Anna had a nap. I was eager to wait for Catherine to arrive with her husband and daughter before deciding on a dinner menu. Anna and I waited until ten in the night, but they didn't show up, and we decided to have something to eat from whatever leftovers we had. By eleven o'clock, Monsieur's car had pulled in, but they had already been to a restaurant on their way, as I heard.

The next morning was a bit busy for me, as I had to prepare breakfast to feed the entire family, including Anna. Catherine had brought some fresh baguettes as well as sausages and pastrami from Paris. I also cooked Spanish omelettes. Soon after breakfast, Catherine rushed to make luncheon items using the stuff she had brought so that the family could head to the beach. Even though I had the call to join them, I stayed home, as Catherine said that Zana could call me, as he would be doing some chores at home. I was told that dinner needed to be something special, as the family was left for the beach. Although it was too early to think about dinner, it was in my mind until I decided what to cook. In the end, my final choice was the scallop of the veal, French style, or *Escalopes de veau à la crème*, served with buttered French beans and creamy mashed potatoes.

In the afternoon, I made jams with freshly picked strawberries from the garden, which Catherine loved to find in the pantry. Unlike the berries we bought from the market, these berries were sweet and delicious. The jam would go nicely with crêpes over a little spread butter. I managed to make two medium-sized jars. My next item on the agenda was to prepare the ingredients for the dinner menu. I started with the preparation of green beans and potatoes soon after eating my lunch, which Catherine left for me from her luncheon box. I also had to thaw the meat and pound veal cutlets to make them thin. The late afternoon was the right time to begin doing so. Suddenly, the phone was ringing, and I picked up to find Zana calling me. It was great to hear him after a long while. I did miss him and Julie, not to mention Fernanda, who had asked Julie about me several times. I reminded Zana about the letter that I expected from Rome, which he promised to send me at once.

The Lamark family and Anna arrived home late, almost at eight-thirty. The veal cutlets were nicely thawed and ready to be pounded flat. This delicate dish, although perfect for invited guests, was simple-to-cook food. Originating in Northern Italy but popularized by Austria as Wiener schnitzel, it could be cooked with two different recipes. The Italian-Austrian recipe used pounded meat dusted with flour and lightly covered with egg batter to be pan-fried and cooked with lemon sauce. The French version was innovative in that the pounded veal cutlets were pan-fried in butter and blended with fresh cream and sautéed sliced Parisian mushrooms. Within an hour, everyone was down at the dining table, and the dinner was served as expected. It was indeed a special dinner, as Catherine hinted. What a happy family and a happy chef; everyone seemed delighted. Anna helped me clean up the table and kitchen, and we were all set to relax with coffee until midnight. We gathered in the reception hall and watched the television until all slipped away one by one. I badly needed a wash before hitting my bed. I knew that the Lamark family had planned to spend time at the beach during the entire week, and thus an early breakfast would be expected.

From time to time, I would join the family to go to the beach, and I should say that the private beach area the Lamark family had rented was very well kept, and there were a few other families sharing the compound with them. It came with beach chairs and parasols, as well as toilet and shower facilities. The beach was also watched by lifeguards. I was not fond of the sun, and on a typical beach day, I stayed under the parasol most of the time. Deauville being a safe beach, I did try to go for dips a few times. Lamark family and Anna seemed to enjoy the sun very much, and they had to protect their skin with sun cream throughout the day when on the beach. While on the beach one day, Geraldine queried about a visit to Deauville Racecourse, and I remembered Catherine saying that she would ask Gerald to take all of us one day. When he heard this, Gerald seemed to smile for a while and promised us a visit.

8

COMPLIMENTS TO THE CHEF

Over breakfast on a Friday, I was pleased to hear about our forthcoming visit to a famous racecourse in the afternoon. l'Hippodrome Deauville-La Touques, or the Deauville Racecourse, was the best and most popular racetrack for thoroughbred horse racing from the time of its founding in the 1860s, when it was simply called the Hippodrome de la Touques. The name stands refers to the River Touques. The Duke of Morny, Charles Auguste Louis Joseph, the half-brother of Napoleon, is said to have constructed this racecourse. From early on, Deauville Racecourse hosted some famous races, including those of Maurice de Gheest, Rothchild, Jacques Le Marois, Morny, and Jean Romanet. All of these races are prestigious Group One events. One of the Group Three races was the Grand Prix de Deauville, which ended the summer season. Deauville Racetrack had a reputation for hosting races throughout the year with hectic summer events. It should be noted that the Calvados region of Normandy in general and the Deauville countryside in particular were considered the key horse breeding areas in France, with several stud farms around. Deauville-La Touques was also a famous horse training centre in France.

Finally, we visited the racetrack on Sunday in August, and I should say that it was the most memorable experience of my sojourn in Deauville.

To the best of my knowledge, this is one of the best racecourses in the world. Gerald explained that it was rather difficult to get tickets for popular summer events during July and August, particularly on Saturdays and Sundays. Since we went on Sunday, it was fully packed and not suitable for families with children. However, we were lucky, and it was a great day, as everyone flocked to see the Grand Prix de Deauville. Thanks to Gerald, we had the best view of the course and were close to the winners' enclosure, where we could closely see the winning jockeys as well as the parading horses.

I hardly remember the races, except a few, but I was in a celebratory mood. There were many international visitors to the course, with English visitors outnumbering everyone else from outside France. I helped Catherine choose a winning horse, as she wanted to spot the lucky one based on instinct rather than rational judgement. When the Grand Prix de Deauville took place, there were many cheers and rapturous noises. As the leading horse approached the winning post, there was a huge uproar when the famous English jockey Lester Piggott lost his whip and grabbed one from a fellow jockey. Although he managed to get second place after First Prayer, ridden by Maurice Philipperon, won the race, Lester got twenty-day ban from racing for that steal. I made a bet on First Prayer and won money for my five-franc stake. So did Madame Lamark. I reckoned that she made a bet of fifty francs.

Apart from betting, winning, and sheer entertainment, I learned something new about how this wonderful creature called a horse ran and how much the rider could influence its running speed to reach a gallop. Anna knew much about racing horses and how they were trained. As an Irish girl, she had worked on a stud farm as a teenager. I began to understand that the canter and gallop were two gaits of a running horse, where gallop was the fastest gait, averaging approximately 25 miles an hour. The canter was supposed to be the normal running speed of a horse, and when moving from the canter to gallop, the rider would spur the horse to lengthen its stride. A wider stride meant faster running, and the horse was to lift off all four legs into a state of suspension, which a novice could hardly notice. Anna tried to show me this during one of the races. After that, my eyes were glued to the fastest horse until the last scheduled race ended. We stayed at the racecourse until the end, and we were able to see the winning horses and riders close to where we stood. The experience at Deauville-La Touques was unforgettable. I would like to thank Gerald and Catherine for giving me this opportunity to visit the famous racetrack. While returning home, Catherine and I stopped at a takeaway restaurant to pick up some dinner, while Geraldine and Anna headed home with Gerald. We bought roasted chicken and chips, as well as some quiche Lorraine for dinner. We were not really hungry, as we'd all had some baguette sandwiches for lunch in the racetrack food court. In addition, there was plenty of snacking between the races.

The next morning, everyone went to the beach as usual, but I decided to stay home. Catherine wanted to show me how to cook one of the French country dishes called boeuf bourguignon, or Burgundy-style beef, for dinner, and she promised to return home early. I thought I could start the preparation in the afternoon, as the beef needed to be thawed and cut. The first step involved marinating stew-cut beef with chopped carrots and celery, along with button mushroom halves, garlic and onion, mustard, bay leaf, cloves, and black pepper, as well as a copious amount of red wine. The marinated beef was cooked slowly in a covered casserole pot or baked in an oven and could be served with mashed potatoes.

Later in the day, I spent a few hours doing some gardening and took a shower, followed by household chores. I made a baguette sandwich with canned tuna and mayonnaise to eat with a salad before preparing thawed beef for the dish. When Catherine arrived home at about six, I worked on other ingredients, such as the carrots, celery, and mushrooms. It was after seven when Catherine put on her apron and joined me in the kitchen. She was delighted to see the prepared beef and told me that she would cook it in a casserole dish first, before placing it in the hot oven. When all the vegetables were sautéed and cooked lightly, the beef was added, and it continued to be cooked over low heat, covered. When the food was almost cooked, we transferred the pot to the oven and allowed it to simmer to ensure that the beef was well-cooked and soft to touch. In the meantime, I prepared mashed potatoes, while Catherine made a delicious vinaigrette sauce. The French would always want freshly made vinaigrette. Suddenly I heard that the rest of the family had arrived from the beach and should be ready for dinner within the next thirty minutes. In fact, the dinner was served at nine, early in the evening. Believe it or not, the boeuf bourguignon was a big hit. It was as authentic as it could be, as noted by Gerald, who was originally from Burgundy Province. This was a compliment to the chef, but I said that credit should go to Madame Lamark. At the end of the day, I understood that Gerald loved this dish and that it was one of his favourites.

The week was to continue with the usual ritual of breakfast, beach, and dinner, and the occasional hosting of guests or eating out. Towards the end of the week, Gerald and Catherine left for Paris on a brief visit, leaving me and Anna in Tourgéville. I was told that they expected a couple as dinner guests on Saturday nights, and Catherine hinted that something with fish would be ideal. Since she left me to choose the menu, I said, 'Please buy some Nordic salmon,' while bidding them au revoir. It was midafternoon when Anna and I grabbed some leftovers from the fridge to eat. While heating up food, Anna asked me whether I would be interested in visiting a nearby stud farm. I wondered what would be there to see the other than horses being bred and trained. She told me that she could teach me how to ride horseback. I thought that was not a bad idea.

We both got onto the bicycles and went to the stud farm located near Deauville Racecourse in Touques. It was one of the oldest thoroughbred stud farms, Haras de Meautry, founded in 1875 by two Rothschild brothers. It was still owned by the Rothschild family. As we entered the farm, I realized that it was huge, with a large stable yard and a century-old building inviting guests as a great place of entertainment for the entire family. From the turn of the century, Haras de Meautry has remained one of the main thoroughbred nurseries on the Continent. Meautry had bred and trained some of the most popular and leading mares and stallions in France.

It was quite entertaining, and I found it a great learning experience to observe how horses were bred and trained. Anna, being an apprentice in this field, took me around and showed me how these wonderful animals were trained. There were families with children having fun, and some of them learned to ride horseback. Anna did hire a horse and started to ride; she wanted to teach me how to ride horseback. When I said no, she went on to do a show jump. I wondered whether two could ride horseback together, but we were not allowed, for safety reasons. Anna told me that the weight of two adults was too much for the horse. Haras de Meautry, being a touristic place, provided all the necessary amenities for visitors, including food and drink stalls. We spent hours at Haras de Meautry until they closed in the evening.

On the way back, we picked up takeaway food from Touques. As we reached home, it looked like it was going to rain. It would have been wonderful if it had rained, but it was just a passing cloud. In the meantime, I badly needed a shower and ran to the bathroom, as did Anna. After a while, we had our dinner in the living room and started watching the TV. Anna made some coffee after a quick serving of ice cream. We watched a 1968 film in English with French subtitles—Stanley Kubrick's *2001: A Space Odyssey*. The film was inspired by the works of the science-fiction writer Arthur C Clarke. I don't reckon we understood the story that time, but it was rather absorbing, with beautiful music and sound. I appreciated it more a few years after reading the script written by Arthur C. Clarke. After a while, we went to sleep, and it was a peaceful night.

The next morning, I wanted to make it different from our usual breakfast, so I suggested to Anna that we should go out for breakfast. She agreed, and we rode to Touques, where we found a cafe that served crêpes for breakfast. They had both savoury and sweet crêpes to order, but I wanted to try something savoury, while Anna wanted something with chocolate sauce. Ultimately, we both ended up eating both varieties one after the other. The crêpes were delicious and crispy. The breakfast was made complete with a good mug of milk coffee. Having accomplished what we wanted to do, we wondered what we should do next. It was too early to return home, and so we explored the countryside until the early afternoon. When we returned by midafternoon, the Lamark family was already home, and I saw Catherine had bought me a large salmon to cook for dinner.

In the late afternoon, I started skinning the fish and preparing it for cooking. The menu was my own but was essentially a fish baked *al-Americana*—southern baked salmon. The whole footlong salmon was baked with potatoes, carrots, parsnip, and halved whole onions around herbs such as rosemary, sage, and thyme, to be topped with cream of mushroom. Catherine was not even bothered to find out how I was going to cook the fish, and that, in fact, remained a surprise until the dinner was served. However, she did tell me that the guest couple would arrive at eight and the dinner was expected to be served at half past nine. Madame would prepare the starters with some new stuff she had brought from Paris, which was a great relief.

I was told that the guests were close friends of the Lamark family and that they lived not far from Rue de la Pompe in Paris. The couple, like the Lamark family, spent their summers in Tourgéville most of the time. They had already heard of me ahead of their visit, and there were some expectations. Catherine had bought a blueberry cake from her local patisserie in Paris. And, of course, the southern baked salmon would be a surprise. At half past seven, Catherine came down to prepare the starters and the hors d'oeuvres table while I was still attending to little things in the kitchen. She had a variety of cold foods, including processed meats and marinated vegetables, such as artichokes and sun-dried tomatoes. I was able to sample a few of them and loved them. In the meantime, I assured Catherine that the food would be ready on time. Gerald joined us later in the kitchen, and he was curious to find out what I was cooking for dinner. However, Catherine jumped in and said, 'A surprise, and in a couple of hours you will know.'

At about eight, when the guests arrived, they were soon rushed to the kitchen to be introduced to the chef. They spoke English well, and I didn't find it difficult to communicate. They were a polite and humble middle-aged couple with a sense of pride in being French who had lived in Africa and the Middle East. The couple was fluent in Arabic and wanted to know whether I spoke Arabic, as they knew that I had worked in Saudi Arabia. I said that I hadn't had any reason or opportunity to speak Arabic, as everyone in my work environment spoke English. Using a few common words and limited vocabulary, I had managed shopping when visiting outside Aramco. They were pleased chatting with me and appreciative of what I was making for dinner.

The guests and hosts all enjoyed wonderful evening nibbling on the hors d'oeuvres and chatting while I was preparing to serve the dinner. At half past nine, I prepared a dinner table, and Anna was very helpful in serving the food. Overall, it was a wonderful evening, and the guests seemed very impressed by the skill with which I had cooked the dish of baked salmon. I told them that it was based on a recipe from the American South but refined by my own ideas. After the guests left, Madame and Monsieur patted me on the back and thanked for the great meal. It was almost midnight by then, and everyone slowly slipped to their bedrooms.

The next morning was near to the end of August, and thus the end of long holiday season. Gerald would be leaving for Paris in a couple days, but Catherine wanted me to stay with her until the next Sunday. I stayed in Tourgéville until Sunday, but Anna wanted to leave with Gerald, as she was about to leave for Ireland the early next week. I was still waiting to hear from Rome about the confirmation of the job offer with a tuition waiver from the American College of Rome. In the meantime, everyone wanted to head to the beach during the final week in Normandy. Soon after breakfast, all went to the beach and joined the family. In fact, the beach remained the highlight of this final week, and I didn't cook much during the week. The following afternoon, Gerald and Anna left for Paris, but Gerald would return on Saturday to accompany us on Sunday. We went to the beach every day soon after breakfast, and on most of the nights, Madame had takeaway food picked up from Deauville, except for one evening when we went dining out.

On Saturday, Gerald returned, as expected, and we had all packed and were ready to say farewell to Normandy. We all woke up late on Sunday morning. I prepared a sort of brunch with baguette sand-wiches using leftover pastrami and sausages. At the breakfast table, I was surprised by Gerald, who had for me a letter from the dean of the American College of Rome. Even before opening the envelope, I knew that it was the confirmation letter that I had been waiting for. What wonderful news it was. I had to be in Rome before enrolment began in the last week of September. I had just three weeks to prepare. When I conveyed the message to Catherine, she simply said, 'Good luck.' In the early afternoon, we all left for Paris, and I bade my final au revoir to Tourgéville. Thanks to Zana, this was a wonderful summer.

9

LA VIE PARISIENNE

Zana already knew that I was to return this week on Sunday, as Gerald had already informed him. It was six in the evening when we arrived in Paris, and to my surprise, Zana and Julie were eagerly waiting to welcome me at doorstep. They might have been waiting for some time. As the car pulled in and the concierge opened the door, I saw Zana and Julie's delightful smiles. I got out of the car to greet them with a huge hug and kisses on the cheeks, as the Parisians do. We all helped the Lamarks unload the luggage so that the car could be moved to the parking area. Catherine called me to say that we could see each other the following day after lunch. I knew that she wanted to settle my payments.

Back on the upper floor, we sat and chatted for hours while Julie kept filling my coffee cup as I drank. I had to tell them of every bit of my experience in Tourgéville. Julie wanted to know about the nature of my job, the recipes I had cooked, and the activities I had done during my leisure time, as well as my friendship with Anna. Strangely enough, neither Zana nor Julie had ever visited Deauville before. This meant that I had to describe them the resort town and its environment, as well as the geographical features of Normandy. Zana had heard of Deauville as a famous racetrack, as he from time to time used to frequent the betting shop in Paris.

Julie was particularly interested in hearing about Anna. She was curious to find out whether I'd had any relationship with Anna, as Fernanda had asked. I had to explain about Anna and her personality in detail and assured Julie that I had never fancied Anna but that she had been good company. I then queried Julie about Fernanda and said that I wanted to see her if she was available tonight or tomorrow. 'She would be delighted to see you tomorrow evening,' Julie said. Later, I came to know that Zana and Julie had already made arrangements to meet Fernanda, as she was anxiously waiting for this encounter. Fortunately, this being the week before everything returned to normality after the summer holidays, everyone seemed to be free.

In the conversation, the major issue was my decision to leave Paris to go to Italy. This was something which Zana and Julie already knew of. I had already told Zana that I didn't desire to stay in France but wished to pursue my studies in Rome. I showed them the confirmation letter, which said the enrolment date was Monday, the twenty-fourth of September. This meant that I would need to be in Rome a few days earlier. Zana thought I was mad, and I was sure that he would try to do whatever he could to jeopardize my plan. This, therefore, warranted a meaningful one-to-one conversation with Zana. In the meantime, Zana wanted to go out for a quick meal and just walk. After a quick shower at about eight, we three walked up to Champs-Élysées and leisurely wandered around the busy alleyways while holding a shawarma and can of cola in hand. As we walked around, we managed to kill time quickly, and when it was almost approaching eleven o'clock, we began to walk back home. In fact, we were in bed before midnight, and nothing was planned for the morning. I did remember, however, that I had to meet Catherine after lunch, meaning at two or three o'clock.

After an unusually long sleep, I got up at midday, while Zana and Julie were still sleeping. As I made coffee, they both woke up and joined the table. While sipping coffee, I wondered what attracted economic migrants to Paris from all over the world. Was it money or being in Paris? Julie said it was a sense of freedom as well as reasonable earnings, not to mention the glamour of being in Paris. When I asked whether she would return to Portugal, she wouldn't say anything. Zana had an idea to start doing his own business with his brother's help, but nothing seemed to have materialized as of now. Would they ever tie the knot as a husband or wife? There was no definite answer to this question. I thought I at least had a solid plan to pursue. In between conversation, Julie did manage to prepare some eggs to go with a baguette for breakfast or brunch. Meanwhile, Zana started to think deeply and mentioned that he wanted to go back as soon as he got permanent residence status in France. I told him that I wanted to have a confidential conversation with him soon after our afternoon meeting with Madame Lamark.

At two-thirty in the afternoon, Zana and I saw the Lamarks leaving Julie behind in the room. Catherine was very appreciative and expressed her sincere gratitude, saying how wonderful the overall summer experience had been. She expressed anger at my not having accepting her offer to stay in Paris, but she was considerate of my desire to pursue higher education and wished me good luck. She then handed me an envelope containing the reward for my travail. She also proffered a note from Monsieur Lamark thanking me for all my good work. Catherine reminded me that the door was open if I decided to come back to Paris. Finally, I thanked her for the great opportunity offered to me and the wonderful summer job. It was a bit emotional and sad, and I left with a big Parisian kiss on the cheeks.

Outside the house, I peeped into the envelope to see how much I had earned from my summer job. It was a huge sum of 5,000 francs, which amounted to 800 US dollars in September 1979. I offered Zana 1000 francs, but he refused to take it. He had been a very good friend; without him, I wouldn't have come to Paris. We seemed to be in the same age group, and we had been friends from the post-high-school days.

As we both walked along the avenue towards the Arc de Triomphe, I explained to him about my ambition and the whole purpose of me coming to Europe. I explained to him the trouble I went through to gain this opportunity, which was not the end itself, but the beginning. I said that I would love to stay in Paris with him so that we could pursue some business interests together, but my mind was in Rome. I said he had my full support if or when he decided to pursue his ambition. I said that Rome and Paris were not far away, and I promised to visit Paris as soon as I settled there. In the end, this made him open his mind and began to think differently. I reminded him that at twenty-six, we were not teenagers but grown-up men. I made a remark saying that Julie was a good fit if he wanted to make a life together with her.

Suddenly, I saw a Cafe and I wanted to have a cup of tea with milk, English style, as it had been a long time since I had tasted tea. Zana suggested that Julie be asked to make tea. As we walked back to the room, we picked up some fresh croissants and *pain au chocolate*, along with a baguette from the baker. Julie was anxiously waiting for our return, as our journey had taken over two hours. As we relaxed, Julie was kind enough to brew tea for us, and we all enjoyed our evening tea. I was very refreshed after such a long time. However, Julie suddenly interrupted this break by questioning us as to where we had been all this time. We had to lie, saying that we spent an hour with Madame Lamark and then went to buy croissants and baguettes, which ended up in a long walk. Julie never thought that I was serious about my ambition and would leave for Rome soon. It seems that she and Fernanda had other plans in their minds.

As we continued to chat about life in general and debate about what the future held, Julie interrupted, reminding us that we had to meet Fernanda that evening at Les Halle. When asked what time we had to leave, she said seven. This would enable us to meet her before eight and have some quick dinner before checking out a discotheque. Zana and I wrapped up our conversation and rushed to get ready, as it was already past six. In about ten to fifteen minutes, we were ready to leave and proceeded to the Metro station. When we reached Les Halle, Fernanda was waiting for us. My attention turned to her immediately, and we embraced each other with the usual kisses and hugs. We even forgot who was around, but we suddenly heard a murmur coming from behind. It was, of course, Julie, protesting that we were ignoring them. It seemed a bit of an emotional episode, but soon we were back on track with the others. The first item on the agenda remained dinner, and Julie and Fernanda invited us for a special dinner at a Portuguese restaurant.

The restaurant reminded me of the family-run operations in Rome that I'd had the opportunity to dine at during my first week in Italy. This cosy little place had a few empty tables, and we managed to fit comfortably. Julie spoke with the waiter in Portuguese and decided to sample some fresh charcoal-grilled sardines as a starter. Seafood is a popular food in Portuguese cuisine; sardines in the summer and codfish in general are considered staples. As for the main dish, we had a few choices, such as the most popular, *Bacalhau à Brás*, a dish made of salted and dried codfish, hot Piri-Piri roast chicken, or a roasted octopus dish called *Polvo à la lagareiro*. Julie and I ordered Bacalhau à Brás, and Zana wanted Piri-Piri chicken, while Fernanda preferred the Polvo à la lagareiro.

The starter meal was served with salad and fresh Portuguese bread, and I enjoyed the fresh sardine, which was gently grilled with copious amounts of Portuguese olive oil. The fragrance and flavour of char-grilled sardines marinated in olive oil was extraordinary. As for my main dish, I had shredded dried cod scrambled with fried potato strings, onions, and eggs topped with chopped black olives and parsley. I thought it was slightly salty. Desalting dried fish remains an important part of Bacalhau cooking. Julie didn't have anything to complain about. Zana enjoyed his red-hot Piri-Piri chicken, which was served with chips and a salad. In Portuguese, 'Piri-Piri' refers to the small bird's eye chilli from Africa. Meanwhile, Fernanda seemed to have enjoyed the octopus enormously. I tried a small piece of the meat, which had been roasted and baked with potatoes, and it was full of flavour, with a distinct taste of olive oil. Overall, it had been a wonderful evening with good company and a delicious meal. Now, it was time for entertainment.

Popping out of the restaurant was a big relief, as it was stuffy and cramped inside the premises. Both couples held hands, and we walked leisurely to the disco, a Latin American nightclub. Being a weekday, there was not much of a crowd even at nine-thirty. That was a bit of a relief for me and sort of comforted me, as I didn't like cramped spaces. In addition, luckily, the music was not as loud as it would be to cater to the Latin American, particularly Brazilian and Mexican dances such as samba, salsa, mambo, cha-cha-cha, *kalimba*, and *karimbo*. All of these dances were rather sensual and tried to express sexuality in some form or another. On the dance floor, Fernanda was clinging to me with incessant bursts of kisses while moving to the rhythm of the music. Most of the dances were easy to learn if one had a trained dance partner, and Fernanda was one such partner. Honestly speaking, I was an amateur who was experiencing most of this sort of dancing for the first time. I should say that I got carried away with Karimbo, a Brazilian erotic dance performed by a couple holding each other closely while gyrating their hips in synchronized movements.

Standing away from the dance floor, while holding Fernanda's hand closely, I was watching a young couple dancing the Argentinian tango. What a beautiful and sensual dance. I thought that one day, I would learn to dance the tango. In the meantime, Julie and Zana seemed to enjoy it very much and kept on dancing without a break. It was almost midnight when we thought of heading home while the Metro was still in operation. Zana suggested that we have coffee and a croissant before reaching home. This was welcomed, and we stopped at a midnight cafe on our way home. At home, we didn't waste time but headed to bed immediately.

In the bed, Fernanda seemed impatient and aroused with energy, triggering sexual foreplay, while Julie and Zana were attending to their own business. At twenty-seven, one cannot blame her for being impatient with a male sexual partner. I had heard before that she'd had a boyfriend in Brazil a couple of years ago, and she was no longer a virgin or amateur. As a certified care worker, Fernanda had come to Paris to learn French and find work there. I remembered her saying that she flirted with a French guy briefly but nothing materialized, as she didn't like his attitude towards foreigners and his sheer arrogance. In her late twenties, she had been discovering herself, and a lasting relationship with the right man mattered to her. I could sense her feeling of love towards me, which I did not want to reciprocate, as I had a mission to accomplish. Nevertheless, this was something to consider on another day. At the moment, expectations were different, and the animal instinct dominated as we two individuals seemed to be drawn together by passion and love.

The next morning, I had a vivid memory of what I had experienced overnight, and I pondered what I should say to Fernanda when I bade her goodbye next week. Since she was off work for the entire week, I had enough time to have an in-depth discussion with her while relaxing on a bench in a park ahead of the weekend. In the morning, although we all managed to get up before eleven and complete the morning rituals, including breakfast, we did not have any plans for the day. Suddenly, one thing came to my mind: I needed to book an overnight train to Rome very soon. I understood that I needed to do this discreetly with the help of Zana but without the knowledge of Julie and Fernanda. Normally, we had to go to the Gare de Lyon station in southern Paris to book a ticket. I had already explained everything to Zana earlier and warned him not to rebel against my plan to leave Paris. Ideally, I could book my trip for Saturday afternoon when Zana returned from work. Julie and Fernanda were to resume working on Saturday and thus wouldn't be free to see us until the following Thursday or Friday.

As Zana wondered what we could do during the day, I suggested a visit to the Palace of Versailles, which lies about ten miles away from Paris, to the west. Fernanda liked the idea very much, as did Julie and Zana. We had to take a train ride for nearly an hour to reach Versailles, so we had to hurry up and prepare something to eat—sort of a picnic lunch to eat while at Versailles. Since Zana had already been to the palace once before, he knew how to get there, and the easiest route for us was to go from Gare St Lazar in the north of Paris. It was a hot and humid day, but in the evening, when we returned, it was expected to be chilly and pleasant. I was therefore warned by Zana to take a light jumper with me. Parisian evenings in September are normally considered colder than the average summer temperatures.

We managed to get to Gare St Lazar by half past twelve to catch the one o'clock train, and we boarded the train on time. I knew half a day would not be enough to see the Palace of Versailles, but it would be at least enough for a tourist gaze. The train cruised through a beautiful

French countryside, and from time to time I spotted a chateau, but we had to pass through a number of stops before reaching Versailles, a commune established by Louis after installing the court and government in 1682. The king was said to have permitted a large court to live close to the palace that established the commune of Versailles.

We arrived in Versailles at two in the afternoon, and after ten minutes of leisurely walking at the palace gate, I said, 'What a massive and impressive palace.' The Palace of Versailles was the main residence of French kings from the time of Louis XIV to the time of Louis XVI, and it remained the model of European royal residence during the seventeenth and eighteenth centuries. There were several architects and sculptors involved in the construction of the palace, starting in 1623, when Louis XIII made Versailles his hunting ground and built the hunting lodge. It was transformed into a chateau in 1634 and then the palace after 1660. Architectural changes and expansion occurred during the royal occupation of the palace in several phases. These include the construction of an impressive garden. The palace had to be restored after abandonment during the French Revolution period. Although Napoleon first used the palace as his summer residence, he didn't live in Versailles. After the Bourbon Restoration in the early nineteenth century, the palace remained as the centre of French culture and arts when it had installed in it the Museum of French History. It was also the place where the treaty was signed to end the First World War on 28 June 1919. The Palais de Versailles and the park have remained a popular World Heritage Site since 1979.

When entering the palace, one can be overwhelmed by the enormity of the task that a visitor needs to sort out if all key attractions are to be seen in a short time. Obviously, we had to plan what we needed to see and what to miss. To begin with, no visitor could miss the most famous room, the Hall of Glittering Mirrors. This dazzling Baroque reception hall which was built between 1678 and 1684 by Jules Hardouin-Mansart, offers a spectacular and grand look for curious visitors. The hall is itself a work of art. This magnificent hall, over seventy metres long, consists of massive ornamental mirrors in eighteen segments. The hall is adorned with gilded statues, crystal chandeliers, and ceiling paint-ings. As a hallway, it remains the passage between another key attraction, the Grande Appartements, which consisted of the king's and queen's apartments. The Hall of Mirrors was also used as a ballroom, concert hall, and waiting room for courtiers who came to see the king and queen. At both ends of the hall were the Salon de Guerre, or War Salon, and the Salon de Paix, or Peace Salon. The Hall of Mirrors faces the Water Parterres, the ornamental pools of the formal gardens of the Chateau. I felt the urge to make another visit to appreciate the beauty of this hall.

Pressed for time, we moved to the State Apartment of the King, which included the royal bedchamber as well as other private rooms used for meetings and official ceremonies. These rooms were named after mythological deities, which made a connection between the king's reign and history. Some of these rooms contained paintings of cele-brated French artists, such as Charles Brun, Charles de la Fosse, and Jean-Baptise de Champaigne. The famous portrait of Louis XIV by Hyacinthe Rigaud is noteworthy. As we passed through the Queen's Apartment, it was easy to recognize the feminine characteristics of the decor where the rooms were subtle and delicate in style. The Queen's Bedroom, which was first created for Queen Maria Theresa, was later improved for Marie Antoinette. The paintings on the ceiling depicted the virtues of a queen, namely compassion, generosity, wisdom, and fidelity. We also stepped into two *Salon des Nobles*, the antechamber of Queen Marie-Thérèse and the Antichambre du Grand Couvert, where Louis XIV served meals with royal protocols, as well as a room for the twelve bodyguards who protected the queen. We were not able to see the king's private suite, including the king's bedroom, as it was not included in the standard ticket price.

Having enjoyed viewing the key attractions inside the palace, we ventured in to see another work of art by a famous landscape artist of the seventeenth century, André Le Nôtre. This park was a human-made per-fection with well-trimmed shrubbery and tidy lawns in geometric pat-terns that provided the foundation for formal French gardens. One could not fail to admire and appreciate the two ornamental pools adorned

by the fountains and statues. The visual effect created by the designers
is marvellous. The symmetrical view offered the Grande Perspective,
which stretched from the pools to the expansive *Allée Royale* pathways.
This led to Apollo's Fountain, where the famous statue of Apollo by
Charles Le Brun can be found.

We did not visit the vegetable garden or *l'Orangerie*, where the king
kept fruit trees. Seeing the garden in itself was a huge task if one wanted
to appreciate and enjoy what was on offer. We had already spent five
hours seeing the palace and garden. Unfortunately, we had to miss a
few other key attractions, such as the Grand Trianon and Petit Trianon.
The Grand Trianon was created by Hardouin-Mansart and Robert de
Cotte for the mistress of Louis XIV, while the Petit Trianon was created
by *Jacques-Ange Gabriel* as a retreat for Louis the Fifteenth and his mistress and later presented by Louis XVI to his wife. The English garden
featured a temple called the Temple of Love. Other attractions that we
had to leave for another visit were the Royal Chappell, Queen's Hamlet
of Marie Antoinette, and the opera house. We also missed the Galeries
Historiques, which exhibited artefacts and paintings related to French
history.

We rushed to the station to catch the train around seven in the evening. As we boarded the train, it was still a beautiful day, but I felt the
chills that a typical September evening would render. While we didn't
have any plan for the next day, I remembered that Fernanda wanted to be
with me sometimes, and thus she invited me to stay with her. However,
we all headed to Rue de la Pompe and decided to grab a quick dinner.
We had a slice of pizza from a food stall at St Lazar and happily returned
to the room. Julie agreed to stay with Zana and Fernanda, and I left
towards Place de Republic, where she and Julie lived.

Unlike the maid's quarters of the sixteenth arrondissement apartments where Zana lived, Fernanda's studio was slightly larger than a
bedsit and had a comfortable living space with a mini kitchen and bathroom. However, it was on the fifth floor of an apartment block mainly
occupied by low-income families. I brought my shoulder bag with me,
which was loaded with all the required clothing and other necessities

to stay overnight. Fernanda and Julie had a single large bed to sleep in. Although the window could be kept open at night, it was stuffy; therefore, we had to turn on the table fan throughout the night. Thus, it was better than Zana's room. First, I wanted to take a shower before heading to bed, and we both stepped into the bathroom together, as Fernanda would not let me alone. I knew it was going to be an extraordinary experience with her under the shower.

In the shower, starting with passionately explosive kissing, we rolled our hands over each other's flesh, diligently exploring the most sensual parts of our bodies. Just imagine the aura and the pleasure when I skilfully moved down to bite her nipple while caressing the most sensitive point of her body, arousing a burst of energy. Fortunately, the shower cabin was sufficiently large. Having reached her climax, she wouldn't let me free for even a minute, and we ended up doing Brazilian samba. What a delightful experience it was.

Back in the room, having prepared ourselves to go to bed, we both sat on the mattress; Fernanda reclined on my lap. For some time, we tried our best to make sense of this relationship. I tried to explain that I had a mission to accomplish and that it was no longer something like shooting at a star or a dream. Although she was an understanding and listening person, her emotions ran deep. The only consolation I could offer was that we would see each other when time permitted. I said that I could be in Paris within a day. She was not planning to leave France any time soon, and even if she did, there was always a chance that we could see each other, and we could try to see if our relationship would last for a year or two. In the meantime, while we tried to embrace reality, we thought that it was time to sleep, so I turned off the light. To my surprise, we were soon back on the lovemaking trail. This time there was a gradual and mature kind of foreplay that lasted nearly an hour. After a while, tired and exhausted, both of us fell asleep in minutes. We did not wake up until 11.00 a.m.

We had our coffee with croissants we had bought the previous day. The coffee was better than what Zana used to make, as it was brewed using an Italian-style percolator. Fernanda told me that Zana and Julie were sometimes expected to visit us in the afternoon which I did not know. Since Julie and Fernanda would be at work from the next day until Tuesday, they had planned to meet us and spend time together. While Fernanda was doing household chores, I took a shower. Later in the day, Fernanda shared her photo album showing her family and friends in Brazil. She had a younger brother, Paiva, living with her parents somewhere in Bahia, a resort town in northern Rio. They came from a middle-class family, according to the Brazilian standard, where her dad worked as a municipal clerk.

'Browsing the photo album can bring back old memories,' Fernanda said. 'It can also make you relax,' I replied. After all, it was a time for relaxation, and we both had a good time together until Zana and Julie arrived at around three o'clock. To our surprise, they came with a lunch basket, with the idea of going for a picnic at the park. They had pre-pared some baguette sandwiches and bought some quiche Lorraine on their way. Fernanda was asked to find mats so that we could sit on the ground at a nearby park and enjoy the food. Zana, however, hinted he would like to go to a quiet place, such as the Bois de Boulogne, which was a bit far to reach from where we were. Ultimately, we ended up in a nearby park and enjoyed a wonderful evening while nibbling on food from the basket and sipping coffee from the flask. We spent quite a lot of time in the park while chatting about almost everything, including my plan to leave Paris. By now, everyone knew that my departure from Paris was imminent, though it wasn't clear when it would happen. At this point in time, I didn't know exactly when I would leave; it depended on the booking and availability of seats on the Paris–Rome night train, the Palatino Express. This was the same train I took from Rome to come to Paris in May.

By late evening, Zana and I wanted to say goodbye, but I had to pick up my shoulder bag, which I had left in Fernanda's place. Thus, we all got up and walked towards her room before we took the Metro back home. On the following day, a Saturday, everyone would be at work except for me. I thought I could spend some time exploring Place de Trocadéro and take pictures of the Tour Eiffel and the surroundings.

Back in the room, we hardly ate anything, instead tidying up the room and discussing my future in Rome. We went to bed rather early, as Zana had to wake up in the morning. He had already prepared the necessary items for my breakfast the next morning and showed me locations in the kitchenette. He knew that he would have left home when I got up.

As expected, I got up around midday and took things easy. It was midafternoon when I finished my shower and breakfast and was ready to leave the room. I had in my possession an old Canon AE camera for which I had to load up a film roll, which in those days we could buy from a souvenir shop in a nearby tourist hotspot, such as the Eiffel Tower. This was the first thing I did when arriving at Trocadéro. I was at ease, and I took time to stroll in the garden below, appreciating what I had seen. There were tourists everywhere, but they were not solo, as I was. Occasionally, I would ask someone to take a photo of me posing near an attractive view. I was familiar with the area, as I had already visited these places, including the Eiffel Tower, with Zana and Julie. By late afternoon, when I reached home, Zana had already returned from work with some lamb to cook in a curry sauce so we could eat it with the baguette. I helped him cook the lamb curry, and we had an early dinner. The curry was delicious according to Zana, but it was based on a simple recipe of tomato and chilli sauce with lots of onions and garlic and supermarket curry powder

Zana wondered what I was planning to do the next day, as it was a Sunday. I thought I would do some window shopping along the Champs Élysées. I thought it was not a bad idea to buy some cheap clothing before I left Paris, but it was not something urgent. Zana warned that few stores were open on Sundays. While I was doing the washing up of the dishes, he went on to make a cup of tea for us both. Soon after enjoying the cuppa, we both went to bed, as on the previous night. I had a comfy sleep and woke late, as usual, to see that Zana had already gone to work. I didn't see him until late evening, as he spent long hours at work on Sunday. On his return, I showed him what I had bought and gave him one of the long-sleeved jumpers as a memorable gift for him and showed the other two jumpers I had with me, one for Julie and another for Fernanda. Zana loved his and he thought the other two were also fantastic in regard to colours and materials.

For dinner, Zana picked up a takeaway burger meal for both of us, which we ate when he came out of the shower. While eating, I reminded him that we had to go to Gare de Lyon to book my ticket, and he nodded and assured me that he would be returning by three o'clock so that we could proceed with our visit to the station to the west of Paris. After dinner, we ended up making coffee and sat on the sofa chatting for a while before heading to bed. In a few minutes, I heard Zana snoring, which initially made me a little uneasy until I fell asleep.

10

AU VOIR BLISSFUL ROMANCE

As I woke up the next day, I saw sunlight hitting the mirror and casting a glittering reflection on the glass window. After a refreshing shower, I made a cup of coffee and sat down holding a croissant in one hand. Later, I went for a walk along Rue de la Pompe and further down the street until I reached the baker, where I got a freshly made sandwich for lunch. While walking towards the room, I sat on a bench to enjoy the sandwich while browsing through a newspaper that someone had left. I was not sure what I was looking at or reading, but by flipping page by page, I was able to read some headlines in French, and I found it difficult to grasp the meaning. Suddenly, I realized that Zana would be home early today, so I had to get home soon. When I returned home, Zana was already in, and in no time, we were ready to leave for Gare de Lyon. We still had time for coffee, which Zana started to make. It would take just thirty minutes to get to the rail station, so we headed toward the Metro after the coffee.

The Gare de Lyon station was rather crowded, but we easily found the ticket and reservation counter. But we had to join the queue first to proceed to the information counter. Instead, Zana suggested that we look at the timetable notice board to determine the departure time of the Palatino and then approach the ticket counter. Thus, we approached the timetable board and found that the departure time was seven in the evening. The legendary night train ran daily and passed through the usual cities and towns in France and Italy before reaching Rome just before midday. The Palatino was expected to pass through Dijon along the Yonne River in the South of France and traverse through the border to take the classic route towards Rome via Bologna and Florence.

When we approached the ticket counter, we were able to get through the queue much faster, and I simply asked the counter clerk for a Palatino ticket to Rome with a sleeper seat on the 17th of September. I was not concerned about the ticket price, but availability mattered to me the most. The reply of the ticket clerk was not encouraging, but sleeper seats or couchettes were available on 14 September. I did not have much of a choice but to buy the ticket, and I paid about 150 francs, which was less than 40 US dollars. I got my ticket with my name printed on it along with the seat and compartment numbers. The European consortium named TEN, or Trans Euro Night operated Palatino Express. Voilà, I was ready for Rome. I was told that I should be on the platform for at least forty-five minutes before the train was to leave.

On our way back, Zana and I were thinking about my sudden departure date which was a few days earlier than I had planned. With 14 September being a Friday, Julie and Fernanda would be at work until the late evening. They would be surprised and shocked to see that I had booked the train for the next Friday when they came to know this on Wednesday evening. Since there wasn't much time, Zana wanted to arrange a dinner for us, and he thought that the nearby pizzeria would be ideal. I heard that the meeting on Wednesday evening with girls was prearranged.

On the Metro, we decided to continue the journey instead of returning to the room so that we could go for a hamburger meal. At l'Etoile, we got off and took a stroll, as we had enough time before dinner. We spent time browsing the wares of street hawkers and being amused by a variety of individual performers demonstrating their artistic skills until half past eight. We then thought that we should get burgers and sate our appetites. When we finished eating, we walked home rather than taking the Metro. It was a pleasant evening, and the walk made us more comfortable before a good night's sleep. Back in the room, however, we could not do without a cup of coffee.

During the next few days, as Zana would be working, I decided to stay home most of the time, preparing myself mentally for my long sojourn in Rome. Occasionally, I went out by myself and revisited a few places I had already seen. The rest of the time, I was busy organizing my trip and packing the luggage. On Wednesday, Fernanda, Julie, and Zana all came from work together in the evening. But before we headed out for our pizza dinner, Julie and Zana left the room, leaving me and Fernanda to be together for a while. Fernanda said she would not come to bid me farewell on Friday as she would be working long hours, meaning this was the last opportunity for us to be together alone. Obviously, we got a bit emotional, but then something else happened. She started to kiss me passionately while stripping off my clothes, which aroused me and triggered my libido. I wondered whether this was because of her sex drive or because she wanted a relationship with me. Regardless, we had a good time satisfying each other's sexual urges. When Julie and Zana returned home, we were all ready to leave for dinner.

At the restaurant, we tried out authentic Neapolitan pizzas with various toppings. I liked the seafood topping, and one with mushrooms and marinated artichokes was also delicious. Having to work the next morning, the girls split from us before 10.00 p.m., and both of them bade me a final farewell. Fernanda was almost to the point of shedding tears but realized that this was just a small part of her life story. Zana and I started to walk home, as it was not far from Zana's room. Even Zana had to get to work in the morning, so we did not spend time sipping coffee.

I had to kill another day or two until I boarded the train to Rome, but it seemed as if it were a weeklong wait. On Friday, I got up before midday. So did Zana, who had a day off because of me. Strangely enough, we didn't even have any croissants with our morning coffee, and Zana had to run a brief errant to the boulangerie. While we had coffee, Zana told me that I would miss the croissants in Italy. However, the Italian version, the *Cornetto*, was even better. Suddenly I was reminded of the staple of Italians: pasta, and particularly spaghetti. I thought we should cook some spaghetti for lunch, which would be quick and easy, as Zana had some on his kitchen shelf. Zana thought it was a good idea, as we had chopped tomatoes and canned tuna as well. 'A teaspoon of masala or curry powder would do the trick,' I said, and I volunteered to do the cooking as I started to peel and slice some onions while we talked about the Italian way of life.

In the afternoon, we wrapped everything up, and I reminded Zana about the sweaters I had bought for Fernanda and Julie. I had totally forgotten about them when the girls visited us on Wednesday. While I was gift-wrapping the sweaters, Zana was kind enough to make a baguette sandwich for me to take with me so I could have an early dinner while on the train. I also wanted to pick up juices and fruits from the stall at the station before boarding the train. Zana suggested that I take a small pillow and blanket with me. The blanket would fit well inside my shoulder bag, but the pillow would need to remain in my hands. Since I just had one medium-sized suitcase, that seemed all right. Backpacks were not common in the 1980s.

We left the room at five in the evening, bidding farewell to the Sixteenth Arrondissement and Rue de La Pompe. Arriving at Gare de Lyon with ample time left allowed me to quickly browse through the fruit stalls nearby. Unfortunately, I could not find what I was looking for. Cherries were out of season, the fruit seller said, but I bought some sweet and crispy seedless red grapes and clementines. Zana bought me a couple of canned drinks too.

The time was approaching six o'clock as we started to move to the platform. It was a bit of a walk to reach the correct platform, where the Palatino was already parked but not yet ready to take on passengers. Zana and I moved to the end point, beyond which visitors were not permitted, and waited until the conductor started letting the passengers in after checking tickets and identities. When they took the barrier down, Zana and I shared a passionate hug and a kiss on the cheeks, as we bade one another farewell. We were almost crying, but c'est la vie. My compartment, which was at the rear of the train, was luckily not far away.

As I boarded the train and reached my compartment, I could see that two of the six passengers were already in and preparing their couchettes, although it was a bit early to do so. I spoke in English, but nothing much of the communication was between us. A few minutes later, another two passengers showed, whom I recognized as English-speaking tourists from Australia. That was a bit comforting, and we conversed in English.

When the Palatino Express started to move out of the station sharply at seven, we still had one couchette vacant, but I thought someone could board at the next station. In the meantime, I used a vacant seat to sit and enjoy the ride while eating my sandwich after changing my attire to pyjamas. My couchette was on the top, so I had to be careful when climbing up and down. As we moved to the time of sunset, everyone moved to their couchettes, and two of them turned off their lights. The Australians seemed to be engaged in reading, and I was the only one who did nothing but pondered about the life that I left behind. Afterall, it was an exciting three months in the summer. It was about friendship, a summer job, a holiday, entertainment, love and sex, arts and culture, and culinary experiences. It was also about France and Parisian life. What else could someone like me have had within a short period of time without spending money? There was also a significant learning curve.

When the train sped through a silent and rather dark enclosure, I began to reflect on key points and events during my sojourn in France. The early days of visiting Parisian attractions, such as the Eiffel Tower and river cruise, as well as the famous Louvre Museum, came to my mind first. I was also pleased to visit the Palace of Versailles, at least briefly, for a touristic gaze before my departure to Rome. I still had a vivid memory of my visit to the notorious street of 'working girls', Rue St Denis in Paris, with Zana and Julie. I also remembered the day I met Fernanda first time over dinner. Although this was not an inadvertent meeting, I should say that we were attracted to each other. The first bodily encounter with her in Zana's room was not something that I would forget. Obviously, my nearly two-month sojourn in Tourgéville, Normandy, was exceptional. Working for Madame Lamark and coming to know her family and Anna, relaxing at Deauville beach, finding entertainment at the racetracks, and engaging in culinary adventure at the Tourgéville home were all memorable experiences. Indeed, it had been like a holiday, not a summer job.

Moreover, while in Paris, our visit to a Latin American discotheque and a rather intimate encounter with Fernanda that night were still in my mind. We both enjoyed the erotic Brazilian dances Karimbo and samba, which involved sensual body movements. Another exciting night, with Fernanda in her studio, would pleasantly haunt me for years to come. Whether it was love and sex or a pure relationship, we did have wonderful time together. One cannot rule out that love and sex can lead to building a solid relationship over time, although neither one of us had explicitly expressed feelings towards the other. However, for now, all seemed complete. I already missed her, but in some ways I felt it was good that she did not come to the station to send me off, considering her emotional status.

While I reflected on my brief French experience, we cruised through rural France, and along the Yonne River, the train moved through the popular wine country of Burgundy and would pass through Dijon on the way. As the train meandered towards the south as the sun set, it passed through green valleys and beautifully scattered French villages. The Palatino Express was staffed by Italian crews preparing to serve dinner on the buffet car, but I didn't see anyone in our compartment joining the dinner table. I thought that it was time for me to join the rest and turn off my light and call it a good night.

Luckily, there were no midnight calls from the border guards when the train crossed the French–Italian border. We all had handed over our passports early on when the conductor suggested to do so during his inspection, soon after the train pulled off. I was not sure where the train crossed the border, but I thought it would be through Modane, to arrive at Piacenza five in the morning. Obviously, the Italian landscape was rather different from the French, as I could see red-roofed villas scattered around the landscape when the blinds were raised. I remember that we passed through Bologna and arrived in Firenze, or Florence, the birthplace of the Renaissance. I knew that, according to the conductor who returned with our passports, the Palatino Express was expected to arrive in Rome by Midday.

Soon after my washroom visit in the morning, I craved a good espresso and croissant. So I headed to the dining car and sat near the window at a table and enjoyed the changing urban and green landscape while sipping coffee and reading a guidebook. Within an hour, we were to arrive at our destination; but in the meantime, I felt hungry and ordered a panini. While eating the panini, I had to fine-tune myself mentally to the Italian way of life. But I was no longer a stranger, and with confidence, I was ready to face new challenges.

When I returned to my compartment, I found only two Australian tourists seated, and I had a brief conversation with them. They planned to stay a week in Rome before travelling to Naples and Pompeii. I did not bother to find out where they would stay in Rome, as I heard them say that they had a friend living in Rome. They were not very interested in my affairs or me, but I did let them know that I was planning to pursue higher studies in Rome at the American College. In the meantime, we were all ready and waiting for the train to arrive within the next half hour. I knew I had to carry my suitcase, shoulder bag, and pillow when I got off, and I would need to walk for five to ten minutes from the train station to reach my pensione. The landlady, Laura, knew that I would arrive around midday, as I had managed to telephone her a couple of days ago.

Section Three

ABODE IN ROME: THE MISSION BEGINS IN AUTUMN 1979

Zain is back in Rome after receiving admission and the promise of a campus job along with a tuition waiver to pursue his studies at the American College of Rome. He also finds a home to live in as a guest with Lucille, a self-employed Jewish American lady in her fifties. This section chronicles his settling-in process in Rome.

11

BACK IN DOLCE ROMA

The sight of the urban landscape and the dome of St Peter's Basilica at a distance through the window hinted at me that we had already arrived in Rome. The train briskly passed through a narrow passage flanked by multistorey apartment blocks and office buildings to arrive at the Termini station. I got off patiently and walked along a long platform to reach the exit. The station was rather crowded and busy, as usual, but I was not a stranger and thus managed to find my way out. 'What a beautiful day,' I cried with a sigh.

I ploughed through the busy and crowded streets along with criss-crossing tram cars and reached the pensione. As I walked inside the corridor, Laura came running from the kitchen to embrace me with a kiss on the cheek. I even heard her saying, 'Bon giorno amico mio,' in Italian. My room was ready, and she knew that I would stay there for some time. This meant that I would be able to pay cheaper monthly rent than on a daily basis. It was a comfortable room on the first floor with a window facing the street. Luckily, the room had an en suite bathroom. The first thing I did was take a shower and nap for a few hours, as I had not slept well on the train.

Although I kept the window ajar, I was able to sleep for almost three hours even with the noisy street below. It being a Saturday evening, I thought I should go for a stroll, perhaps window shopping. I came down and had a brief chat with Laura, curiously enquiring about lodgers in the pensione. She said that some foreign migrant workers remained there along with a few bag packers from Scandinavia. While chatting, I saw Musa and Albert walking in. They were migrant workers from Mauritius who had come months ago. Laura also told me that a few boys from Ceylon had come to join a ship as sailors. Interestingly, Laura did not know that I was also from Ceylon. I kept this secret for a while, but it often seemed difficult.

When I returned from my leisure walk, it was almost half past nine, and the sun had already set. With my street food that I had eaten while out, I was full, and the dinner was not in my mind. I thanked Laura for the spacious and comfortable room, although it was noisy at times. Laura told me that she had a few good rooms vacant as there were not many tourists in September. This also meant that renting for long-staying migrant workers or transient travellers was the only option to cover expenses and make a modest profit. I agreed with her and said it was a smart move. With her broken English and my rudimentary Italian, we managed to converse. Laura was a single woman who had been widowed some years prior, and she had been helped by her elder brother and a dedicated servant. While enjoying the homemade espresso, I spent almost an hour chatting with Laura and her brother, Mario. My brief nap in the afternoon helped me stay awake, and it was almost midnight before I went to sleep. I didn't intend to get up early the next morning either, as it was a Sunday.

After long hours of sleeping, refreshed and enthusiastic, I thought of going to the famous street market in Rome called Porta Portese, where one can find anything one wants. Porta Portese itself represented an ancient city gate built in 1644 at the juncture of Via Portese and Via Portuensis. The flea market took place along a few streets around Via Portese every Sunday. I heard about the flea market from migrant workers whom I met at the hotel before I went to Paris. The flea market was located in the ancient Trastevere neighbourhood of Rome, and Laura showed me how to get there via trams and buses. I had to rush to get there at least by midday before it ended in the midafternoon.

In September, it looked like Indian summer, which I would call sunny and mildly breezy. I thought it was a pleasant day to be out. As I approached the flea market neighbourhood, I could sense the air as if I were passing through a crowded bazaar. I didn't know where to start, but I kept walking slowly, browsing at each stall. One thing is for sure: I didn't come here to do antique shopping or buy any electronics. As the winter approached, I wanted to get some inexpensive winterwear, such as coats and boots and a couple of good sweaters.

It took some time for me to stumble through the packed bazaar and find the clothing section, although I could see one or two stalls outside the designated area. Obviously, when I found the right place, I found plenty of choices in terms of variety and price. Bargaining and haggling for discounts is a common practice. Finally, I had got what I wanted, except for a pair of boots. I had plenty of time before autumn ended. When the traders started to pack up and dismantle their stalls, I knew that I had to get back, so I walked towards the tram car stop. On the way, I had a couple of *Suplies*, or rice balls stuffed with cheese, as I could not have anything for lunch. With shopping bags in my hands, I did not bother to spend another hour or two sightseeing but boarded the tram car.

After arriving at the hotel, I went to do some errands, as I needed groceries, including tea bags and milk, as well as biscuits and other sundries. Laura had given me a kettle to boil water, as well as mugs and a plate. Although I didn't have a fridge in the room, I was allowed to use Laura's kitchen. I even bought cheese and rustic Italian bread. I was aware that it was easier and less expensive to eat street food, such as pizza, pasta, roast chicken, and deep-fried croquettes or cutlets. When Laura saw my grocery bag on my return from the supermarket, she shouted, 'Mama Mia!' but helped me organize my stuff in one side of the kitchen cupboard. She even volunteered to make a plate of pasta when she saw a spaghetti pack in my grocery bag. That was very kind of her, and I thanked her, but I insisted that she share the meal with me.

The next morning, my attention was directed at the college. I thought I didn't need an appointment but could try my luck. I was there ten in the morning, but it took almost an hour for the dean to show up. When he entered the hall, he immediately recognized me and greeted me. In a matter of fifteen minutes, I was called in to meet him. Surprisingly enough, Michael even remembered my name and said 'Zain, welcome back to Rome.' We then had a quick chat as he started sarcastically teasing me about my experience in France over a cup of coffee. Luckily, he seemed to be free in the morning hours, and he wanted to go over my enrolment as a student of economics and liberal studies and then the nature of the job that I would be expected to do. Michael pointed out that my main role was to help the college management with student services, for which I would be paid three hundred US dollars in cash every month. I didn't need to pay semester tuition fees, which amounted to $1,000 US dollars a semester. He also assured me that by the next year, I might be entitled to free lodging in an accommodation facility at the college.

Michael also briefed me on the organizational structure and hierarchy of the college, what my responsibilities during the enrolment period were, and the preparations to be carried out before the classes started the following week. Familiarization with the college environment and getting to know the staff remained essential. I was later introduced to the director of the college, Barbara, who spent over half an hour chatting with me about the history of the college and its current affiliation with a university in West Virginia. Barbara noted that the college recruited about 50 students every year and the current enrolment was about 140. With a few full-time staff members, the college made use of needy international students like me as part-time employees. Most of our students were the sons and daughters of diplomats and UN representatives of the World Food Organization in Rome. However, some Italian students had attended international or private schools. Barbara also pointed out that recently they'd had some Middle-Eastern students, mainly students from Iran who had fled the country after the revolution.

Susan was one of the Iranian students who worked at the reception desk. Barbara introduced her by saying she was the person I should speak to if I wanted to know more about the college and students. At first glance, Susan seemed to have a pleasant personality. Later, another South American student, Katarina, from the office, shook my hand as we passed through the corridor. In the common room, Barbara introduced me to a few American exchange students from a college in Texas who had come to spend a semester in Rome. In fact, I remembered meeting them when I made my first visit to the college in May. They had completed their summer school and had to leave Italy soon. She continued by saying that she expected another batch of exchange student to arrive the next week from Texas and that I should help them settle slowly in Rome. This would involve working with Barbara to find accommodation and other essential services for the exchange students, as well as taking them around. Since I was new to Rome, I thought I would seek help from Susan, who had been in Rome for more than a year.

Technically, I started my work there on the same day; I was asked to sit with Susan at the reception desk and learn more about the college and Rome. It was a wonderful opportunity for me to get to know her, and by the end of the day, we had become close friends. During the day, the reception desk was bombarded with phone calls, as well as new students seeking admission and course information. Thus, I learned quite a lot about college offerings as well as the American higher education system instantly. In the meantime, some current students came to re-enrol, and Susan seemed to know every one of them. Since course advice and enrolment were mainly carried out by either Michael or Barbara, we had to maintain their appointment books as well. 'What a huge experience for me in less than one day,' I said to Susan. We stayed until seven in the evening and left the building when Michael and Barbara came down to close the door.

Susan offered to buy me a pizza slice from the nearby pizzeria while heading to the bus stop. She showed me the local trattoria, where students normally got together for lunch, and we picked up a slice of pizza as we walked. She said she lived with a retired American lady as a lodger in Trastevere, the old part of the city. As we split following a goodnight kiss, she reminded me of the office's hours and said she normally would arrive at the college at nine in the morning these days.

It was almost ten in the evening when I reached home, and Laura wondered why I was so late. I had to explain to her about my new job at the college, and she seemed pleased by the outcome. For the time being, I almost felt as if I had settled in Rome.

On the morning of the next day, Susan and I were at the college by nine. By midday, things were a bit hectic with more phone calls, as well as existing students visiting the college. In the midafternoon, Barbra offered panini. Now I was getting used to the type of work I was involved in, but I was still learning more about the course specifications and requirements. The admission and entry requirements for the degree course were simple and straightforward. Anyone who had graduated from an international or American school with a high school diploma, who had an Italian secondary school qualification called *Maturita*, and who had level of English language proficiency as assessed by the dean could seek admission. We faced problems only when the candidates were from outside the country or were mature adults without any formal entry qualifications. Assessing these students was a difficult task which only the dean could handle.

By the end of the day, we both dashed off at six in the evening and headed for a walk. Susan suggested that we go to the Spanish Steps and stroll around the shops or sit and enjoy the evening before going back to our rooms. I thought that it was a long walk to get there, but I learned that there was a short underground passage. It was a pleasant evening, and the Spanish Steps were rather packed. We got ourselves gelati in cones and climbed up the steps to sit in a quiet corner so that we could chat and get to know each other. Susan was living in England long before the Iranian Revolution, where she was put in a boarding school by her father. Her mother escaped the revolution and fled to England, where she had lived ever since. Unfortunately, her father could not escape and seemed to have suffered emotionally. I didn't delve further to find out how she ended up in Rome, but I thought it was perhaps because of her boyfriend Sayed, who was half-Italian and often visited her during the weekend. Susan told me that her sister Ruby was also studying at the college, and she promised that she would introduce her and Sayed during the weekend. At about nine in the evening, while walking towards Via Quirinale, we found a trattoria to have a plate of spaghetti before taking the bus home.

At the pensione, I found some time to chat with other occupants from several countries, including a few from my own country. While most of them were mainly economic migrants, a few were on transit, waiting to board ships as sailors. All of them were quite adaptable and resilient, and they often stayed together, sharing rooms, with at least two per room. I learned a lot about Rome from them, and I also helped Laura manage their stays, as I could communicate with them in English. Most of the migrant workers were overstaying their visas, but the Italian authorities didn't bother as long as the migrants didn't commit any crimes.

Thinking about my life, I considered that I had almost settled in Rome and my priority remained the American College of Rome. I knew my life would revolve around college from now on. This prompted me to explore other alternatives in terms of accommodation, but it seemed premature to leave the pensione before securing my financial status. I thought, however, that I should speak to Susan to explore alternative arrangements whenever the time was right. In the meantime, I peacefully spent the first week at the college and stood firmly to face new challenges as a student as well as a staff member at the college.

As the week came to an end on Friday, before the college shut for the weekend, I had the chance to meet Sayed, Flavio, and Ruby. They came all together at about five in the evening, and luckily, Barbara and Michael were also ready to leave. Susan introduced me to them as a new student as well as a college staff member. Flavio was an authentic Romano who was born and bred in the vicinity of the ancient city. He lived with his parents in a town called Rocca Priora, which was about thirty minutes away from the city. Both Sayed and Flavio drove their own cars and seemed to be attached to their toys. When we left the college, Susan suggested that we all should go to the old port town of Rome called Ostia Antica.

Flavio looked friendly and inquisitive, while Sayed seemed a bit socially reserved. Ruby seemed talkative and sarcastic at times. Susan said that as we were all students, I was bound to meet Flavio and Ruby frequently at the college. Flavio, who was a product of the International School of Rome, spoke English fluently with a British accent. It was fun and entertaining to interact with them. In Ostia, we walked along a sandy beach and went to a seaside food stall where we could indulge in eating batter-fried seafood, including calamari and prawns. Later, we spent the time playing games and trying out our luck with slot machines in a low-key amusement park. We left Ostia at 11.00 p.m. I joined Susan and Sayed in their Alfa Romeo, and Ruby went with Flavio, who drove a classic Volkswagen. It was already midnight when Sayed dropped me off at the hotel. Susan wanted me to come and see her in Trastevere on Sunday, but I didn't promise. Nevertheless, she drew up a map with her address on a piece of paper in case I decided to visit her.

The door was already closed, but I had a set of keys to enter the pensione. Some of Laura's guests were still awake and chatting, but I bade them goodnight and went straight to the room. Soon after a warm shower, I was able to sleep well; in fact, it was almost midday when I woke up in the morning. With a fried egg and toast and a good mug of cafe latte, I sat on the couch to relax and enjoy reading an old copy of *The Economist*. I decided not to leave the hotel, as I was expecting the first call from Zana and Julie, who had promised to call me when they got together with Fernanda on the weekend. However, it was a long wait; Zana didn't call me until ten at night. He called from a public telephone booth and told me that they had found a way to make cheap trunk calls from a public booth. Zana wondered how well I was and whether I had made any friends. When I said that I was very well and everything had gone well with the college and the job, he was really happy and passed the receiver to Fernanda. I told her that I missed her so much and was thinking about her every night when I was alone. She started to cry, and Julie had to comfort her. When she tried to say something, the line was cut off. I waited for some time, but they didn't manage to call me back. I spent the rest of the day chatting with hotel guests who normally rested during the weekend or visited one of the meeting places. I was also invited to join them on Sunday, but I was not sure whether I wanted to join them or visit Susan in Trastevere.

The next day, after a late breakfast as usual on Sunday, I decided to visit Susan in the evening hours. I already knew how to get to Trastevere using a tram car which passed through the next street. But I decided to leave the pensione after six in the evening. When I arrived in Trastevere, I queried a shopkeeper as to the way to the Piazza Santa Maria, which was easier than I thought. Susan lived in a house just in the Piazza, and it was a two-story building which could have been built during the pre-Renaissance period. The square was vibrant and busy, with restaurants and bars around. The Fountain of Santa Maria, in the centre, dated back to the early Christian era and was definitely one of the oldest in Rome. I was told that the current version of the fountain reflected the work of Bernini and Fontana in the 1600s.

In the square, I looked around and saw one of the oldest churches in Europe, the Basilica Santa Maria, from which the piazza had taken its name. It is said to have been built when Christianity was first accepted in Rome in the early years, but the current structure dates back to the Romanesque period of the early eleventh century. I could have spent hours gazing at the piazza, but at seven in the evening, I knocked at the door, and the lady of the house, Sally, opened the door and invited me in when I introduced myself as a friend of Susan. I heard that Sally used to work with Barbara, looking after the library. She had two lodgers, including Susan. In the evening, Sally invited a few guests for a polenta dinner, and I was an uninvited guest thanks to Susan.

Susan was indeed happy to see me, and she explained to me how polenta, a traditional cornmeal dish, was made and served. Well-cooked lamb chops in ragu were served on a bed of stone-ground yellow maize flour paste cooked with hot water and butter. As tradition dictated, the entire family would get together to eat. Chilli and sautéed vegetables, such as green peppers and sliced mushrooms in the sauce, could make the polenta a wonderful dish for dinner. Sally's Italian friend had cooked the polenta paste using her expertise by carefully stirring the maize flour in boiling water without making lumps and then adding butter and cheese. In fact, homemade ragu contains garlic and onion, as well as Italian herbs, such as oregano and parsley. A dash of cumin and turmeric was added to enhance the flavour.

By half past eight, all guests were in and the dinner was served. Earlier, everyone had the opportunity to check Sally's hot mulled wine. At a large dining table in the middle of a large square hall, all sat around to fork out the polenta. What a delicious meal with a bunch of cheerful people around. This was, in fact, my first time getting together in Rome. Sally's friends were in their late forties and early fifties, and the discussions were mainly about Rome and Italian art and culture. All of them were Americans living in Rome, except for the one who cooked our dinner. Since Sally's house opened onto the piazza, we could pull out our chairs and sit outside the house on the square, and a few of us did so.

Debora and I, along with Susan, sat outside and enjoyed a nice evening overlooking the basilica on the opposite side. When I queried as to the origin of the church, Debora poured out the entire history. The original floor plan and the structure of the wall dated back to the time of early Christianity in Rome—somewhere around AD 340, she said. However, much of the current building was erected during the Romanesque period in the early eleventh century, and the interior mosaics were from the twelfth and thirteenth centuries. In the meantime, Susan assured me that a visit to the basilica was included in the Rome study tour which Michael did every semester with the exchange students.

Any dinner in Italy wouldn't be complete without an espresso. Although I could have stayed chatting up until midnight, I decided to leave soon after the coffee was served. Susan reminded me about the hectic morning we would have, as the classes were scheduled to start while the existing students would continue to come for enrolment. When I walked back to the tram stop, I was able to board the approaching tram car immediately. I was home within thirty minutes.

12

WELCOME TO THE AMERICAN COLLEGE OF ROME: FALL OF 1979

The fall semester at the American College commenced on the last Monday of September 1979. This meant that the classes had begun. Obviously, there was one class for freshers and another in the afternoon for sophomore students scheduled for Mondays. Since the American degree programme consisted of four years of studies, the college had to schedule the classes to achieve a balance between the early-year modules and the junior and senior year modules. This could be achieved by stretching out the classes between Monday and Friday. With my advanced standing, Michael gave me classes for junior-year modules, which placed me with Susan and her friends in one or two classes. However, introductory subjects, such as the introduction to art history, could be offered in the sophomore year. In addition, most exchange students from the USA would fall either in junior-year or senior-year classes, all of which had been scheduled for Thursday or Friday. I had to take three modules: Principles of Economics and Principles of Marketing on Thursdays, and Art History on Tuesdays.

On the first day, the new students had to attend a one-day induction, and I had to help Michael organize this event in the form of a workshop and seminar. This was a very good learning experience for me, as the newly enrolled students had to be informed about the course structure, module specifications, assessment methods, and American degree framework. In addition, workshops and seminars helped them engage and get to know each other. There were approximately thirty students in total, including a handful of adults and some from Iran and Libya. A few from other countries were also included, including India, Bangladesh, and Kenya. We served coffee, biscuits, and pastries during the coffee break, as well as sandwiches and drinks during lunch hours. Barbara and Michael interchangeably made presentations, and Susan and I, along with another couple of staff members, spent time chatting with the new students to make them comfortable. We also invited a few junior-year students and senior-year students to get to know each other. Overall, it turned out to be a wonderful day, and everyone was pleased.

By the end of the day, I had met a good number of freshers, but I could remember only some of them by name. Among them were the tall, attractive Molinari sisters, Mona and Lisa, and the two cute but chatty daughters of a South Asian diplomat, Nasrin and Fouzia. The American teenager of a diplomat, Benjamin, was another interesting character. As for lecturers, I also met two tutors, Dr Mogni and Professor Bota. The college had a team of lecturers, mainly academics from Italian universities and a few executives from international firms or organizations stationed in Rome. Michael often taught modules in art history, humanities, and liberal studies. As most of these tutors were not often available during the daytime, some of the classes had to be scheduled for early evening hours. This meant that the college was sometimes kept open until eight in the evening.

It was almost 8.00 p.m. when we left the college, and on the way out, we stopped at Mario to have something to eat. Barbara offered to join for a quick dinner, and we could not resist. It consisted of a simple pasta dish and a slice of pan-fried chicken breast. After dinner, I walked home leisurely while Susan took a bus home. Before we split, Michael reminded us about the next morning, comforting us by saying that it wouldn't be as hectic as the first day.

The second day was less hectic, as expected, but I was able to meet with some of Susan's junior-year friends. Although a few students from the senior year came for continuous enrolment, Susan did not seem to consider them close friends. Raymond, David, Daniel, and Laura, as well as Anne, Someya, and Zaid were some of those who showed up. There were a few more Iranian students that I was destined to meet through Susan. Flavio, whom I had already met, and his brother Alex were also expected to come in the afternoon. It was great meeting them and getting to know some of them, leading to building a sense of identity and friendship.

As for my work and responsibilities, I didn't have to worry too much, as I was scheduled to work only twenty hours a week. I was supposed to be at the reception desk for only two days and would spend another day and a half attending classes. I attended my first class of each week, which Michael taught, on Tuesday afternoons. The rest of my responsibilities included helping Barbara and Michael to attend to and support the needs of exchange students from Texas who were to arrive by the following week. Susan put in more hours than I, working almost every day at the reception desk except during her class hours. A few more students had been given job opportunities in college. During the first week, however, we had to work more hours than usual. In some sense, I thought the college was my home; whether I worked or not, I was bound to spend most of my time at the college.

By Thursday, I had met almost all of Susan's friends in class. Marketing and Economics, both at the introductory level, were taught by the same tutor, who was a highly qualified economist attached to an international organization. El-Sabry was an American-qualified Egyptian lady with years of business and management experience. I thought I was a star in the class, as Susan and the crowd were clueless in both economics and marketing. Since the degree programme at the college didn't offer business or economics majors, these introductory modules provided the necessary foundation in these areas. There were about fifteen to twenty students in the class, but only a few of them seemed to have acquired the basics to enjoy these modules thoroughly. And I was one of them.

On Friday evening, to celebrate the start of the new semester, Susan organized a get-together at Mario for dinner. We were to be ten in total, but a few failed to show up. Susan and I, along with Flavio and his brother Alex, as well as Susan's sister Ruby, with her boyfriend, Charles, assembled at the college to meet with the rest at the restaurant. Susan's boyfriend, Sayed, was also expected along with David, the youngest among the crowd. At Mario, Daniel and Anne were already waiting for us. Daniel was an interesting bloke originally from Palestine whose dad worked for the Food and Agricultural Organization in Rome. Anne was a Jewish American girl living in Rome with her parents. 'What a fascinating group,' I thought to myself.

Mario, being a family-run trattoria, had just a few tables to accommodate some twenty-five diners. Mario himself was the chef, and the rest of the family members worked at the restaurant. The dinner menu was simple, but a pasta dish and main dish along with salad and bread remained the staple. *Fettucine al fungi* in tomato sauce was served for the primo as soon as we all sat. Two jars of red house wine and rustic Italian bread were already on the table. There was a lot of talk over the pasta meal, and obviously the topic was new students. Some of them had already seen a few freshers, and a handful of names popped up in conversation, with impolite descriptions of how they looked and behaved. The South Asian sisters and their unique accent, the courteous but rather pretentious Italian sisters, and an American bloke who seemed obnoxious were themes of gossip. Daniel was so excited and curious to find out more about the Italian sisters. Flavio, with a sense of English humour, told Daniel that he would need to carry a stool with him if he wanted to kiss them, meaning that they were tall.

When Mario's dad, who served the meal, asked if he could bring the main dish, we immediately nodded. The pasta was delicious, although it was served with tomato-based sauce. Susan explained to me that traditionally, mushroom sauce was made with cream instead of tomato sauce. Within a few minutes, we were ready to tackle our main dish, which was *Pollo Cacciatore*, or hunter's chicken, served with a green salad. This traditional dish is often cooked with skinless bone-in chicken thighs or breasts in white wine and chopped tomatoes. It was a lovely dish, and we enjoyed it. As Mario's father did not leave the premises before midnight, we were not rushed out of the restaurant, but it was past eleven when we wanted to say goodnight. Susan, with Sayed, gave me a ride home, and Daniel took David home, as he seemed a bit tipsy.

As nothing had been planned for the weekend, I was able to sleep well and relax throughout Saturday. Some of our occupants at the pensione invited me to join their Sunday get-together at a pub near St Peters. Migrants usually spent time chatting and drinking in the evening on Sundays. The pub landlord also allowed them to bring potluck food. Two guys from Sri Lanka invited me to join them, and I did. It was not bad, and I met a handful of migrant workers from several countries, such as the Philippines, Columbia, Brazil, Mexico, Pakistan, and India. I was able to enjoy food from these countries, and I enjoyed the company, which was very different from that of my college friends. There, I came across an attractive girl from Sri Lanka who claimed that she knew the boys at the pensione and sometimes visited them. After a moment, the two guys who had brought me here interrupted us to introduce her to me as Shani. Shani, who had a college degree, had ended up in Rome as a migrant worker, and she said that she was working for a French diplomat's family as a babysitter. Shani seemed pleasant and spoke good English compared to the rest of the crowd.

It was indeed a fascinating experience to meet people from different countries, but surprisingly many of them were just economic migrants without any specific goals to attain. Shani told me that she was tricked by a con artist who promised her lucrative employment in a company. She ended up with nothing and was stranded in Rome. Italy did not have strict visa requirements for many nationals, and many came to Rome simply with a return flight ticket and some dollars in their pockets. Shani asked me whether I would come next week, but I didn't make any promises other than saying that she could always see me at the hotel. I was aware that South Asian girls were emotionally sensitive and that men would always try to protect them even if they didn't have any intentions.

At about ten-thirty, I was the first to leave the pub, and I reached my pensione within half an hour.

The next morning, the business at the college remained normal as expected, and there was not much to do other than answering phone calls or speaking to students to sort out their problems. Susan was usually good at answering phone calls, and she was also good at speaking basic Italian. On Wednesday, Barbara and I went to the airport to pick up exchange students who arrived from the USA. There were a dozen adults (five men and seven women). They were short-stay exchange students from Texas Lutheran College in San Antonio. Barbara noted that they were not regular students but from an adult exchange programme who were interested in Italian history and culture. We accompanied them to Rome from the airport and housed them in a nearby pensione. It was more than an average pensione which served breakfast to the guests and offered a decent room with an attached bathroom and a comfortable bed. Lunch and dinner were on their own, and thus I had to show them the college neighbourhood and amenities, including restaurants. Mario was indeed one of them.

Our guest students attended Michael's History of Arts class on Tuesdays and special seminars, arranged by the dean, during the week for four weeks. In between, they would be taken on a number of study tours in Rome, visiting key historic attractions. Their calendar included dates for visits to Pompeii and Florence, although these were not meant to be serious study tours. I was supposed to accompany Michael when they visited Florence and Pompeii. I also joined them during the Rome tour. Michael planned to hold an induction session on Friday. Michael and I had already prepared several materials, including a basic guidebook and a map of Rome with a list of all key attractions and places of interest. We planned to take them for an induction tour of the city on Saturday.

I knew that my leisure time was getting shorter, with the tasks assigned to me for the next month. On Friday, the induction session, which lasted almost four hours, went well, and the guest students were extremely happy and excited. On Saturday, I met the students at the pensione and took them to the famous square, Piazza Venezia, overlooking the huge building called the Wedding Cake, a neoclassical monument which was built in the late 1800s to honour Victor Emmanuel II, the first king of Italy after unification, also known as the father of Italian unification. This was the centre of Rome, with Capitoline Hill behind and the great Coliseum on the side. I thought this was a good starting point for the induction of ancient cities. The induction tour was not meant to be a study tour, and Michael also did not join us. I was the tour guide, and I was free to decide what was to be shown and where we were to visit.

We visited a few places of interest which were good for a touristic gaze. After I had shown them the Colosseum, Roman Forum, and Capitoline Hill, we proceeded to the Trevi Fountain, the Pantheon, and then the Spanish Steps, where we paused for a while to appreciate the landscape and to gaze at the crowd flocking to Via Condotti. I briefed them by saying that some of these places needed to be revisited with Michael as a study tour and that the museum at Capitoline Hill was a place of high priority. What amazed me the most was the enthusiasm shown by the visiting students, who had good knowledge of these attractions. My next stop was the ancient neighbourhood of Trastevere, where I had visited a few times, including my visit to see Susan, who lived in Piazza Santa Maria. In fact, it was the right time to have some quick lunch, and I suggested that we should grab a panini or a sandwich to save time rather than spending two hours for a lengthy Roman lunch. Kevin, who seemed to be the eldest of the group and the de facto leader, was very much supportive of my idea. Therefore, we took a quick break as we arrived at Trastevere to grab something to eat. Some opted for a slice of pizza, while others picked up a panini from the nearby cafe.

At Piazza Santa Maria, I pointed at one of the oldest churches in Rome, the Basilica di Santa Maria, and reminded them that this could be included in the study tour with Michael. I also showed them the *Jewish Ghetto,* which was not far from Trastevere. I hinted that the Jewish quarter hosted a few good restaurants, and in fact, a few of them were already interested in making a visit. Martha wanted to know whether I could recommend one, and I showed her the one where I had dined with Massimo during my first week in Rome. But I hinted that other restaurants could be as good as this. Some even suggested that they should try it in the evening after the tour. The next item on the agenda was St Peter's, in Vatican City, which was not far from where we were. At about four-thirty in the afternoon, we stumbled to the tram stop and headed for our next destination.

Some in the group were rather amazed on sighting St Peter's Basilica, with its expansive piazza and monumental structure. The basilica was still open to the public, and people were lining up to enter the museum to see the Sistine Chapel. The impressive colonnades and panoramic view of the church would make anyone blink with amazement. This is what most of the guest students seemed to experience when entering the Vatican compound. The students knew more about St Peter's and the museum than I knew, and they wanted to see in person what they had learned. I assured them that this would be included in Michael's study tour. In the meantime, I briefly explained what I knew and how to get around. I also pointed out that the Vatican Post was very popular with foreigners living in Rome, as they were very prompt and efficient compared to the Italian postal services that often failed to deliver mail on time. This prompted many guest students to send postcards home or to friends in the USA.

By the end of the day, I wanted to ensure that our guest students were satisfied with their introduction to the city. I made efforts to show them the other key attractions and how to get there by using public transport, which was relatively inexpensive. I also warned them to be alert when in crowded places or when using public transport, as pickpocketing remained prevalent. I even recommended that they should try to be together rather than being alone when visiting places or travelling in the city. I ensured that they could return to their hotel from anywhere if they were lost. They all carried the hotel's visiting card with an address so that they could get home by cab. In the end, when I said I wanted to get back home, they invited me to join them for dinner at the Jewish quarter. But with a polite apology, I told them, 'Next time.' However, before I left, I showed them how to get to the Jewish quarter and return to their hotel using public transport. I was confident that they would be fine by themselves, as they seemed to stick together as a group. All of them were middle-aged, and eight were couples.

We were already in the third week of the semester, and my life as a student and college staff member seemed to have passed smoothly. At times, I would join the study tour with the exchange students, which Michael appreciated very much, and he wanted me to help him with the Saturday tour to Tivoli scheduled for the next weekend. This was a one-day excursion open to any student interested in joining. The following Saturday, Michael planned to take the exchange students to Pompeii for a one-day excursion. Two weeks later, he would visit Florence for two days with one overnight stay. I was supposed to join Michael on both the tours.

One Tuesday, Michael took the entire class of the History of Arts to the museums at Capitoline Hill, a group of art and archaeological museums in Piazza del Campidoglio. The layout of the piazza dates back to the renaissance period in the sixteenth century. It was the creation of great renaissance artist Michelangelo. The founding of the museums can also be traced back to the same period, when Pope Sixtus reserved a collection of bronze statues to the people of Rome. In one of the buildings that houses the museum, Palazzo dei Conservatori, we found some famous statues, such as the she-wolf and the sucking twins, Romulus and Remus, which were adored as symbols of Rome. The courtyard of the palazzo hosted visitors with the remains of the statue of Emperor Constantine and the equestrian statue of Marcus Aurelius. On the second floor of the palazzo, one could find the works of masters such as Titian, Caravaggio, and Rubens.

The Palazzo Nuovo, the second building of the museum, housed classical sculptures, including the *Dying Gaul* and *Venus Capitolina*, as well as the sculpture group of *Love and Psyche*. Here, the one that fascinated me was the statue of Aphrodite, *Afrodite Calipigia* which Michael described as Aphrodite with a beautiful buttock. Michael was such a good narrator who knew how to feed the art enthusiasts as a chef would garnish a plate of food and make a wonderful presentation to hungry diners. Michael ended the tour with an hourlong visit to the Roman

Forum, where he left the students to spend time exploring the ancient Roman history based on his lecture notes and class-based seminar.

Back at the college the next day, I had an opportunity to brief Susan about my search for an affordable accommodation instead of spending the rest of the semester at the pensione. While she promised to look for a place to put me up as a lodger, she also suggested that I insert an announcement in the English daily called the *American Daily News*, as it was free to place an ad for students seeking accommodation. Since I was busy with classes and study tours, as well as helping Michael prepare for the Tivoli excursion the next Saturday, I decided to do this the following week. In the meantime, for the rest of the week, I would spend the time preparing the list of students interested in visiting Tivoli and collecting a small fee to cover the cost of the trip, including a light lunch and ticket prices for museum entries. I was expected to hand this in to Michael by Thursday evening. I was told that half of the cost would be absorbed by the college.

For this entertaining day trip, Susan and her friends also showed interest, but the seats were limited to just forty, which was the capacity of the coach. However, we managed to find seats for all those who had signed up. In the morning, I counted the total number of visitors at forty, including Michael and me, as well as exchange students from Texas. In the morning, after nine, as the coach ploughed through the city and then the hilly road towards Tivoli in the East of Rome, I could see the hilltop houses with patches of lush green vegetation and grazing sheep. The coach ride was less arduous than expected, and we reached Hadrian Village and the archaeological site of Villa Adriana in less than an hour. As we arrived at the coach park, I told the exchange students to be with me as much as possible, as it was a vast area that spread across acres.

Hadrian's Villa is not just a villa but a vast area of about 120 hectares of land with many pools, fountains, baths, and ruins of temples and libraries. It was a huge compound with a complex of buildings set out in classical Greek, Egyptian, and Roman architecture, a sign of Hadrian's love for different cultures and the lands he visited. Built in the second century AD by the great Roman emperor, it was to become a World Heritage Site in later years. Today the site comprises ruins and the archaeological remains of the complex. It was first built as a summer retreat, later to become Hadrian's official residence. Several buildings were dedicated to administrative functions when Hadrian ruled the Roman Empire. During this time, it could have been a vibrant mini city, with thousands of people living in Tivoli.

With Michael's onsite mini lecture explaining the historical significance and pointing out the various building sites, we began to spread out. The Maritime Theatre, Hospitalia, imperial palace, Piazza D'oro, thermal baths, Vestibule, and Canopus were the key sites we explored. However, our time was limited, as Michael had warned us not to spend more than a couple of hours there. Archaeological evidence showed that the villa was built stage by stage after Hadrian became Emperor in AD 117 and completed in AD 138. During his time of official residence, it was opulent and enormous, the largest of all Roman Emperors' villas. Historians claim that many of the missing statues and much missing marble were taken to decorate the renaissance garden of Villa d'Este, which was built centuries later. When we got together after spending more than two hours at the site, we headed towards the Tivoli Centre, where the coach was parked. It was already lunchtime, and before we entered the Tivoli Gardens, Michael had to run to the restaurant to see whether we could be served lunch within the next half hour. Fortunately, the answer was yes.

As the September sun shone on the cobblestone streets of Tivoli on our way to the restaurant that Michael had booked for lunch, the aroma of fresh basil and garlic made us walk faster, tantalizing our senses and beckoning us inside. The restaurant was located on a quiet street a short walk from the town centre and had a charming outdoor seating area shaded by parasols and surrounded by flower pots. The restaurant was bustling with activity, with servers rushing between tables, carrying crusty Italian bread, plates of steaming hot pasta, and flavour-emitting meat dishes. Restaurant walls were painted with murals depicting scenes of the Italian way of life and culture. The sound of lively chatter and gossip with laughter filled the air as we were shown the tables to be seated.

As we settled into our seats at two long communal tables in a pleasant atmosphere underneath a canopy of grapevines, with ripe grapes
hanging over our heads, we could sense the warm breeze and sounds
of chirping birds in the nearby trees. The servers brought plates and
rustic bread, along with jars of cold *limonaatta*. We had either *spaghetti
al-carbonara* or *cacio e pepe* to choose from as the primo. The carbonara
consisted of raw beaten eggs and finely grated Parmesan cheese, whereas
the cacio and pepe had crushed black pepper and finely grated *Pecorino
Romano* cheese. Both are classic pasta dishes. For the main dish, we had
a plate of ossobuco—braised shanks of veal cooked in white wine with
diced carrots.

In order to make it cost effective and easy to prepare and serving to
the large group, Michael limited the number of dishes in the menu to
choose from. If anyone didn't like veal, he or she could ask for roasted
chicken. Some picked cacio e pepe and roast chicken, but most ordered
carbonara and ossobuco. A few of the students also enjoyed a glass of
house wine, for which they had to pay separately. As we approached
the end of the meal, some continued to enjoy chatting and relaxing in
the warm sunshine, feeling lazy but satisfied after their delicious lunch.
Some even ordered desserts, such as tiramisu and gelato, for which they
paid extra, to complete their meals. It was a superbly delicious meal, and
the students had a fantastic time enjoying the convivial atmosphere of
the restaurant. But this did not last long, as Michael was soon calling
us to proceed with our planned trip to the Villa d'Este, the famous
renaissance garden.

I thought our visit to the Villa d'Este in Tivoli would be an exciting
and educational experience. As we arrived at the entrance of the villa,
we were greeted by the impressive facade of the Renaissance palace,
which took us back in time to the historic era. The villa, a magnificent
Renaissance palace built in the sixteenth century, was known for its
stunning architecture and incredible water features, and we were amazed
by the grandeur of the estate, especially the gardens.

At this point, Michael reminded us of his lecture in the class
the previous week and asked us to follow him if we wished to be

guided. Michael started the tour with a visit to the sixteenth-century palace, which was the home of Cardinal Ippolito d'Este. He went over the opulent frescoes and artwork that adorned the walls and ceilings, followed by an impressive collection of antique sculptures and furnishings.

Next we ventured into the gardens, where we explored various terraces, walkways, and fountains. When we entered the area, we were greeted by the sheer beauty of the gardens and fountains. The group stopped at a beautiful oval-shaped fountain with cascading water and a variety of sculptures, the Fontana dell'Ovato, and then the Rometta Fountain, which depicted scenes from ancient Rome. I was really carried away to another world by the intricate fountains, beautiful sculptures, and cascading waterfalls that were spread throughout the garden, which was beautifully landscaped. I was also stunned by the technology and engineering skills that used to harness the river to design and build water systems that powered the fountains and cascades.

The visit provided many people with a unique opportunity to experience the beauty and grandeur of Renaissance art and architecture in real life. For some, it was just another Italian garden; Villa d'Este gave me the opportunity to gain an appreciation for the meticulous craftsmanship that went into creating the Renaissance villa and its gardens. Throughout the tour, Michael made us learn not only about the history and significance of the Villa d'Este but also about its importance as a symbol of Renaissance art and architecture. Our visit to the Villa d'Este and Tivoli in general was a memorable and enriching experience which offered a glimpse into the grandeur and glory of the Italian Renaissance.

Having returned to the coach park, I counted the number of students and guests, but surprisingly, I found that some of them were missing. It was Susan and her group of four friends. While we were with Michael following his trail, Susan and Flavio, along with Daniel and the Molinari sisters, had stepped away to enjoy the villa on their own. I knew that some of the students had visited Villa d'Este previously. In any case, it didn't take much time for them to appear in the coach park. Back in

the coach, I could feel that there was something unusual going on, and
Susan was trying to pacify the Molinari sisters while Daniel and Flavio
were arguing about something. I felt that Daniel may have been a bit
silly with the sisters, as he had a crush over Mona. Soon, however, things
returned to normal as we pulled out of the parking area.

13

A HOME IN ROME

Back at the college the following Monday, things were less hectic. Michael had arranged a couple of study tours, including one of the Sistine Chapel at St. Paul's for the exchange students, but I was not keen to join. Susan reminded me about placing an announcement in the *American Daily News*, the English daily of Rome. I found out where the office of the publisher was located and managed to draft a twenty-word announcement, as the maximum word count allowed was less than twenty-five. By midweek I had placed the announcement, which read, 'An American College student is seeking accommodation in exchange for some flexible hours of household chores.' The college telephone number was provided as a contact number, along with Susan's name. I wanted the announcement to continue for four weeks, as permitted by the publisher, and it was free of charge. I was not very optimistic but said to myself that only time would tell whether I would get any calls.

In the meantime, a week had passed, and Michael was preparing for the next tour with the exchange students. It was to Pompeii, and it would be a one-day trip without an overnight stay. This meant leaving Rome by a minibus early in the morning, which would take nearly two hours to reach and return by late evening. I had already promised I would join them, and it had been planned for the next Saturday. Michael told me that this tour was to be repeated with overnight stays the following semester with regular students as part of the module called 'Western Civilization through Arts and Monuments' for the junior-year students.

On Saturday morning, we left Rome early, at seven-thirty, and arrived in Naples before nine-thirty. The exchange students seemed very excited and enthusiastic, and our tour of Pompeii started at ten after a quick break to relieve the bladder. It was a wonderful morning in October with sunlight shimmering over the ruins. We were warned to prepare for long hours of walking with suitable boots or trainer shoes, as well as to carry a bottle of water and some form of packet lunch in our backpacks. Michael had to purchase the ticket for fourteen of us, and once ready, we were in full gear to start the tour.

Our first stop was the Pompeii Amphitheatre, which was used for gladiator fights and other festivities and performances. Michael took 10 minutes to explain the history and significance of the Amphitheatre and commented that it was not any different from other Roman amphitheatres. On this occasion, he also briefed the students about the chronology of events in Pompeii over the last 2000 years, from the time of volcanic eruption to excavation. Pompeii perished from the ashes of the erupting Mount Vesuvius in 79 AD., on the 24th of August. This was one of the most catastrophic events in history and had a devastating impact on Pompeii, which was buried under volcanic ash and pumice. The Vesuvius eruption was a two-day event with a massive cloud of ash, pumice, and toxic gas thrown into the sky on the first day, and fast-moving pyroclastic flows consisting of highly destructive clouds of ash, rock fragments, and gas on the second day. According to scientists, the speed of the flows could have reached up to seventy miles per hour with a temperature of over five-hundred degrees Celsius that engulfed the entire city, burying it under several metres of volcanic material.

After the mini-lecture at the amphitheatre site, we moved to see the Forum of Pompeii, which was the city's main square. It consisted of the remains of the basilica, the courthouse where legal proceedings were held, and the Temple of Jupiter. Michael noted that the temple was dedicated to the Roman god of the sky and thunder. After exploring the forum with site-specific descriptions by Michael, the group split up to take a quick break. There were cafes and food stalls around for anyone who wanted coffee or snacks. Some opted to enjoy the food they had carried in their backpacks. We had decided on a place to meet after the break which was relatively easy to find. In any case, I had to keep an eye on the movements of the guest students. We all had red flags attached to our backpacks to easily identify each other.

After half an hour, we met in front of the famous Casa del Fauno, the House of Faun, which was one of the largest and most impressive houses in Pompeii. It was named after a bronze statue of a dancing faun found in the house, which could be seen in the National Archaeological Museum in Naples. According to historians, the House of Faun was built in the second century BC during the Samnite period and is considered the most luxurious aristocratic palace in the Roman Republic to be preserved from the Hellenistic period. Although the eruption of Vesuvius was a devastating event, its ash, which fell in layers, helped preserve valuable artworks, including mosaics. Michael pointed out that after a period of excavations, most of the valuable artefacts were moved to the museum in Naples. The group also visited the Pompeii baths, which were used for public bathing. Baths were an important part of Roman society and were used not only for relaxation and hygiene but also for socializing.

As the last item in the itinerary of the Pompeii tour, we visited the Pompeii gardens, which were once used for private residence. This was full of the remains of several villas and gardens, without exception of the Villa of the Mysteries, which contained well-preserved frescoes depicting ancient Roman rituals. Wrapping up the tour by sunset offered us enough time to look at Naples and enjoy a delicious pizza in Naples, which is considered the birthplace of pizza. At the coach, while chatting with the driver, Michael quickly pointed out the cultural traits of Naples and its inhabitants and the beauty of the city itself. Naples Bay provided a beautiful landscape, particularly at night, and picking a good and authentic pizzeria overlooking the bay remained Michael's aim.

The driver suggested that we check one of the traditional longstanding pizzerias called Pizzeria Lombardi a Santa Chiara. Within half an hour, we were on a hilltop overlooking the Bay of Naples. The coach meandered through the narrow roads and arrived at Lombardi, and it was an authentic place to enjoy pizza in Naples. All pizzas were made *al-forno* in a traditional stone oven, using fresh ingredients. The air was full of flavour emitted from fresh tomatoes, mozzarella cheese, basil, oregano, and virgin olive oil, which made all of us crave a slice of pizza.

The menu at Lombardi was simple, as all of the pizzas had a standard crust base with tomato sauce and mozzarella cheese, which is a traditional margherita pizza. Customers could order their preferred toppings, including seafood, such as clams, prawns, and anchovies; meats, such as salami, prosciutto, and pepperoni; and fresh vegetables, such as onions and mushrooms. A fresh egg cracked in the centre was another addition if anyone preferred. Fortunately, everything at Lombardi was fresh except for the cured meats, olives, and marinated vegetables. I ordered a *Pizza alla Pescatore*, or seafood pizza, consisting of fresh anchovies, prawns, and calamari with marinara sauce. I also wanted to add fresh mushrooms and sliced onion. Everyone tried their favourites, and some shared between two or three, which gave them the opportunity to taste more than one pizza.

We were extremely happy and a big thumbs-up for the driver's choice of restaurant. Because we had to pay for the meal, we all chipped in for the driver. At eight in the evening, we were set to leave Naples so that we could arrive in Rome at ten at night. On the way back, some of us dozed after a busy and tiring day. As we arrived in Rome, I had to pick up a cab to go home, as I also felt a bit tired and sleepy.

On Sunday, I wanted to visit Susan, but unfortunately, I had to attend to my household chores. The next morning, business as usual at the college continued. Midweek, Barbara asked me whether I could volunteer to help her do some wall painting in one of the spare rooms, which I could not refuse. The spare room was to be used as a classroom, and the college ordered desks and chairs. In fact, a couple of Iranian students had been offered financial hardship funds in exchange for some hours of work. I acted as a supervisor to help them paint and perform decoration-related chores. We started this paint job on Friday afternoon and finished it on Saturday, and the classroom was ready for use on the forthcoming Monday.

Michael was preparing for a weekend trip to Florence with the exchange students. In the first week of November, they had just a couple of weeks left before returning to the USA. Again, this would be just a sightseeing tour rather than a study tour. Michael pointed out that an extensive study tour would take place the next semester in line with the scheduled course module. He said my attendance on the trip would be helpful but not required. They planned to go to Florence, the birthplace of the Renaissance, on Friday, and return on Sunday morning. They would have the entire Saturday to visit the key attractions and to hear briefly about the birth of the Renaissance in the late 1400s. Michael pointed out that it would be a Florence-only trip and not Tuscany at large, and that he could easily manage by himself.

In mid-November, on a Wednesday, I received a call from an American lady regarding my newspaper announcement. First I thought that it was another call like the one I had received the previous week when a woman called me to say she was prepared to offer me some hourly paid household chores but no accommodation. But to my surprise, this call was different. She lived alone and had a spare room, but I needed to take care of her dog. I thought about it for a while and said I would be prepared to take up the offer after meeting her at her house. So I made an appointment to see her on Saturday, after four o'clock. When I said this to Susan, she was pleased and wished me good luck. She went on to make fun of me by saying that being single, the woman could be looking for a companion. I took it very lightly and said, 'You will find out next Monday.' After a while, we saw a few new Iranian students who walked towards us to say they were planning to invite a few people for an Iranian dinner. There were about ten to twelve Iranian students at the college in total, including a colonel who had fled Iran with his daughter just before the revolution. Susan had met all of them before but didn't know them except a few. Susan thought that it was not a bad idea to join them, and she and I agreed to join them on Friday.

In the evening, still in college, we decided to do a marketing coursework assignment which we had to hand in the day before the class started. The college library was kept open until 7.00 p.m., and we went downstairs, where the library was located. Susan's landlady, who was covering for the librarian, agreed to stay with us until eight. We managed to do some good work and collected useful materials to help us start writing. Since the assignment was about a promotion campaign, Susan seemed excited, but I had to show her how to plan and come up with an advertisement campaign for a newly introduced car by the German giant Daimler-Benz. My project was different—something about a new breakfast cereal to be introduced in Italy by an American company. We left home soon after 8.00 p.m., but I was determined to finish writing the project before going to bed.

In the marketing class the next day, El-Sabry was not happy, as not all students submitted their assignments. As a mid-semester assessment, we also had to make a five-to-ten-minute presentation in the class. Out of the fourteen students, only eight managed to present their projects, and Susan and I were among them. In fact, Susan and I attained the best marks, while Flavio received a borderline pass. Daniel did not submit his and seemed cross with me, as I hadn't helped him write. But I promised to help him to do so the next week for his late submission. After class, Daniel and Flavio wanted to go for a movie and then dinner. But I declined, and they all went to see the movie. I reminded Susan about the Iranian dinner on Friday night, and we agreed to see each other at the college in the late evening.

I got to the college on Friday rather late after midafternoon, when Michael and the Texan students had already left for Florence. I joined Susan at the reception desk and spent a couple of hours chatting and speaking to the students or answering phone calls. Susan, being an Iranian herself, likely knew what sort of food to expect at Hossain's house that night. She brought some Iranian sweets along. As we had to take a bus ride lasting at least thirty minutes, we decided to leave the college by 7.00 p.m. Of course, we had to walk for a few minutes to catch a bus.

At Hossain's, we were the first guests to arrive, but in less than thirty minutes, the house was full of people, roughly fifteen in total.

There were no special foods except a few. But we found a variety of dips and finger-foods which we could put our hands in and try out. There were tantalizing flavours to tease tongues. Saffron-flavoured rice pilaf cooked with juniper berries and sliced almonds, and topped with a layer of burned sliced potatoes, attracted my attention. It was laid out as if it were a cake; the guests would use a spatula to break off and serve a portion. I sprinkled ruby-red pomegranate seeds over rice. There were several mezes on the table, including yogurt, cucumber-onion dips, and roast aubergine dips. Lightly spiced oven-roasted lamb and chicken wings were also placed on the buffet table, along with freshly prepared and cut crudités. There were no complaints whatsoever except that it was stuffy and full of smoke. I was an occasional smoker in the seventies, but this was too much, and from time to time, I had to step out to get some fresh air. Another problem was that everyone chatted in Farsi, the Iranian language. Susan probably felt my discomfort and suggested that we take off just after ten. Again without a car, we had to return to the town by bus. Luckily, we didn't have to wait long for a bus, and we were back home by 11.00 p.m.

I was unusually early to get up for a Saturday; perhaps I was thinking about my meeting with the American lady in the late afternoon. I had already searched and found the road on the map, and I knew how to get there by walking, as it was not far from the pensione. I didn't tell Laura that I was looking for a place to move out, but she knew it was not sustainable for me to stay in the pensione for a long time. She also knew that I spent most of my time at the college, and she hardly saw me during the day. In any case, she was nice to me.

In the late afternoon, around half past three, I left the room so that I had enough time to walk what I thought would be a couple of kilometres. Later, I realized that it was a matter of fifteen minutes of walking to get there, but I did not want to knock on the door before four o'clock. So I spent some time checking out the neighbourhood and arrived at the doorstep on the second floor of the apartment just after four. When I rang the bell, a lady in her fifties opened the door to invite me in while shouting at the dog behind her to lie down. I introduced myself as Zain

Baba, and she said, 'I am Lucille.' Finally, I saw the lady, whom I was eager to meet. At first sight, I thought there was some chemistry between us, and the welcome I received proved this to be so. Lucille pointed out that she had been renting a three-bed apartment for the last four years. She was a single woman living with an Alsatian dog called Peakeo and Olga, a housekeeper who was on and off. Olga frequently stayed out with her cousin.

Lucille wondered where I was from, and when I told her I was from Sri Lanka, she responded by saying 'Oh, *Ceylon*, I used to know your former prime minister, John.' She was referring to Sir John Kotelawala, who was the third prime minister of Ceylon after gaining independence from Britain in 1948. Lucille had become acquainted him while in London and, in fact, had stayed in his house in London as a guest. This was great news and was the end of the story, and as a Ceylonese person, I didn't need any more references. We had a long chat over a cup of tea, though she still preferred coffee. Lucille was a Jewish American lady and had been living here in Rome for over fifteen years. As I understood it, she worked as an estate agent of some sort for diplomats and executives of multinational and multilateral organizations. Although Lucille worked from home over the phone, she had to go around the city to show houses or inspect them before listing them in her book. Thus, she was looking for someone to take her dog out for a walk at least twice a day, which I was prepared to do, although it seemed a bit of a challenge for me because of Peakeo's sheer size. But, as he seemed to be a well-behaved dog, I didn't expect any problems in controlling him.

Lucille showed me around the house and briefed me about the house rules, but she didn't treat me as a housekeeper. Since Olga was often in and out of the house, I was expected to help her with household chores, which I didn't mind. I did tell Lucille, however, that I wished to move in December first, which was ten days away. This would give me ample time to speak to Laura and leave the pensione amicably. In the meantime, I also stressed that as a student and college staff member, I needed some flexibility. Apart from some special assignments, such as helping Michael with excursions and study tours, my working hours at the college were limited to three half-days. This meant that most days in a week, I would be free to walk the dogs in the evening or night, and almost every day in the morning before leaving home. Lucille noted that in my absence, either she or Olga could walk Peakeo.

In the end, I thought that was the best arrangement I could expect in the pursuit of my dolce vita. Housing was free, and I had a job that paid my expenses as well as a good lifestyle, which I wouldn't have ever expected when I first stepped on Italian soil the previous summer. I was grateful to Susan for suggesting that I place an advertisement in the newspaper, so I thought I would go and visit her on Sunday with chocolates to express my gratitude. I made a call to her host's landline phone to see if she would be home on Sunday, as she might have planned to be out with Sayed. However, luckily, Sayed had not come to visit her this weekend, and she seemed pleased to see me the next day.

In the evening on Sunday, I bought a box of Baci chocolates and headed towards Susan. When she heard me say, 'I found a place to live,' she sarcastically replied, 'So, the American lady liked you.' I tried to assure her by saying that in looking at the fifty-year-old, I could imagine her being my Roman mum. We sat and chatted about the arrangements with Lucille and the job I would be expected to do in exchange for a room in her house, which was not far from the city centre. Susan seemed extremely happy, and we thought we should go for a leisurely walk along the Tiber and then find a trattoria for a light dinner. The walk along the riverbank was indeed pleasant, and we finally ended up crossing the bridge and reached the Jewish ghetto to find an eatery. We avoided fancy restaurants and spotted a modest trattoria which did not have a menu. Diners there had to eat whatever the chef served. We were asked whether we wanted a pasta dish first and meatballs as the main dish separately, or both together in one dish. We believed that it would be much easier to serve both in one. We were served a plate of penne with spicy meatballs in sauce on the top. Here, minced beef balls with Italian herbs were lightly fried and cooked in a spicy tomato sauce, which provided an exotic garlic and chilli flavour.

The meal was good, delicious, simple, and fast. I walked Susan home after dinner and returned to the bus stop to catch the bus back to the pensione. It was half past ten when I reached the pensione, and I was met by Laura at the reception desk. I thought it was a good time to chat with Laura about my plan to move out by early December, while everyone was planning for Christmas. Laura and her brother were chatting about decorating the reception area and the hall for Christmas. They usually erected a large Christmas tree with lights and ornaments by early December, but this time they wanted to put it up one week earlier than the previous year.

As we approached the last week of November, the students were already chatting about the festive season. Even Texan exchange students back from Florence were excited about returning home for Christmas by the next Saturday. The exchange students seemed to have had a wonderful time in Florence, and they told me that their visit to the Uffizi Gallery remained the highlight of the tour. This important museum contains a valuable collection of members of the Medici family. As one of the most visited Italian museums, it was said to have held a collection of priceless works from the Italian Renaissance. The exchange students also visited the nearby Museo Galileo, which is a museum of the history of science, and the famous Ponte Vecchio, a medieval stone arch bridge over the Arno River. This was the only bridge in Florence that remained intact after World War II. When I asked them about their overall experience in Italy, most of them thought that time had been tight for them and they would return to Italy in the near future.

14

THE FIRST CHRISTMAS: ROME 1979

It was good to sense a wonderful feeling of festivities and celebrations during December in Europe. In Italy, the birthplace of Catholicism, it seemed much more prominent than elsewhere. For me, this was an extraordinary first-time experience in Europe. At the college, Susan and I were thinking about our holiday, and Barbara had already published the Christmas and New Year holiday calendar. All teaching and assessment ended one week before Christmas, and the college would be shut until the first week of January. Susan and I decided to stay in Rome during the festive season, as it didn't seem convenient or affordable to travel anywhere. We also heard that Michael and Barbara were planning to host a Christmas lunch in their homes, and we would be invited.

Meanwhile, we had other plans for the festive season, including a couple of parties and dinners already in the pipeline. Susan and Flavio remained a catalyst in this regard, and Daniel would be very supportive when it came to organizing parties. While Sally, Susan's host, was keen to let us hold the New Year's Eve party in her place, Susan and Flavio were also planning to celebrate the dawn of the new year in an outside venue with disco dancing. Susan assured me that before the college closed for holidays in mid-December, we would come to make our final decision.

In early December, the streets of Rome were already lit with festive colours, and Christmas trees in some piazzas remained attractive for shoppers who would pause for a while to take a glimpse. In the evening, it seemed a real joy to stroll through the streets as the shops were still open. Quite a few times, after college hours, Susan and I strolled through one of the busy street under the pretence of Christmas shopping. For a newcomer from South Asia, Christmastime in Rome was not at all bad, even though the weather was not always conducive. For the first time in my life, I was having the experience of walking with a female friend holding each other's hands. We enjoyed the walk in the beautiful but brisk and mildly chilly weather, with our winter hats and sweaters on and our necks wrapped by scarves. It was also a wonderful feeling to visit Vatican City during Christmas, particularly in the evening. One could feel the air of *Natale* as one entered the St Peter's Square. Thousands of international and Italian visitors came to see the Vatican during the Christmas period. Most of these visitors could have been on their first visit or a sort of pilgrimage.

The last week of the semester at college was a slow-moving week. Some international students had already left Rome to celebrate Christmas in their home countries. While Barbara suggested the idea of hosting a Christmas party at the college, it never became a reality. 'Perhaps next year,' I said to myself. However, for that Tuesday evening, the college secretary had booked Christmas dinner at a restaurant in the city, and about twenty students, including guests, had signed up to join. Michael was expected to join the dinner too. 'At a reasonable price for a three-course dinner with dessert and house wine, it could be an enjoyable evening,' I said to myself.

Christmas dinner essentially looked like an American or rather British-style event, with guests wearing headbands and pulling Christmas crackers, as well as the overall ambiance. To start with, antipasti would suit American or British tastes. We had mulled wine along with the assorted cheese and olives. But the dinner menu was typically Italian, and we were served *Lasagne Al-forno* with Bolognese sauce as the primo, followed by roasted veal, along with carrots and oven-roasted potatoes.

Traditional Italian bread and house wine, both red and white, were also served to accompany meals. Being a Tuesday evening, the restaurant was not entirely packed as usual and was therefore less noisy, giving us the liberty to chat loudly, with an occasional burst of laughter. Daniel and David were, in fact, showing off their colours to the girls in the group, but the Molinari sisters were not impressed. They seemed to enjoy good conversations with us and our company. Before we left, we had tiramisu as a dessert and espresso to complete the dinner.

In 1979, Christmas day fell on Tuesday, and we had a week more to pass by. The college was to shut from this week, and I was still to move out of the pensione. I could not move out as I had planned at the beginning of the month, although I had made a few visits to Lucille during the last couple of weeks. In fact, I stayed over a few nights, and my room was ready, with all necessary furniture. I didn't have much to carry with me—only a couple of luggage items and handbags. Since Lucille had given me bedding, such as pillows and duvets, I didn't need to buy anything new. Susan even promised me that she could give a hand when I had to move my belongings, but Lucille said she could pick up my luggage in her Fiat Cinquecento, which sounded much better.

On 21 December, I bade farewell to Laura and moved to Lucille, but I promised to visit the pensione time to time. At Lucille's, Olga and Peakeo welcomed me as we both entered the home. Olga made me a cup of coffee, and she was about to cook some dinner for all of us. She had already erected a small Christmas tree in the corner of the living room, which made the house glitter in the evening. Lucille was not particular about religion, but she wouldn't miss any parties or celebrations. Christmas remained at a time of joy for everyone, and so it was for Lucille. Olga, being a Catholic, was ready to go to her native village somewhere in Trieste, near Venice. In the meantime, Lucille's dinner calendar seemed almost full during the current week, and I understood that she had also been invited to Christmas lunch. Thus, I would be alone myself at home for dinner after Saturday, but I had been invited to Susan's for Christmas Eve and for Christmas lunch with Michael and Barbara. Since we were determined to go out for New Year's Eve, Sally decided to organize the Christmas Eve party with a buffet dinner.

As I settled in with Lucille, I was getting used to taking Peakeo out for a walk twice a day. He quickly learned to deal with my attitude, and I found him well-behaved. I didn't usually get up before nine-thirty in the morning, as I didn't have any classes or work to attend during holidays. So I went for a walk with Peakeo after coffee but before breakfast. In the evening, I took him out at 10.00 p.m. In an urban environment, it seemed difficult to control Peakeo when he tried to sniff everything that he smelled. However, this was a good opportunity to meet new people, and everyone wanted to say bon giorno when they saw someone with a dog. The other dog walkers were particularly interested in chatting with me. However, at times, I got into trouble when another dog tried to confront Peakeo. At home, he was an adorable animal, and Lucille kept him clean and healthy with regular check-ups.

On the evening of the twenty-fourth, I took Peakeo for an early walk at eight, when Lucille was already on her way out. This evening, when the Nativity displays were completed by adding the baby Jesus to the scene, most would flock to St Peter's Square. Some would even spend the entire evening at St Peter's until Midnight Mass. In the meantime, at Sally's, Christmas buffet dinner would be ready by nine, as the party kicked off at ten. I was told that it would be a low-key event with soft music in the background. However, when I got there by half past nine, there were just a few friends of Sally, fewer than ten people, eating and chatting. Susan warned me that the invitees were mainly middle-aged people or even older folks of Sally's age.

Within an hour, however, we had about twenty people having a wonderful time together, nibbling whatever they could find on the buffet table. Sally had cooked some lasagne and roast lamb, and there were plenty of antipasti as well as lots of wine brought by the guests. As usual, the ambiance was pleasing, with many Christmas ornaments floating around a spacious living room. I had already met most of the people during the last summer get-together at Sally's. A chatty Jewish student from the college was also present. Margie, who lived with her diplomat parents, frequently visited Sally. Susan expected Sayed and her sister Ruby to show up but they didn't until I left the party at half past twelve. Margie gave me a ride home, and in fact, I was home before Lucille walked in an hour later. Luckily, Peakeo didn't bother me, insisting on going out. He usually had a way of telling me that he would like to go out by patting my foot.

On Christmas Day, I was up early on and cooked a breakfast of eggs and toast for Lucille and me. It was rather misty in the morning when I took Peakeo for a walk but turned out to be chilly and sunny later in the afternoon. Both Lucille and I had to get ready for the Christmas lunch. Michael and Barbara expected the guests to be there at one o'clock for lunch. There was enough time for anyone to visit St Peter's in the morning to get a glimpse of the pope and hear him addressing the mass and showering his blessings on the devotees.

The lunch at Michael and Barbara were something special, but there was just a handful of guests—only eight of us. Susan had arrived before me, and she even seemed to have helped Barbara with preparation. As I arrived, a glass of warm mulled wine helped me feel comfortable near the traditional fireplace. We had all the traditional antipasti to start with, and a wonderful baked penne dish with Bolognese sauce as the first dish. Once that had been completed, Barbara carved out thin layers of perfectly roasted Tacchini Ripieni, a traditional stuffed roast turkey. The stuffing consisted of breadcrumbs and finely chopped onions, celery, carrots, spices, and herbs, all of which was mixed with wine. Of course, winter vegetables, such as artichoke hearts, roasted potatoes, and carrots, were also served. Christmas crackers and gifts were also exchanged. For desserts, we had some tiramisu, which Barbara had created from an old recipe. The end of the meal was completed with a traditional Italian espresso made in a percolator, served with a delicious panettone. I realized how wonderful Barbara and Michael were as hosts. We moved from the dining table and sat on the sofa while sipping the coffee and engaged in all types of conversations, including the Christmas highlights in Rome. Michael brought about the topic of extended Christmas celebration on the twenty-sixth day of December, which the locals called St

Stephen's Day. It was the day when they visited Christmas markets as well as nativity displays in churches. With more panettones and coffee, we spent long hours chatting at Barbara and Michael and took off just before seven.

On St Stephen's Day, Susan and I went to the famous Christmas market in Piazza Navona, which is known for Bernini's Fountain of the Four Rivers. Unalike other piazzas in Rome, the shape of the Piazza Navona seemed strange but unique. It didn't look like a square but was structured in a *U* shape which stood above the Roman chariot-racing track built during the time of Emperor Domitian in the first century AD. Unfortunately, most of the stadium consists of a ruin today, although a good part has been well preserved.

The market was opened from the eighth day of December to January 6, from ten in the morning until two in the afternoon. It was fully packed at eleven in the morning. We took our time browsing while stumbling through the crowd, gazing at what novelties the market had to offer. It was so nice to be wrapped up in a rather cold but crispy and misty day, browsing ornaments and foods from all over the region. The Church of Sant'Agnes in Agone was also popular with locals visiting the market. At the piazza, the Christmas market occupied the entire square with stalls on the long sides and a roundabout and nativity scene, as well as the balloon sellers in the centre. Before leaving the market, Susan bought a pair of leather gloves and I bought an artisan panettone for Lucille.

When I woke up the next morning, Lucille was already busy cleaning her room. She also took Peakeo for a walk, so I didn't have to rush. After a good, warm shower, I made breakfast for both of us. At twelve mid-day, it was a lunch meal rather than breakfast. Lucille said she wanted to spend some time cleaning up the clutter in her room during the weeklong holiday. At times, I attended to some of the household chores during the week, but on Friday, I went to see Susan after visiting Laura for a Christmas coffee. Lucille knew that she had to take Peakeo for a walk if I didn't show up before ten in the night. In the city, the streets were almost empty, and I could hardly see any traffic, but public transit was functioning with limited services during the entire week.

I took the tramcar to Trastevere and walked on empty roads to reach the piazza where Susan stayed. To my surprise, Sayed and Ruby were at Susan's and were planning to visit Flavio, who lived with his parents thirty minutes away from Rome. Susan and Ruby wanted me to join them, and I agreed. Rocca Priora, known as one of the Castelli Romani, was a historic small town situated at the feet of Alban Hill outside the city in the southeast of Rome, not far from Lake Albano.

It was a beautiful ride along hilly slopes with lush green vegetation and patches of vineyards. Flavio didn't seem surprised to see us. He would perhaps have expected an impromptu visit such as this from us. Susan wanted to drag Flavio out and go for a ride somewhere, such as to the lakeside. But Flavio's mama wouldn't let us go without a meal. Flavio's sister Antonia too was keen to see us stay for dinner. So we went around for sightseeing, including the vineyard in Frascati. When we returned, along with the usual Roman antipasti, dinner was served. The primo was a simple but delicious plate of spaghetti with *Aglio, Olio,* and *Pepperoncino* laced with chopped canned anchovies. Here, cooked and strained pasta was simply tossed in prepared olive oil with chopped garlic and chilli pepper. We served quail cooked in red wine with olives, capers, and fresh tomatoes as the main dish.

Before leaving Flavio, we were reassured that he had everything arranged for the New Year's party at an exclusive club in the outskirts of the city, for which only a limited number of tickets were sold. Flavio counted a total of twelve from our side. The ticket price included only one free drink. We decided to meet at Susan's place about 10.00 p.m., after dinner, before going to the venue. Flavio was to collect the money on the evening of the thirty-first before we headed to the party.

Sayed drove us home straight away, and I was home before 11.00 p.m. Luckily, Lucille had already taken Peakeo for a walk. Lucille said that she had made a sandwich for herself and that she wouldn't mind having coffee. So I made coffee for both of us. This was the first time after Christmas that we both sat together for a chat, and we spent about half an hour talking about each other's Christmas experience over the coffee and a slice of panettone I had picked up from Piazza Navona on

St. Stephen's Day. Lucille asked me what my plan for New Year's Eve was, and I let her know about the planned party with my friends. She had been invited to join her American friend for the family evening. They wanted Lucille to come along with Peakeo, and I was also invited.

On the night of the thirty-first in 1979, Rome was no different from the rest of the capital cities in the world. At five in the evening, celebrations had already started with firecrackers and illumination. I heard that a large public celebration was to take place at Piazza del Popolo, where we could see spectacular fireworks, listen to music, and dance. The old part of the city, such as the Trastevere, Testaccio, and Ostiense neighbourhoods, where nightclubs and discotheques were found, would see an influx of revellers after nine in the night. Following the years after the dolce vita era, discontent Italian youths had been searching for some sort of direction in life, and discotheques were seen as an ideal escape route to kill their pastime. In the late seventies and the early eighties, Italian discos gradually adopted rave music and songs influenced by the New York and London disco scenes. The albums of the Bee Gees and Pink Floyd were common in the late 1970s. The Piper, a popular nightclub close to the exclusive neighbourhood of Rome on the north side, was a pioneer in this regard.

The disco bar that Flavio had chosen for our New Year celebration was situated south of the Ostiense neighbourhood called the EUR, a relatively modern suburban enclave built by Mussolini. At nine, as planned, we assembled at Susan's and drove to the disco, which was in a secluded area with many parking spaces. There was not much formality, and as we entered and left our coats at the cloakroom, we could see the decorated dance floor with a rave-disco ambience, along with a posh bar serving drinks and things to nibble on. We were told that Asti Spumante was to be served as the clock struck twelve o'clock. The ticket price included the cost of the fizzy wine and another additional drink at the bar. The ticket price, however, seemed relatively expensive compared to the market price, if I remember correctly.

We were fast approaching midnight, and the environment was relaxed, except for the blasting sound of the music, with about hundred or so people present in total. Along with a few popular local songs, the

DJ took his liberty to play the Bee Gees album from the trendy film Saturday Night Fever. This 1977 film starring John Travolta as a dancer became a symbol of soul-searching disco kids everywhere in the West. Songs such as 'Night Fever', 'Stayin' Alive', and 'Jive Talkin" from the Bee Gees album were popular hits, and we had the opportunity to revel in these songs. I was dancing with Susan, Anne, Ruby, and a friend of David, Katarina, who was a fantastic dancer. Daniel seemed a bit out of his mind and went after almost every woman on the floor. He almost started a fight with a man when Daniel attempted to approach his lady while she was sitting on a chair to rest. Susan intervened in the scene and made the couple understand the nature and character of Daniel.

While we were anxiously waiting to hear the clock strike midnight, there was an announcement from the DJ saying that he was going to start the countdown for the last sixty seconds. I was holding my Asti up with Anne and David, ready to toast to the New Year with a kiss and hug. We all were holding our Asti, and when the DJ declared, 'Buon Anno,' everyone had a sip of the fizzy drink. After exchanging kisses and hugs for a few minutes, we were all joined by the crowd dancing around, holding one another, and singing. It took another thirty minutes before the crowd started to leave the disco bar slowly. When the barkeeper asked us to stay put for a while, we stayed seated, and to our surprise, we were served a mini panini with an omelette. We were the last few people to leave.

In a matter of minutes, everyone split from one another to get home. I went home with David and Katarina, as they had to pass through the city centre. Katarina seemed sober, and she drove us home carefully. When I got home, I sensed that Lucille had not arrived yet; I thought she would arrive home with each passing minute. I made myself a cup of coffee and kept myself awake for almost an hour, but Lucille didn't show up. But before I jumped on to the bed, I heard the door open. 'Buon Anno,' I said, and she repeated the greeting as we both exchanged kisses and hugs. She described her New Year's Eve as a family event, and she had enjoyed a wonderful evening. As we went to sleep, Peakeo lay down to sleep as well. I welcomed 1980 as a wonderful year ahead—another slice of Dolce Vita.

Section Four

THE YEAR 1980: A TASTE OF THE GOOD LIFE

For Zain, 1980 is an unforgettable year. Life in general looks promising and enjoyable. Unexpected encounters of love and romance, fascinating and enriching study tours, and the joy of mingling among peers with exposure to the Italian culinary tradition and delicious meals are all on his plate to be explored throughout the year. Christmas with Debbie and Marinela in Padua and cultural and leisure visits to the North-East add further joy to the year. Zain enjoys the taste of Dolce Vita.

15

THE YEAR OF LOVE
AND ROMANCE

The arrival of 1980 delighted all of us, undoubtedly, and we welcomed the new year gracefully—some of us with a few resolutions. Whether we would succeed in accomplishing them or not remains to be seen; after all, we had one whole year ahead of us to make them happen. On the first day of the year, I woke up rather late, at half past eleven, and took Peakeo for a walk immediately, as he was wagging his tail when I got out of bed. Lucille seemed deeply asleep, so I made myself a cup of coffee to start the day. Soon I was in the kitchen, preparing breakfast before she got up. As Lucille preferred jam and toast, along with eggs, I made an omelette with mushrooms, onions, and tomatoes. We also had some gorgonzola and other varieties of Italian cheese to go with the rustic bread which Lucille brought the previous night. Not to mention chilled orange juice. By the time I made breakfast ready, Lucille was already up and noted that I had made an omelette, which she liked very much.

Lucille and I sat and enjoyed breakfast while chatting about a number of things, such as my New Year's Eve party and the resolutions I had made. Completing my studies successfully remained my top priority. She seemed very supportive and assured me that I had a home and a second mother in Rome. This made me very happy, and I had wonderful feelings after hearing this message on the first day of the year. Lucille wanted to hear about my progress in the college, which I thought involved a huge learning curve in general. My examinations were conducted by the second week in January. I pointed out that I did not expect any problems with my courses, and informally I knew I had achieved good grades. In fact, I expected a distinction in the economic and marketing modules. In the next semester, Michael had me enrol in only two modules, International Business and Western Civilization through Arts and Monuments, which provided six credits over two semesters, including the summer term. Lucille already knew that I could be called up to go with Michael on study tours during the semester and that I might be away from home for a couple of days.

It was indeed a long chat over breakfast, and nobody was in a rush. It was the first time I had seen Lucille relaxed and easy, and she was not prepared to do any work for the entire day. She asked me whether I would want to visit the countryside for a ride in her *Cinquecento*. I thought that would offer wonderful experience with Peakeo in the countryside, and I agreed. In a matter of an hour, we got ready and were on the move. Peakeo occupied the entire back seat, which he did all the time when we went out with Lucille.

When thinking about where to go for a countryside walk, I would get into time-wasting exercises, as Rome had an unimaginable number of options to choose from. Some of them were close to Rome, while others were at least an hour and half from the city by car, such as Lake Bracciano, Frascati, and Grottaferrata. We could even choose a picturesque town, such as Tonfa, near Rome. However, the purpose of our visit was just an escape and an outing to enjoy nature rather than to appreciate history and heritage. The trip would offer opportunities for Peakeo to enjoy the countryside as much as possible. Based on these criteria, we decided to go to the Veio Regional Park, which would not only offer plenty of space but also help immerse us in beautiful and gorgeous natural environments and everything near Rome.

It didn't take hours to get to Veio Park, but just over thirty minutes. When I sighted the beautiful nature with thousands of acres of woods and pastures, it was almost like an epiphany, and I exclaimed, 'Awe!'

while Peakeo jumped out of the car with excitement. We parked the car on a cliff near the roadside, overlooking the pastures, and descended the slope slowly with Peakeo on a leash, as it would be quite risky to let him free. I did hold him firmly when he tried to pull down fast, as he rarely saw this sort of an opportunity to escape and run freely in nature. Lucille took her time to leisurely walk down, and as we descended the hill, it was something like seizing the moment. It was indeed mesmerizing to touch and feel nature. We had a small ball to play with Peakeo, but I still managed to hold him on the leash and ran with him while Lucille kept throwing it around.

The Veio Park was an ecological treasure with a wealth of flora and fauna. In addition, the park had abundant historical and archaeological treasures. It could also be a place for day trips with picnic baskets, which we missed, as we never thought of it. We could have enjoyed a wonderful picnic lunch while watching calves and horses grazing pastures freely. In fact, there were many day trippers in the park, some well prepared with picnic lunch baskets. In the past, the park was an Etruscan city, and it was full of ruins, including those of the Temple of Apollo. The park had a well-preserved Roman monument, the Villa of Empress Livia, the wife of Augustus. Veio Park also allowed us to see the Sorbo Valley waterfall and the Sanctuary of the Madonna del Sorbo, hence the name. We were able to drive around to briefly see these attractions.

On the way back, we stopped at a roadside cafe and had a panini at approximately four in the afternoon. It was a beautiful, sunny day, but the air was crispy and cold. When we returned, it was almost dark, and Peakeo did not need to walk. The first thing I did was brew a good cup of espresso, and Lucille wanted it doppio, or double, with a slice of panettone. I wouldn't ask anything more. As for dinner, I could try some fried breasts of chicken and chips, which Lucille wanted with a bowl of salad. Late in the night, at about half past nine, we had our dinner, and I took Peakeo out before hitting the bed. Lucille would sleep much later than usual. She wanted to browse her calendar and plan for her business visits in January. In fact, she had two appointments for tomorrow, with an Asian diplomat that involved a visit to the outskirts of Rome to show a house. I bade her good night and went to sleep. What a wonderful first day of the year!

The American College was scheduled to open on the third of January, which was a Thursday. Barbara asked me and Susan whether we could be available to come, and we agreed to be there after ten. When I went there, I was alone with Barbara, and Michael was absent. Susan did show up after midday. I was pleased to have her company. Michael was expected to show up late in the afternoon so that we could have a meeting for the next semester's preparations. Thus, we were free until afternoon, but there were a few students visiting the college asking for course and admission information. Since the college had a rolling admission policy, students could be admitted for both semesters as well as the summer semester, which was much shorter but intensive. However, the September sessions usually had the highest student intake.

At just three in the afternoon, Michael came with some snacks and called us for a meeting. He was busy preparing the class timetable for the semester so that classes could start on the twenty-eight of January as planned. With some croquettes, rice balls, and chips, we continued to discuss the issues of staffing key positions, such as the reception desk, as well as helping students with administration. Michael said that freshman classes would be available only if we could gather twelve students, but Barbara thought we would end up admitting at least fifteen students for the new semester. About six exchange students were expected from Texan Lutheran College to spend the entire semester in Rome, Barbara said. They were regular young adults who could transfer their accumulated credits to the US college. I was also expected to help Michael with his study tours related to his two-part module of Western Civilisation through Arts and Monuments. 'It seems like an exciting semester,' I said to Susan. By the time we finished the day, it was nearly six and we were ready to head home.

For the next couple of weeks, things started to move smoothly, and we were somewhat busy dealing with admission enquiries over the phone, while some students visited for registration. All our current students also needed to enrol in the new semester, as some of them who were on an instalment plan had to pay their tuition fees as well before enrolment. In the meantime, our class colleagues, such as Flavio, Daniel, Raymond, the Molinari sisters, and the South Asian sisters, all had made their visit to the college during the weeks before the classes commenced. We were all excited to see them back, not to mention the exchange of trivial but symbolic New Year gifts and kisses. This was something that I was not expected to see, but I received gifts too. All in all, it was a wonderful experience, and the college environment was exciting as the students moved around chatting and listening to the gossip.

On Friday, a few days before the classes began, Barbara wanted me to join her to pick up and welcome new Texan students. Barbara had an eight-seater van that we and the four students could easily fit in. Of the six expected students, only four joined us. At the airport, I displayed the placard with the American College of Rome sign so that the students could easily identify with us. The exhausted students who made their way out at the exit gate were easily able to find us, and we introduced ourselves. Among them, three were girls, and my eyes immediately turned to Sandy. The group leader was Phil, who looked to be the studious type. We helped them load their luggage into the van and drove it back to the city. They all wanted to have a nap rather than eat anything, so we took them to the hotel near the college that we had arranged. It was the same pensione we had arranged in the previous semester for the exchange students. It was nine in the morning, and I was supposed to meet them in the late afternoon to take them for a meal, which I did at five. I then showed them around, including the cafes and restaurants. They were also introduced to Mario so they could have early dinners.

The first day of the semester was quite hectic, but everything went well. To our surprise, freshmen enrolment was higher than expected, and we had some more Iranian students joining the college. A few of them were adults and enjoyed advanced standing to join the sophomore year. The exchange students from a Texas college in San Antonio, were enrolled mainly in junior-year and senior-year modules and therefore had classes on Wednesdays and Thursdays. All of them even enrolled in the first part of the art history module History of Western Civilisation through Arts and Monuments. We enrolled almost twenty students in this module. Since I had to keep an eye on Texas students, I spent most of my time during the week with them taking the four on an induction tour of the city. This gave me the opportunity to get to know Sandy a bit more and to build confidence since I had a crush on her.

The following week, I invited Sandy for a dinner date on Valentine's Day, but she agreed to come with me for a drink. Using Valentine's Day as an excuse, I carried some flowers when I went to take her out. She was shocked and said, 'It is indeed a surprise.' Even the other girls had strange looks on their faces when they saw me with flowers inviting Sandy for a Valentine's Day date. I said to myself, 'Who cares; if she likes me, she will come.' Anyway, we went out on a drink date, and I realized why she had been so hesitant to give it a chance. Sandy had a boyfriend who seemed serious about their relationship. Also, she was just twenty years old, while I had just had my twenty-seventh birthday the previous December. I didn't expect someone from rural Texas to be promiscuous. It was a good meeting, and we had a good understanding of each other that helped us build a healthy friendship for the time being. When I took her to the pensione, I was thrilled to get a real kiss, which made me think that there was still something out there to hope for.

Back in the college, as the semester progressed, I was exposed in the Arts and Monuments class to the nitty-gritty of understanding the history of art, including Western art and architecture, starting from the classic Greek and Roman traditions dating back to the end of the Hellenistic period and after. In Italy, the protected ruins in Sicily and excavated historic sites in Pompeii and Rome provided a powerful platform to study the significance and history of lost civilisations in Western Europe. As part of module-led study tours, Michael had promised to take us on site visits to Sicily and Pompeii this semester. During the summer semester, although intensive, we could continue to follow the second part of the module, where the contents would be Renaissance, Baroque, and Classical arts and architecture. We were told that site visits to Florence and Venice during summer remained the highlights of the course. Study tours involving site visits were quite fun, and normally all students were welcome. Most tours were affordably priced, but as I was a staff member, they would be free for me.

On the home front, Lucille seemed busy taking new clients to show houses for either purchase or rent. With our busy schedule, I ensured that Peakeo received the necessary attention. Luckily, Olga was back, and the dinner was mainly done by her, but occasionally I helped her out with some experimental dishes. On Sunday in mid-March, when everyone was home, I volunteered to cook some Italianesque mutton curry with boneless cubes of mutton. I sautéed sliced onions with garlic and ginger in olive oil, and then I added cubed meat, along with Indian curry paste. But to make it Italian, I added chopped tomatoes along with pesto sauce before leaving it to simmer with the lid closed. To go with the curry and rice pilaf, I cooked cut fine green beans and sliced carrots together in olive oil seasoned with a dash of salt, crushed hot peppers, and cumin. We all loved it.

As the month ended, we stepped into April, and Rome was in an Easter mood. In between classes and other responsibilities, I spent hours every week with the Texas students, showing them around the city, in addition to a couple of study tours with Michael in Rome as part of the Arts and Monuments module. In fact, I tried to be with Sandy as much as possible. I liked her, her naivety, and her outgoing personality. After all, she was attractive and had been an engaging student in her high school. I managed to convince her a few times to go out with me to see a few tourist hotspots, including the famous park Borghese. I noticed that at first she was a bit apprehensive when it came to going out with someone like me, as I was not of the same ethnicity as her. Also, I knew she needed to feel secure and comfortable. But after going out a few times, she seemed comfortable to be with me, and she seemed to be getting closer to me.

Easter in Rome is a memorable experience. Good Friday, a national holiday, fell on third of April. As the entire city was closed and calm, only a limited number of public transit networks were in service. It was an ideal day to relax and, perhaps, visit the Vatican to hear the blessing of Pope John Paul II. In fact, I had promised to take Sandy to the Vatican on Easter Sunday to hear the Pope's Urbi et Orbi address. However, I did not have any plans for Friday, and at home, Olga was preparing to cook some fish for lunch, which seemed to be a Catholic tradition. I was impressed to see a colourful fish dish of Mediterranean sole on *Puttanesca* sauce. Sole fillets were carefully baked in a sauce made of fresh tomatoes, onions, garlic, and fennel, with herbs and spices.

On Sunday, I woke up early so I could see Sandy at the pensione before nine. When I arrived at the pensione, she was already up and ready so that we could leave for the Vatican before it became crowded for the midday sermon. We somehow managed to get there early on, before the Easter morning Mass began. Any first-time visitor to the Vatican is awestruck on sighting its architectural landscape, which consists of both renaissance and baroque styles. St Peter's Square, designed by Bernini; the dome of St Peter's Basilica, which the renaissance master Michelangelo designed; and the baroque facade of the church all warranted our attention. Meanwhile, Sandy was curious to know how a pre-Roman obelisk from Egypt had come to be here, in the centre of the square. Historical evidence showed that it was brought to the eternal city in AD 37 by Emperor Caligula, who initially erected in his private garden but later moved it to the site of the basilica.

St Peter's Square was packed when the Urbi and Orbi message was delivered by Pope John Paul II at twelve midday on April 6. The pontiff presented this from the balcony of St Peter's Basilica, and he blessed Mary, ever virgin, and the saints, including the holy apostles Peter and Paul, and begged for God's mercy for all of us. Sandy, although not Catholic, was pleased to be there and hugged me passionately when everything was over. Meanwhile, Sandy's friends at the Pensione, although they would celebrate Easter Sunday in Texas, were not keen on visiting St. Peter's but stayed in their rooms. We both slowly moved out of the Vatican and found a Pizzeria outside St. Peter's Square. Sandy offered to buy a slice of pizza, and we sat outside and enjoyed the bite with a sip of the cola.

Later on, we enjoyed walking leisurely along the Tiber after visiting the site of the tomb of the emperor Hadrian, which was built in the year

AD 134. The emperor's ashes were kept along with those of his wife and adopted son. The mausoleum was converted into a castle by popes in the 1300s and continued to be used by several popes. Pope Nicholas III was said to have connected the castle to St. Peter's Basilica by a covered corridor later. The archangel Michael was believed to have appeared atop the castle at the end of the plague in 590. Hence the name Castel Sant'Angelo. Sandy, although not obsessed with art history, was very interested in the history of Rome. This made me happy, as we seemed to have enjoyed seeing something together. While indulging ourselves in the discussion of Roman history, we both walked quite a bit towards the city centre until we got onto a tramcar on the way.

It was almost six in the evening when we got to the hotel, and I returned home immediately after so that I could take Peakeo for a walk. But when I arrived home, Olga had already walked the dog, and I didn't have to rush for anything other than for my evening cup of tea, which I usually enjoyed when I was home during the weekends. To my surprise, Olga brought a *Colomba* Easter cake, which was not very different from Panettone. I enjoyed my cuppa with a slice of Colomba with Olga. The Christmas and Easter cakes were made using the same ingredients, and the output was almost the same, except that the former contained raisins and trimmings of mixed candied fruits, and the latter contained only candied orange peel. Another difference could be the almond coating with sugar pearls in the dove-shaped Colomba. Olga prepared dinner as Lucille returned home after visiting a friend. Meanwhile, I went to a shower after attending to my personal chores, such as ironing clothes. Since the college was shut until the next Monday, I thought I should go and see Susan during the week, but Sandy and friends would also be looking for me to visit some places.

One midweek afternoon, I called on the pensione and told the Texan students to get ready for a city tour the next day and headed towards Susan. I walked all the way to Trastevere, as it was a beautiful day. Susan had been out with Sayed and had just returned home when I knocked at her door. Sally, who opened the door for me, was cheerful and sipping wine. She suggested that I join her, but Susan wanted to go out to see an

Italian film. I couldn't say no, but I joined her for the film. I wouldn't remember anything except that it was a funny film which would have made children very happy. Soon after the film, Susan invited me for some pasta which she wanted to cook, but I had to rush home, as Lucille was out and I had to take Peakeo for a walk. Olga didn't like to go out in the night very much.

On Thursday, as I had planned, I took Texan students around the city. Since they had an entire semester to spend, Michael had asked me to take them around and show the key attractions of Rome, as the study tour could not cover everything. They all had tourist guidebooks and were pretty well aware of the places of interest, which we could list in a number of specific categories for simplicity, such as Historic Rome, the Old City, Catholic Rome, piazzas, churches, and museums. Most of them were found to overlap. These students had already seen several of these attractions, such as the most important Catholic site, the Vatican, and St Peter's Basilica. The other three important churches for visitors were St. Paul Outside the Walls, Santa Maria Maggiore, and San Giovanni in Laterano. They had also seen famous landmarks, such as the Roman Forum and Colosseum, as well as the Spanish Steps. But they still had not seen the Pantheon and the Trevi Fountain, as well as the old quarter of Trastevere. Therefore, I decided to start from Piazza Venezia and walk towards Esquiline Hill to visit San Giovanni in Laterano, which was one of the major basilicas, as well as the cathedral church of Rome and the church of the bishop of Rome, or the pope. Thus, it ranks above all the other churches in the Roman Catholic Church. We also looked at a fourth-century baptistery and the medieval cloister located on the piazza. Sandy and her friends were very much impressed, and although Southern Baptist by faith, they seemed still very much interested.

In the same quarter, not far from the current location, another important church merited a visit. It was Santa Maria Maggiore, which was built in the year 800 and is situated on top of the hill. As we entered the basilica, we could see the impressive mosaics, as well as the glittering layers of gold which adorned the interior. The pope was said to hold an evening service on Corpus Christi, to be followed by a procession to Santa Maria along Via Merulana. This happened every year on Thursday, eight weeks after Easter Sunday. As we came down slowly and walked through the alleyways, we ended up on the piazza to find the Fontana di Trevi, or Trevi Fountain. It was midafternoon but was rather breezy, making it cooler than usual. It was initially designed by Bernini for Pope Clement XII, but was built fifty years later, in the 1700s. This baroque-style fountain became famous among international visitors after the release of movies such as Fellini's *La Dolce Vita* in the early sixties. I did not see any half-dressed women sunbathing in April at the fountain, but the piazza was packed as visitors threw coins, hoping to return to Rome. Sandy and Ben, as well as Caty, all threw their coins; but I didn't throw any, as I had done so once before. The statues of the fountain, next to Neptune, symbolize health and abundance.

The piazza of the Trevi Fountain was a fascinating site, and visitors loved to hang around for some time. So we spent almost half an hour browsing the statues and taking photos. When we reached Piazza della Rotonda, Sandy and the friends were amazed to see the massive ancient but well-preserved structure of the Pantheon. It was built by Emperor Hadrian in year AD 126 on the site of an earlier temple built by Agrippa, whose name can be seen in the front inscription. It had been a Roman temple and then a Christian church since the seventh century, and it has remained almost intact until today. Among the prominent people buried in Pantheon were two Italian kings and their wives. We were also curious to see the hole in the centre of the dome, which was thought to be designed according to architectural norms. The third-largest masonry structure with a dome after the Hagia Sophia, in Istanbul, and St Peter's, in the Vatican, it attracted numerous visitors, including the students of architecture and engineering.

When we were done with the Pantheon, Sandy and others were whispering, but I could hear them saying 'lunchtime'. There were plenty of eateries at which to grab a sandwich or panini around the Pantheon, and I took them to a popular joint along the alleyway next to a gelati parlour. It took about fifteen minutes to get our paninis, and we sat on the bench on the piazza to eat. After lunch, I badly needed an espresso, but Sandy wanted ice cream from the gelati joint. A good half-hour was spent before we proceeded to the archaeological site Largo di Torre Argentina. Archaeologists unearthed four Roman temples, the Theatre of Pompey, and the Roman public toilet at this site. Historians believed that the great emperor Julius Caesar was assassinated in the senate house next to the Theatre of Pompey on the Ides of March in 44 BC. The remnants of history were still visible from the ruins of buildings, some with frescoes that had lain untouched for ages. It was strange that the city authorities didn't pay much attention to this historic site.

By the time we finished seeing the intended places of interest, it was almost time to call them a day, but we still had to visit the old town of Trastevere. So we began walking down towards the riverbank to reach the historic Jewish quarter. Passing through this fascinating quarter, we spotted a number of restaurants and bars already flocked by guests. I pointed out a few restaurants which I had already visited and suggested that anyone interested in dining out could come on another day. As we progressed across the oldest Roman bridge, Ponte Fabricio, to Isola Tiberina, or Isle on the Tiber, which was again part of the ghetto, I showed them a few places of interest, such as the synagogue. Across Ponte Cestio, another old Roman bridge, we crossed the river to Trastevere. By now we had already seen some of the old parts of the city, such as the Jewish quarter. The numerous restaurants and bars, as well as historic piazzas and buildings, including the Church of Santa Maria in Trastevere, were part of the overall experience in this old quarter, which my guests appreciated very much. Discretely, I mentioned to Sandy that I wanted to take her out for a dinner in Trastevere later on another day, and she agreed. In Trastevere, I didn't take Sandy and friends to visit Susan, although she lived very close to where we were. Susan had no idea that I fancied Sandy either. Hoping to visit Susan on the weekend, I decided not to disturb her. We managed to get back to the pensione before eight in the evening, and I was home for dinner with Olga and Lucille.

16

THE SICILIAN TOUR

We were back in business at the college on Monday after the Easter break, and it was business as usual. I heard that Michael and Barbara had visited New York during the break. A week away from the college for them sounded like a million-dollar loss, as they had to catch up with several important lost appointments and chores. On the other hand, they seemed relaxed a bit and showed a lot of enthusiasm with a go-getter attitude. Moreover, talking about their nine-year-old son, Barbara said, 'John was very pleased and had a fantastic time with his cousins.' Meanwhile, Michael warned me, saying that we had a lot of things to catch up with and should work on planning the study tour that had been scheduled for the first week of May. I already knew about this tour, and in fact, I was eagerly waiting for this trip, which was expected to be fun-filled and exciting.

In the early afternoon, Susan and I took a quick break to go down and grab a sandwich from a nearby cafe. There we had a few minutes to sit and chat, and when I said that I had wanted to visit her during the last weekend but had not been able to, Susan noted that it was good thing I did not visit her, as she was away in the countryside with Sayed. When we returned after the lunch break, Susan shared with me fresh cherries that she had brought from the countryside. It was a bit early for the cherry season, but it was not uncommon to see cherries occasionally in late April. They were small but delicious, and I loved them. As we sat at the reception desk chatting, we had a few Iranian students come up looking for somebody to help them with their coursework. Most of them had problems with written English, and they seemed lazy about completing their assignments. Susan directed them to contact a couple of seniors who would, perhaps, be willing to help. The rest of the afternoon was easy, and I left the college early, while Susan stayed over until late evening.

In our midweek class on the history of arts, Michael briefed us on places of interest to visit in terms of classic Greek and Roman arts and architecture. Although I had visited Pompeii before, I had never had the chance to see Sicily. As he spent an hour or so explaining Greek architecture, Sandy seemed to be carried away by visualizing the beauty of Greek temples. Subsequently, there were discussions about Greek gods and mythology. Michael loved to link everything about Western civilisation to Greece, and the explanation would stop there. Anything beyond Greece, although there existed apparent links to Egyptian, Mesopotamian, and Persian civilisations, would normally be set aside. He was always careful not to cross the line; after all, he was an art historian, and he was right to stick to Western arts and architecture. After the class, Sandy said that she got hooked on the idea of visiting Greece, and she was already planning to visit Europe again after graduation.

In the afternoon on Friday, Michael and I sat together and discussed the itinerary for the study tour, which included two overnight stays in Sicily: one night in Agrigento and the second night in Taormina. Although everyone was welcome to join, we had to plan for forty students to achieve the maximum capacity of a standard coach. I believe that travel and meal expenses were included in the price, but the students had to foot the hotel expenses for two nights. The next week, I began to publicize the tour for the students and collect money on a first-come, first-served basis. Since we planned to cover all of Sicily, we needed to leave Rome seven in the morning, as we were to take the boat from Naples to Palermo. If we were to travel on the road, we would have had to cross the Strait of Messina to reach Palermo. It would have been tiring for the drivers to drive for ten to fifteen hours. Once in Palermo on the following morning, the coach would head towards Catania, along the southern coast of Sicily. Seeing an ancient Greek village called Erice, near Palermo, and visits to the ancient Greek historic sites at Selinunte, Syracuse, and Agrigento, as well as a trip to Taormina to have a glimpse of the still active volcano Mount Etna, were included in the itinerary. We had planned to leave Rome on the last Friday of May and return on Monday, arriving at Civitavecchia in the late morning by an overnight ferry from Palermo. The trip did not include a visit to Pompeii, but Michael decided to take TLC students to the historic city at another time during a weekend in early June.

When I informed Susan and friends, they seemed excited about the Sicily trip, so were Sandy and her friends. I big poster that I made about the study tour was already on the wall, and some of the students started to pay the deposit towards the trip by midweek. Michael had assigned a deadline for payment as the twenty-fifth of May, as he had to confirm the number for hotel booking. By Friday, I had twenty-five confirmed passengers, and at least another five would be enough to hire a large coach. A few Iranian students and South Asian girls were also expected to participate. As the news spread, I expected this number to exceed thirty.

In the following week, on the twenty-fifth, we had counted the number of students who had paid as thirty-two. Therefore, we closed the file and Michael immediately went to confirm the number to the hoteliers in Sicily and book the ferry rides. In fact, the deal allowed us to enjoy three free rooms, which Michael and I, as well as the coach driver and his helper, who would be another driver, could occupy. The college would pay for Susan and Barbara, who could also accompany John. Another student came late to join, but Michael promised to confirm this after communicating with the hoteliers. Since we still had a few more seats left, we could have admitted another one or two, but this depended on the availability of rooms in our hotels and the boat. In addition, our booking was based on double occupancy, which meant that two people occupied one room. In some cases, single-bed occupancy would be required, for which a supplementary charge would be incurred.

I had already told Lucille about my trip away from Rome on the weekend, starting from the next Friday. Luckily, Olga agreed to take care of Peakeo during my absence. I also warned Lucille about my summer engagement during July—August, as Michael wanted me to help him with a small group of exchange visitors coming from the United States. This required me to be away from home a few times. The college had already arranged to rent a house with five bedrooms in Trastevere during the summer to house these visitors. I had a chat with Lucille, who seemed supportive, and Olga promised to stay in Rome during most of the summer months. Lucille was also aware of the fact that I could even be offered free accommodation by the college anytime from September, in which case I would be moving out from home.

On Friday morning, I was up early on and arrived at the college site even before the coach came in. But Michael and Barbara, along with John, were already at the site. Within the next ten minutes, we had almost half the crowd gathered at the cafe nearby, and this included Susan, Flavio, Daniel, and the Molinari sisters. To our surprise, the coach was already there but had parked in the next street, as coaches were not allowed to park on Via Piemonte. I immediately directed the students to go to and take their seats. Susan and I managed to reserve some seats for us and for Michael and Barbara, as well as John. When everyone was seated and the necessary luggage had been loaded, I took a headcount, but four students were still missing. Fortunately, it did not take much time before we departed at half past eight in the morning with everyone on board.

After a smooth coach ride, we arrived in Naples, the City of Pizza, and our itinerary for the day included a visit to the National Archaeological Museum, where we could see the artefacts from the Pompeii excavations, along with other national treasures. Of course, a pizza lunch at an old pizzeria was also on the agenda before heading to the Port of Naples to take an overnight boat to Palermo. We were told that we needed to be at the port before five o'clock. Michael said that Naples was famous not only for pizza but also for opera and theatres. Unfortunately, we wouldn't spend more than a few hours there. The coach drove straight to the museum site, and we were offloaded.

The National Archaeological Museum of Naples enjoyed a world-famous status, and the first two floors were dedicated to exhibiting artefacts from the two famous ancient cities that were buried by the volcanic eruption of Vesuvius in AD 79. We had a couple of hours to browse through the collection of the Pompeii and Herculaneum excavations. The highlights of the museum were *Pan and a She-Goat*, sculptures depicting sexual acts, frescoes of sexual intercourse, and a mosaic from House of the Faun, in Pompeii, in which Alexander the Great fights the Persians. In addition, there were other objects from antiquity, such as the Farnese collection from the sixteenth-century excavation of the Baths of Caracalla in Rome. Some of the collections of Roman erotic art—both frescoes and sculptures—from the excavation of Pompeii and Herculaneum, displayed at the archaeological museum, had been kept in the secret cabinet, or Gabinetto Segreto, before being moved to the museum.

By the time we finished seeing the museum, it was almost half past one in the afternoon, and we were rushing to get to a restaurant for a pizza lunch. Naples, as the birthplace of pizza and the pizza capital of the world, had hundreds of authentic pizzerias on offer to locals as well as to visitors. Choosing one pizzeria from among the several best and oldest remains a real challenge for any discerning traveller. After all, Michael knew better, and he suggested that we should try out the Don Antonio pizzeria in the Materdei district, which started as a wine cellar in the year 1901. The pizzeria was located in Via Materdei in a historic working-class area that offered the real Neapolitan experience, and the premises were adorned with photos of celebrities and accolades. Michael was quick to point out that it had been featured in the film of the Dolce Vita period *The Gold of Naples*, in which Sophia Loren plays the role of a young pizza maker. At the restaurant, we agreed to have a buffet-type lunch, where everyone could try out a number of varieties by slice. Owing to the sheer number of eaters to be served in the group, it made sense for us to choose this option. In the end, we all loved it, and my favourite was the seafood pizza. Some opted to have a glass of house wine to go with the slices.

As we headed towards the Port of Naples, the traffic was horrendous, but we made it on time to board the ferry, which left Naples in the late evening. The agent booked the cabins on the same floor, which also had a restaurant, a bar, and a lounge. All cabins were double-bed cabins and had a few family units. Some of us were already ready for fun, but all of them had been warned by Michael to be well behaved, particularly regarding the consumption of alcohol and behaviour with female students. They were free to buy any food or drinks on board with their own money, but breakfast before six o'clock was served free of charge. I was keen on keeping an eye on Susan and her group for antisocial behaviour, but by default, I was one of them. I was also keen on being together with Sandy whenever an opportunity arose. In the meantime, I was busy with Susan sorting out the cabins for the rest of the students and guiding them to the correct cabins. All of us had already been informed about how to be alert and respond to any emergency situation before boarding the ferry.

The boat had already started to sail, and some of us were at the lounge at half past ten. Daniel and Flavio were flirting with Mona and Lisa. From the Texas students, only Sandy was with me, and Susan was also teasing Daniel and Flavio. I should say, luckily, most of the students had already gone to sleep, but a handful were hanging around. We all had a wonderful time chatting and gossiping about the other students. When Mona and Lisa took turns leaving the group, there were only a few of us chatting. I had to accompany Sandy to her cabin, which was a family unit, and the rest of the girls were already asleep. Just outside the cabin, Sandy and I stood embracing and kissing for the first time, and this was indeed a memorable experience. As she entered the cabin, I moved on to my cabin, which I shared with Ben. The sea was not as rough as expected, and the ride was relatively smooth.

By six in the morning, some of us were already at the lounge bar, waiting to pick up a breakfast pack, which contained a croissant, a fresh drink, and an apple. We asked the participants to purchase coffee from the vending machine. The boat was expected to arrive and land in Palermo just after seven o'clock, and we arrived on time as planned. Somehow, with all the students up and ready, we managed to get out of the boat by half past seven in the morning. Fortunately, most of us were able to have breakfast in the boat and thus did not need to spend time outside the boat. However, we could not see much in Palermo early in the morning except for the palaces and churches from outside. Therefore, we proceeded to our next point of interest: Erice, an ancient Greek village. Michael assured us that we could visit some of the key attractions, such as the cathedral, a Norman castle, St John of the Hermits, and the botanical garden, or Villa Giulia, when we return to Palermo to catch the ferry back. Erice was 'Eryx' in Greek, but the village in the old days was said to have been inhabited by Phoenicians before it gradually became Hellenistic.

Several invaders occupied Erice from early on; therefore, the village on the mountaintop of Erice exhibited distinguished heritages. After the Arabs conquered it in the year 1831, the name changed to 'Cebel Hamid', or 'Hamid's Mount'. After the Noman invasion in 1167, the name changed to 'Monte San Giuliano', but later in the twentieth century, the name was again changed to 'Erice'. In the north of the city, we found the remains of ancient walls erected during the time of the Phoenician and Elymian settlements. In addition, in the city we found two castles, one from the Saracen period, Pepoli Castle, and another, Venus Castle, from the Norman period, which sat on the top of the hill. The students enjoyed the visit, although it was in the early morning.

From Erice, we continued our journey south towards Selinunte, one of the most important archaeological sites in Sicily. We passed Mazara before arriving at Selinunte. The Arabs landed in Mazara del Vallo in AD 821 and used it as a base for further expansion of the island. They ruled the city for over two hundred years. During the Arab era, Mazara became a thriving commercial hub and a centre of learning. Soon after, the city grew quickly, with a diverse mix of people from all over the Mediterranean region. Arabs built schools, mosques, and libraries and contributed to the development of the city culturally and economically. They also introduced new agricultural techniques. The Norman invasion put an end to Arab rule in 1072, but Arab heritage continued to flourish, and the city remained to enjoy a significant number of people of Arab descent.

We arrived at the archaeological park of Selinunte in late morning. Michael gave us a brief overview of the ancient history of Selinunte. It remained a fantastic place to explore the ruins of an ancient Greek city that dated back over twenty-five hundred years. The Greeks from Megara Hyblaea colonized the place and founded the city in the seventh century BCE. It quickly prospered, and by the fifth century BCE, it became one of the most important colonies of Greece. Afterwards, students split to explore the ruins of Selinunte and visited the Temple of Heracles, the largest temple built in the sixth century BC. Today it is considered one of the best-preserved Greek temples. We also visited the temples of Athena, Poseidon, and Demeter.

At the site, we had some free time for a lunch break as well as for other necessities, such as using the washrooms or having coffee. After lunch, we visited the Acropolis at the highest point in the city, which offered breathtaking views of the Sicilian countryside. We also had the opportunity to visit the Temple of Apollo in the acropolis. When we returned to the base, we were tired and exhausted, but in the meantime, we seemed happy and content after having seen some of the wonders of the ancient past. Sandy was immensely happy, and we thought it was a valuable learning experience. We had learned about the history and Greek architecture in general, and of this once-thriving metropolis. All of us were also able to appreciate the stunning beauty of the surroundings as well as the site, which was located on a hilltop overlooking the Mediterranean Sea.

From Selinunte, we headed further south towards Agrigento, where we could visit the Valley of the Temples, a world-famous heritage site. This ancient Greek site features a number of well-preserved temples and ruins. In the early afternoon, we arrived at *Agrigento*, and it was sunny, as this was in the middle of the summer. Before checking in to the hotel, we headed to the Valley of the Temples. As students of Michael's art history class, Sandy and I were very interested in seeing some well-preserved Greek art and architecture. Michael had been teaching art history for years, and we were lucky to have him here with us. The heritage site was home to seven ancient Greek temples, some of which were the best-preserved Greek temples in the world, including the Temple of Olympian Zeus, Temple of Concordia, and Temple of Hera Lacinia. These were incredibly well preserved, and they offered us a fascinating glimpse into the culture and history of ancient Greece. We spent the afternoon exploring the temples and learning about the history and unique architectural features of each temple. Sandy seemed to go crazy as she was so fascinated with the collection of temples in well-preserved condition.

Michael then called us for a brief lecture on the sites of the temples. First he explained that the Temple of Concord was the best-preserved Greek temple in the world. Sandy and I were amazed by the symmetry and beauty of the temple. We then visited the largest temple, the Temple of Heracles. We were all impressed by its size and unique architectural features. Sandy and I were able to walk around the temple and admire the intricate details of the architecture.

By the early evening, we all looked tired but were hopeful of a restful night at the hotel. There were a few more places of interest that we could have visited, such as the Archaeological Museum of Agrigento, San Gerlando Cathedral, and the Roman Theatre. However, time remained a limiting factor. As we checked in to the hotel in the evening, we were told to come for dinner at the hotel restaurant at half past eight. After a quick shower in a relaxed atmosphere, all went down to the lobby so that we could enter the dining hall where the restaurant staff and servers were eagerly waiting for the guests to be seated. This restaurant at the hotel, I was told, boasted a very good reputation for seafood; they used freshly caught fish and fresh local ingredients to cook. This part of the Sicilian cuisine and food culture definitely had an influence from the diverse mix of people and cultures that had colonized the island.

The restaurant menu contained many authentic Sicilian dishes, but we were allowed to pick from a handful of selected items as a group. As an antipasto, most of us chose *aubergine caponata*, which remains one of the most famous and favourite starters in Sicily. The recipe for caponata varied from city to city, or even household to household, but always contained fried aubergine or aubergine, pine nuts, raisins, and vinegar. Celery, onions, tomatoes, capers, and olives could be added to it before serving as an antipasto at room temperature. A few of us were also brave enough to try fresh uncooked red prawns, or *gambero rosso*, from Mazara, which all famous restaurants in Italy loved to serve. They were served raw with a dash of lemon juice and olive oil. Everyone could taste local cheeses, olives, sun-dried tomatoes, and batter-fried anchovies.

For the primo piato, we had a pasta dish and chose either the bucatini or linguini. We were also given a choice of popular local sauces, either *Cavatelli alla Agrigentina*, made with aubergine and aged ricotta or creamy pistachio sauce, like the pesto sauce made with cheese, basil and olive oil. I tried the latter, which was delicious and varied. The main dish in Sicily had to be fish or seafood, and the most popular item was sardines. Sicilians cooked sardines in a variety of ways, but the most famous recipe involved stuffing sardines with pine nuts, raisins, and breadcrumbs before baking them with olive oil. We were offered a choice of either *Sarde Beccafico* (stuffed sardines) or *Panelle* (a Sicilian meat roll). Sicily also had a fair share of *dolce* and desserts. One of its famous was cannoli, a deep-fried pastry stuffed with creamy ricotta cheese. We were given a choice of either cannoli or cassata, a Sicilian sponge cake made with citrus, fruits, chocolate, marzipan, and ricotta cream. Most of us chose the latter. I tried cannoli from Sandy, who was seated next to me.

After dinner, some students wanted to check out the night bar and lounge. Some even suggested going out to a disco, but I did not feel like venturing out; after all, most of us were tired and exhausted. I believe Daniel and Flavio went out with some girls. Sandy and I spent an hour or so at the lounge, sipping a drink until midnight. Michael wanted us to be up and ready by eight in the morning, and thus we thought of hitting the bed as soon as possible. I shared a room on the ground floor with Ben, whereas Sandy had to go upstairs. As time would be tight in the morning, I decided to shower before going to sleep.

The next day, we wanted to visit the town to have a glimpse of the cathedral, amphitheatre, and museum, but much time to spend at the museum was not on the agenda. Luckily, we all managed to gather on time at the coach, but, unfortunately, a few could not find time for breakfast. They had to manage with a cornetto and coffee. In the coach, Michael briefly talked about our next destination, and in general he was pleased that the students had learned a lot about Greek art and architecture during their trips to Agrigento. While taking a gaze at the city, we managed to visit the Roman Amphitheatre. However, within an hour, we left towards Syracuse, which was a thriving Greek city in the old days, some seven hundred years before the Christian era. Syracuse was the most important and powerful city-state in the Mediterranean during the old days and remained the capital of Sicily during the times of the Greeks, Romans, and Byzantines, as well as the Aghlabids, who moved the capital to Palermo during their two-hundred-year rule starting in AD 878. In the year AD 1085, the Norman invasion ended the Muslim Emirate of Aghlabids in Sicily.

Syracuse, from an early time as a Greek colony, attracted intellectuals, poets, philosophers, and scientists. This tradition continued even during the Roman and Byzantine periods, as well as during the Aghlabids' time. It was considered not only one of the most important cities in the region but also one of the most beautiful to live in and visit. The great mathematician Archimedes was born in Syracuse, approximately 300 BCE. Owing to its geographic position in the East Mediterranean with the Cape of Ortygia, the city also remained a commercial hub under the various rulers. After the Aghlabids moved their administrative centre to Palermo, and at the onset of the Noman conquest of Sicily, and particularly Palermo, the importance of Syracuse diminished gradually. However, in later years, Syracuse was prominent during the Norman, Swabian, and Spanish periods. In 1693, the city was damaged by an earthquake but was rebuilt to remain an important Sicilian city.

It was already lunchtime when we arrived in Syracuse, but we decided to take a coffee break in the city centre, as some of our students
had missed their breakfast. Later, we visited key archaeological sites, such
as the Temple of Apollo, Temple of Athena, and Roman Amphitheatre.
Syracuse remains a beautiful city even today, and its beaches are popular
among tourists. This is not to mention its delicious food. Of course, we
had planned to take our lunch in a couple of hours, but unfortunately, it
would be quick, as Taormina was waiting for us. After the coffee break,
we went on a sightseeing tour of the coast, including the beachside on
the small baroque island of Ortygia, which could be reached by two
bridges from the mainland.

The sight from the Cape of Ortygia, overlooking the Ionian Sea,
was stunningly beautiful. Ortygia, the historic centre of Syracuse, was
considered one of the most beautiful destinations in Sicily. With three
millennia of Greek heritage and those of other invading empires, it offers
everything one needs to see within a short period in one place. We started
with the *Mercato*, which showed off colourful, delicious fresh fruits and
vegetables, and then proceeded to take a look at the baroque Church of
Syracuse, a cathedral that was built on the site of a Greek temple. We
stopped at Santa Lucia Alla Badia and Palazzo Borgia del Casale on the
way to Piazza del Duomo. While we thought we should find a place to
have some quick lunch, Michael suggested that we go to the historic
and picturesque Jewish quarter, where we could visit the puppet museum, the Museo dei Pupi. We also found the famous Antica Giudecca,
a friendly eatery that served Ortygia's street food. *Arancini*—massive
freshly fried rice balls filled with ragu, aubergine, or spinach—were my
favourite; they were much bigger and better than those in Rome. They
also served pizzas with various toppings, as well as meat and vegetable
dishes. Students found that this eatery was godsent in a timely manner.
As we finished eating, we were told that it was time to leave Syracuse, but
we insisted that we take a quick stroll on the beach before we departed.
On the way, I also managed to sneak into a *pasticceria* to get *granita*, a
Sicilian favourite usually served with breakfast.

Finally, by midafternoon, we were set to leave Syracuse, and we headed towards Catania, a city famous for its baroque architecture and vibrant atmosphere. However, we did not have a plan to stop and visit any attractions, although the Cathedral of Saint Agatha, which stood on Piazza del Duomo, was stunning. However, with a brief stopover at the piazza, some ventured into taking a coffee break, and others, including Sandy and me, got some gelato. Naturally, green pistachio-flavoured ice cream was my choice, while Sandy opted for strawberry and vanilla. It was smooth and delicious, and the pistachio flavour was authentic and natural. It was indeed a brief stopover, and we had a chance to admire the baroque architecture of the buildings, including the cathedral. Our next destination was Taormina, a beautiful town that stood on a hill overlooking the ocean just north of Catania.

We arrived in Taormina in the late afternoon, and we still had time to visit some attractions, such as the Teatro Greco, which dates back to the third century BC. Along with some other site visits, we decided to do some sightseeing in the beautiful town before visiting the hotel. This gave us plenty of time to see Mount Etna before proceeding back to Palermo in the morning. Although Taormina was a historic town with stunning scenery and several places of interest, we managed to see only a few key attractions, such as the Roman Forum, Byzantine Cathedral, and Jewish Ghetto. We went through the main street of Corso Umberto, which was flanked by shops, cafes, and restaurants on both sides, and later ended up in the main square of the town, Piazza IX Aprile, or Square of 9 April. We did not venture to visit the small island located off the coast, a popular spot for swimming and sunbathing, but climbed up to the hilltop to see the Church of Madonna della Rocca. What a stunning view of the town and its surroundings. It was beautiful. Back in the town centre, we spent some time at the Villa Comunale, a public garden with plants and trees, as well as statues and fountains. There we found some nice places to sit and relax.

Around seven in the evening, we arrived at a hotel which gorgeously stood overlooking the Ionian Sea. Susan and I, along with Barbara, helped the hotel staff to check in smoothly and the students to find their rooms, and Michael announced that the dinner was to be served at nine o'clock sharp. Rooms were allocated as in Agrigento, and I shared the room with Ben from TLC. During the time of collecting the room keys, students were also given the menu card so that they could be prepared to order their meals when they came down for dinner. While the usual Sicilian antipasti were available to start with, we could pick a pasta dish from a choice of seafood lasagne or Sicilian-style *spaghetti all' arrabbiata*, which is a spicy tomato sauce with garlic, basil, and dried red peppers cooked in olive oil. The lasagne contained seafood, such as prawns, clams, and squid, cooked in white béchamel sauce.

As we sat down for dinner at the restaurant after having enjoyed the antipasto buffet, we simply had to wait for the primo we had already ordered. I had ordered seafood lasagne. I thought that the majority had chosen this dish, as we were warned that arrabbiata sauce could be hot and spicy. As for the main dish, we had three options: grilled swordfish *Salmoriglio* (a swordfish steak grilled with a dash of olive oil, lemon, and herbs, as well as crushed hot pepper, served with grilled fennel and courgette); stuffed sardines baked with a dash of olive oil and herbs, which we'd already had in Agrigento; and *Courgette Ripieni*, or stuffed courgette with minced meat prepared from delicious tomato sauce cooked with olive oil, garlic, and herbs. The stuffing also contained raisins, pine nuts, and breadcrumbs. Of course, my choice was swordfish, but I was also tempted to try stuffed courgette; I had a bite from Susan's, who sat next to me. Even Sandy had picked swordfish.

We were generously served local wine from start to finish, and some of our students took advantage of it to get drunk. Local wine from grapes grown in the volcanic soil of Mount Etna was at the top of the list. Nerello Mascalese and Carricante Etna Bianco, as well as other wines, such as Catarratto Bianco, Zibibbo, and Grecanico, were some of the red and white wines offered at the restaurant. In addition, the famous sweet wine of Sicily, Marsala, was served with desserts.

After a sensuous and rather fulfilling dinner which lasted a couple of hours, our students were ready to party, and Daniel suggested that we head to the disco next door, which was operated by the hotel owner. Michael warned that if we overslept and missed the excursion to Mount

Etna, the coach would not return to the hotel to pick up anyone. The planned departure time was seven in the morning, soon after breakfast. This meant that we did not have much time to enjoy the disco. Most of the students still went to the disco and had a wonderful time, and as always, I was with Susan and the group, but Sandy was an addition this time. Susan noticed my close relationship with Sandy, including on the dance floor, but she seemed supportive. As always, Daniel and Flavio were with Mona and Lisa, and I could feel a sense of intimacy between Flavio and Mona for the first time. Susan, after watching all these events unfold and perhaps feeling a bit jealous, left the disco early on. Sandy and I also left after a while. We bade one another goodnight with a kiss and headed to our rooms.

In the morning, after a buffet breakfast, we all headed to the coach, and nobody stayed away from the excursion. Mount Etna, an active volcano, often erupted, spilling out molten lava. Mount Etna was a short drive from Taormina, and we started our excursion early in the morning soon after breakfast. It being the highest mountain in Italy, we could see it from far away. Visitors could hike to the summit or up to a certain point to see the stunning views of the volcano and its surroundings. A visit to Mount Etna remains a must for every visitor to Taormina. Michael had arranged to take us on a guided hiking tour of the volcano, and we enjoyed the incredible views and explored the lava caves while stopped over for a wine-tasting session along the way back, all within a couple of hours. Most of the students avoided hiking, but it was a pleasant walk on a rather chilly morning. All in all, we were back on the road before eleven o'clock and headed towards Messina for a quick lunch on the way to Palermo. When we started in Palermo two days prior, Michael assured us that we would have enough time to see some of the key attractions before we boarded the overnight ferry back to Rome. This meant that our lunch break at Messina was very short, and in fact, we managed it with a sandwich or slice of pizza and drink.

As we arrived in Palermo, Michael made an announcement to stress that we needed to be ready to board the ferry before half past eight. We also were to look after our dinners independently before boarding the ferry. Finally, we were given a rundown on a few key attractions that we should visit with him in Palermo in the midafternoon. Palermo Cathedral, the Norman Palace, and St John of the Hermits were at the top. If time permitted, we were to visit the botanical garden or Villa Giulia after taking a stroll in the streets of the historic centre. Palermo, a beautiful and vibrant city of culture, was full of attractions, including architectural treasures and sprawling street markets, with several places to eat and drink. Michael took us to the Norman Palace first.

What was interesting for a visitor like me was the history of Palermo, which could be traced back to the time of Greeks and then the Byzantines and Arabs. The invasion of the Arabs in the early ninth century and then the Norman conquest in 1060 laid the foundation for most of the architectural treasures seen in Palermo. The Norman Palace, or simply the Royal Palace of Palermo, was the seat of the kings of Sicily, which stood at the highest point in the old city. It was initially built by the emir of Palermo in the ninth century. Cappella Palatina was a good example to demonstrate the influence of Arabs, Byzantines, and Normans. Our next place of interest was the Cathedral of Palermo, an important architectural treasure. Arabs built a Muslim mosque over a basilica, which was later rebuilt or converted to a Christian church by the Normans in 1184. As in the Norman Palace, the cathedral also demonstrated the heritage of various rulers of the city. Koranic verses were engraved on a column.

Sandy and I liked the Monastery of St. John of the Hermits, which was a mosque turned into a monastery. A Norman king is said to have converted the mosque into a monastery of the Benedictine order in 1132. After seeing the monastery, we headed to Villa Giulia, also known as Villa del Popolo, an urban public park next to the botanical garden. The garden had a square pattern and was separated from the surrounding area by a wall. It contained human-made lakes, bridges, and sculptures along the pathways. It was a peaceful and serene place for us to rest and enjoy beauty. We had plenty of time to enjoy the early evening, especially in the vibrant city centre, where we strolled along the street markets, and some of us even had an early dinner, while others picked up takeaway food to consume on the boat. As expected, we all managed to get to the

Palermo Ferry Terminal on time before the ferry gate was opened, as we had to go through the necessary rituals concerning sea safety issues in case of any emergency. It was going to be a twelve-hour journey, as we were told by the ferry operator, so we would arrive at Civitavecchia an hour before midday. The college was scheduled to be closed the following day so that students could rest before returning to class on Tuesday.

Barbara and Michael needed some help guiding the students to their cabins, which were allocated as in the hotel, as all of them were double-occupancy rooms. As soon as the students checked in to their rooms, they could visit the lounge for a drink or consume their takeaway dinner, and most of them did come to the lounge. However, Sandy and her friend did not come, as they wanted to sleep early after a long, tiring day. I joined our usual group of friends, led by Susan, for a drink and gossip. Daniel and Flavio were not enthusiastic, as Mona and Lisa didn't join us. At the lounge, when David, the youngest in the group, curiously asked me about Sandy, Daniel and Flavio started to gossip about her and me, but Susan immediately cut it off by changing the subject. Meanwhile, the ferry started to move, and we were warned that the ocean would be slightly rough when traversing the Terranean Sea after midnight. After an hour, we decided to call it a day and went to sleep.

I did not wake up the next morning until nine o'clock, and I could feel from the deck that the sun was strong. Most of us did not have breakfast, as we were all sleeping. Within a couple of hours, we were scheduled to touch the land. When I went to the lounge, seeking something to drink, I was welcomed by Michael and Barbara, who had morning coffee. I was offered coffee and a cornetto, which seemed adequate to start the morning with strength. We had a chat reflecting on the entire Sicilian trip and how much we had enjoyed it. I was told that from Civitavecchia, we still needed to travel a bit to Rome, which would normally take an hour by coach. Meanwhile, on the deck of the lounge, we chatted about the rest of the semester, which had almost ended.

Back in the college, it was assessment time, but Michael still had to take the few Texas students to Pompeii without me. He planned to do this the next weekend. As the boat approached the shore, we headed to the cabins to pick up our luggage. By now most students had already come to the lounge with their belongings. In the meantime, they all had been instructed on how to disembark and gather at the terminal until the driver moved the coach out of the ferry terminal so that we could board. During the coach ride to Rome, most of the students fell asleep. Perhaps they had all had a sleepless night on the ferry. However, I was upbeat, and so was Sandy, who sat next to me. Susan, Daniel, and Flavio all seemed tired.

In Rome, the driver stopped several times to drop off some of the students on the way. It was almost midday when we arrived at the college site in Via Piemonte. Michael and I made sure that everyone was up and ready to get off the coach so that they could pick up their luggage before the driver pulled off. Sandy and her friends made their way to the hotel, and I promised to see them the next morning at the college. Only Michael, Barbara, and their son John were left out along with me and Susan. Flavio and Daniel left to pick up their cars so that Susan and I could get a ride home. However, I insisted that I could take a walk, as it was not far from the college. So I said arrivederci to all and started walking home. At half past twelve, I arrived at home while Olga was preparing spaghetti for lunch. It was a good time, and I said as much to her. Peakeo was happy to see me and was wagging his tail. Lucille had gone out to show a house to some executive working for the European food giant Nestlé.

The evening at home was quite relaxed, and I spent it watching television after taking Peakeo out. Lucille took several hours to return. She had gone to do some errands after showing a couple of houses to clients. She was delighted to have a contract signed by one client. By sunset, we all sat down to have the dinner which Olga had prepared. It was grilled chicken and buttered French beans, along with roasted potatoes on the side. We enjoyed the simple but fresh and delicious food over a glass of Valpolicella. Of course, the dinner was not complete without a home-brewed cup of espresso. Lucille and I had a long chat, as she wanted to know the places we had visited in Sicily. It was strange that she had never been to Sicily even though she had been living in Italy for several years.

However, she had visited Naples and Pompeii a few times. After listening to my rather exaggerated descriptions of cities and villages and the story underpinning their significance, she seemed excited and wanted to visit. Suddenly we saw Peakeo wagging his tail. Lucille wanted to take him for a walk, and I joined her. It was half past ten when I finally managed to go to bed.

The next morning, it was business as usual at the college and was quite hectic. Surprisingly, everyone showed up in classes. This was the final week of the semester before the study week. Some were already struggling with their coursework, and even I had a couple of assignments to submit. My aim was to obtain all As, including in the History of Arts module, which was about the study of Western civilisation through art and monuments. This week's class was the last session, and Michael explained what was expected and how to plan and execute the coursework assignment in an essay format. Susan and Flavio already had sought my help to write their essays. Although most students received passing grades, it seemed extremely difficult to score an A, especially from Michael. I was sure to get an A in International Business—which, again, most students found difficult. Most of the Middle Eastern students found their coursework difficult, as well as the exam, but with academic support provided, they usually managed to get by. Some definitely failed and repeated their classes.

In the meantime, as we approached Friday, Michael was preparing to take Sandy and friends to Florence. On Saturday, although I was not joining them, I woke up early to pick them up from the hotel and bring them to the Termini rail station at half past seven in the morning so that they could join Michael. With a one-night stay in Florence, they could enjoy visiting key attractions, such as the famous Uffizi Gallery and Ponte Vecchio, and return to Rome before dusk on Sunday. The highlight of the study tour was renaissance art and architecture. Florence was the birthplace of the Renaissance. Michael was precisely on time to catch the early-morning train to Florence, for which he had already purchased a group ticket. As the train departed from the platform, I headed home, hoping to sleep for a few more hours.

The semester ended after the examination and coursework sub-missions. We all remained anxious about the outcomes. In general, the semester was a fruitful one, and the study tour to Sicily was a plus. The next semester, the fall of 1980, was scheduled to begin in mid-September, if everything went as expected. Meanwhile, Michael and Barbara had no time to relax, as we had the summer term to prepare for. The summer courses were short courses, mainly in the field of arts and culture, in-volving on-site visits to places that we had already seen during the study tours. In addition, summer classes were arranged only for visiting mature adult learners from the United States; therefore, formal assessments were generally not necessary. The adult learners arrived before the end of June so that they could start classes in July which would continue for six weeks. As a team member, I was expected to help Michael and Barbara mainly during site visits.

By midweek, Sandy and her friends were expected to leave Rome, either travelling in Europe or heading home. Sandy and Caty had plans to visit France and Monaco and seemed so excited to visit Paris for the first time. They wanted to fly to Paris and travel around it. Caty would take a flight home from Paris, while Sandy planned to visit Monaco with another friend who would join her in Paris. Sandy had promised to stay with me for a week in Rome before departing to US by the end of July. I would be temporarily living in a furnished house that the college had already leased to accommodate visiting students who were expected to stay for six to eight weeks. The house, located in the north of Rome near Parioli, had four bedrooms, and we expected two couples and two single women to come from the US this week. Susan and the group wanted to host an end-of-semester party for friends, which was to take place in a week or two.

17

SUMMER OF 1980: A CLOSE ENCOUNTER

In July, we were already in summer. The college was technically closed for regular teaching, and the premises looked rather empty and calm. Susan said she would be in Rome for a couple weeks in July, and she was expected to come to the college during the first two weeks. This would make my life slightly less boring. Students would still visit the college for various reasons, including checking their results. New students would also visit the college for enquiries about their courses and admissions. On the first Friday of the month, Barbara and I went to the airport to pick up visiting adult learners from the US. This time, we picked up the guests and took them to the house that we had leased, where I was also expected to live for two months. Barbara had arranged a servant to do the housekeeping on a daily basis. Two of the four rooms were allocated to two couples, one to single women, and the remaining one for me. There were three bedrooms on the second floor and one bedroom on the ground floor. George and Sally chose the first room, while Dan and Pat took the second room. Cathy and Debora, both single young ladies, occupied the third room. My room was on the ground floor.

Michael had drawn up a study plan for the visiting students from Texas, with just three lectures or seminars every week for five weeks. As usual, he planned to deliver short courses in the history of art, Greek versus Roman architecture, the Renaissance Era, and Italian culinary tradition. The first three were delivered by Michael himself, and the last by an Italian culinary expert. These lectures were complemented by a brief visit to Pompeii and Florence, as well as site visits in Rome. The culinary expert, Alberto, arranged to take them to a handful of restaurants in Rome serving food from different regions and to show them how to prepare the dishes, but practical sessions were not planned. I wanted to join them whenever convenient and available to do so.

Among the visiting students from Texas, Cathy, a junior-year student, wanted to continue a semester in Rome after her summer classes. Also a recent divorcee, she wanted to spend a semester abroad. She would most likely spend a semester with us at the college. The two couples and Debora appeared to be in their forties or fifties and were interested in the arts, history, and culture. I was expected to help them settle in Rome with some introduction to the city, as I had done previously. Although I had my own room in a leased house, I would not move there until late June. I had already done a bit of introduction, including introducing them to Mario, our usual hangout. On the next weekend, Michael arranged to take the visiting students to Florence so that they could be exposed to renaissance art and architecture.

The next week, early on Monday, I left home to accompany the Texan students to the college, as they would have needed some guidance on commuting by bus and getting to the college. Michael and Barbara were already at the premises, and we had a sort of an orientation session over a light breakfast. As adult learners, they were curious about what they were supposed to do and learn. We gave them the study plan and site visit plan, as well as the itinerary of excursions. In the afternoon, Michael had a couple of hours of seminar introducing the subjects of Greek and Roman arts and architecture. I was manning the reception desk until Susan appeared at midday. Luckily, for lunch she had brought some pizza slices and rice balls—or supplies or arancini, as the Romans and Sicilians called them, respectively.

Susan and I had the opportunity to catch up with each other and to discuss her holiday plan for summer as well. She had planned to stay in Rome until the end of June and later spent time with her boyfriend as well as her mum and younger sister, who had arranged to visit during July. As Michael wanted her to return in August to help with student enquiries before the fall semester started, Susan was to be back in the college during August. The college was normally shut for two weeks during the last week of July and the first week of August. However, I had no plans for any holiday except spending one week with Sandy on her return from France in late July. Discussing the get-together party that she had proposed earlier, she wanted to host this at her house with Sally after her mum and sister arrived in mid-July. Susan said that Flavio and Daniel, as well David, had planned to go abroad for a short holiday in early August. Normally it is extremely difficult to see anyone spending time in Rome at this time. Even shopkeepers, excluding hospitality service providers, shut and take their annual entitlement in either July or August. The entire city is deserted in the summer.

In the evening, I took the visiting students for a walk along Via Veneto and then to the Spanish Steps, and Susan joined us. We spent an hour sightseeing and walking to Villa Borghese Park. None of them wanted to spend time or money eating out, so I decided to take them home. Susan split us early on as we reached the Spanish Steps. It was dinnertime when I went home, and Peakeo was already wagging his tail, telling me it was time to take him out. I wasn't fussy about dinner, so Olga prepared a cream of mushroom soup with chicken, which I had after a long, hot shower.

As Susan and I were kind of locked in at the college until the end of June, we normally made sure that one of us would come to the college in the morning before ten. By midday, we would join together to plan our lunch or other activities for the day. A few students, in fact, showed up to see their grades, and potential students came to ask about admission and courses. Meanwhile, Michael and I worked together to prepare for the fall semester. Barbara wanted to carry out some maintenance work while the college was empty in early July. Furnishing classrooms with new carpets was one item of this work, and they had already started the groundwork, such as pulling out the existing carpets and taking measurements. This was another area I was supposed to supervise while my job was progressing.

In late June, I moved out of Lucille's and occupied my room at the leased house with visiting students from Texas. It was sad to leave Peakeo behind, but I assured Lucille that I would be back when the summer was over. Luckily, my new house had all the pots and pans for cooking, as well as cutlery for serving. That meant I could cook my meals and invite some friends for dinner. However, our Texan friends were not interested in cooking their meals; instead, they dined out whenever they were free to do so. Most of the time, they went to Mario, and I occasionally joined them. But I loved cooking, and so did Susan, and we joined a couple of times to cook before she left on a brief holiday. In July, I was by myself most of the time but visited the college until the last week of the month, when we got a two-week break. In the third week, Susan came to the college with her mum and sister. They came from England during a brief one-week break, and Susan invited me for her summer get-together on the following Saturday, only a couple of days away. I was told to bring homemade dishes to another potluck-type dinner party.

On Saturday morning, I did some errands and started cooking my dish, which was an aubergine-based Ceylonese dish cooked with plantains or green bananas. Since plantains were not available in the market, I had to substitute potatoes. I named it curry moussaka. The dish consisted of deep-fried aubergine and potato cubes cooked with sliced onions, garlic, and tomato, to be oven-baked with mashed potatoes spread on the top. I thought that it would definitely make a difference as a potluck dish. In the evening at seven, I arrived at Susan's, and I was surprised to see that everyone there was already sipping on their wine glasses. Of course, we had a few Iranian students, all of whom had brought some food, though not necessarily anything Iranian or Persian. However, Susan, with her mother's help, had prepared a special Persian dish called *fesenjān*, which was a sweet-and-sour chicken stew. This dish was ideally served over rice, as in Iran, and seemed common in northern Iraq. It is traditionally cooked with ground walnut and pomegranate sauce. We also had lamb curry and some home-baked pastries. Flavio and his sister had brought apple pie. There were a lot of antipasti to be eaten, including deli items, such as Russian salad.

There was a cordial and convivial atmosphere. Everyone had a wonderful time chatting and sipping wine, which was served in plentiful amounts. Almost all those present brought a bottle of wine with them. As expected, Sally invited a few American friends who were chatty and festive. Sara, who appeared as if she were in her early thirties, was attractive and looked gorgeous in her summer skirt. We had a long conversation on almost everything from politics to religion—which I hated when I came to face an evangelical Christian. Daniel seemed a bit flirty with her at first but didn't like when she seemed dogmatic. But by the end of the party, she became tipsy, and Sally had to rescue her. When the party came to an end after midnight, the food table appeared to be empty, and everyone seemed appreciative of the opportunity to participate in such a wonderful party with delicious food. Of course, Susan and Sally deserved credit. I thanked them before leaving with Daniel, who willingly gave me a ride home at one thirty in the morning.

The summer heat in July was intense, and Rome seemed to be empty, except for the tourists. On Friday during the last week of July, I picked up Sandy, who was returning from her European tour. She had travelled via the same night train that I took the previous year when I returned from Paris. As expected, Sandy stayed with me and shared a room. Initially, she felt a bit shy to be staying with me while there were other students from her college in the same house. Sandy thought she was lucky, as she didn't know the people and had not met them before at the college in Texas, and she wanted to keep a distance from them as much as possible. Most of these students from the US South were devout Christians, and Sandy thought she looked as though she could be the daughter of either of the visiting couples. This meant limiting the number of interactions and avoiding potential opportunities to meet them face-to-face while in the house. Sandy was to stay only a week in Rome, and luckily, the visitors would be out most of the time on study tours in Rome and outside excursions with Michael. Sandy was scheduled to fly home the next Saturday, a week from the following day.

My first night with sandy was exciting, but I was very much a well-disciplined man who could be romantic in behaviour. I knew how to tame my desires and deal with a tender young girl who had just turned twenty-one. Describing her casino visit some time back, Sandy regretted that she had not been able to gamble, as she had not yet been twenty-one years old. But now she seemed mature for her age at twenty-two. I was told that back home, she had several suitors seeking dates. As she was a conservative Southern Baptist, I was not surprised to hear that she was still a virgin, even though she claimed to have had a boyfriend. I had already made up my mind not to take advantage of her, although she was willing to share her intimate space with me during her brief sojourn to Rome. I opted to take it easy, as the Americans say.

In the evening, we had dinner at a local restaurant where they served trattoria-style food at an affordable price. After a simple fettucine with ragu sauce, we enjoyed a plate of *pollo con pepperoni*, which was a chicken dish cooked in tomato sauce with green peppers sautéed in olive oil, herbs, and garlic. As we walked home, we were holding hands while I listened to her talking about the recent European tour. It was a leisurely walk, as it was still daylight. We were cautious of not being intimate when approaching the house, as we may have been spotted by our Texan visitors. At home, we both relaxed at the sofa with a good cup of coffee, which Sandy liked with cream. I was behaving as if we were good friends and showed no signs of any ulterior motives other than an in-depth discussion on Parisian attractions and museums which I was already familiar with. As dusk fell, Sandy wanted to go for a shower before heading to bed.

As she walked in after the shower with a decent but rather revealing nightgown, I thought she would not hesitate to share the bed with me. In fact, I felt she would have expected this when she decided to stay with me. However, despite the temptation, I showed her bed and lay down on the sofa. In a way, there seemed to be a sense of relief in her mind. I didn't even make any effort to kiss her but simply said goodnight. Surprisingly, she approached me and gave me a goodnight kiss. Since we weren't going to do anything serious tomorrow other than visiting the shopping district, we planned to get up late. After her long nighttime train journey, Sandy wanted to rest a bit longer than usual. In the end, I thought I did a very good job by doing what I did without looking for any adventure during the first night.

The next morning, we got up at half past ten, both feeling as if we had had a very restful sleep. Luckily, the rest of the occupants in the house had left on a study tour with Michael. After coffee and cornetto, we started to make breakfast. I made an omelette with grated cheese and mushrooms, onions, and tomatoes which I had bought from the market. I ran to a nearby boutique which had fresh bread, while Sandy helped me prepare the breakfast table. It was quite a fulfilling breakfast, which we both enjoyed. During breakfast, we were still chatting about Sandy's European tours. Although France and Paris were not-to-be-missed items on the agenda, Sandy also visited London, Amsterdam, and Munich. Her journal was full of notes and remarks which she intended to show her mum when she returned home. She had really enjoyed her trip, and luckily, she seemed to have enjoyed the company of her friend from Texas during the trip. For middle-class Americans, visiting Europe on a cultural tour or sending their children to study in Europe was considered something to be proud of and remained a status symbol.

In the late afternoon, we leisurely walked to the Spanish Steps, where one could find a number of shops and boutiques to browse along many alleyways and streets. Via Condotti was also located in this district. We also spent time chatting on the stairs of the Spanish Steps, along with the rest of the tourist gazers. We also licking at some tasty gelato, which Sandy loved. Sandy and I walked around quite a lot, popping in and popping out of fashion boutiques. We could not miss a visit to the most famous street for wealthy shoppers, Via Condotti, where one would find all the popular designer clothes. Armani, Versace, and even non-Italian brands, such as Christian Dior and Yves St Laurent—we could easily find them here. Sandy picked up a few things as gifts and bought some sexy white lingerie for herself on sale. As one would expect, the prices were touristic and inflated here, and unlike in the market or elsewhere in the city, bargaining for discounts was not the norm in this district.

By the time we had finished shopping, it was almost eight in the evening. However, with bulky shopping bags in hand, it was not convenient for us to have dinner at a dine-in restaurant. We decided to get takeaway pizzas and eat at home. At a nearby pizza stall, I ordered a large seafood pizza, and we took a short walk, as we were told that it would take at least half an hour to be ready. The streets were still busy with a bustling crowd, and some shops were still open. We entered a shopping gallery to do some window shopping in a safe environment. Sandy complained that her legs were tired and required massaging tonight. I thought she was hinting at something, but I kept my mouth shut, and after a while, we turned back to pick up the takeaway pizza. We arrived home just before 9.00 p.m. and saw that the rest of the crowd was also back. One of the couples was busy preparing dinner, but we managed to slip away after saying good evening. We needed a wash before the pizza dinner. After a quick wash, we indulged in our seafood pizza with a glass of soave.

Halfway through our dinner, we heard someone knocking at the door. It was George from upstairs, who had been in the kitchen when we arrived. He needed assistance with one of the kitchen appliances. He saw us with pizza in our hands and asked me to finish eating and take a look at the oven, which would not turn on. I left the room then and there and showed him how to turn on the oven. In my room, we leisurely continued our meal. The pizza was excellent, with many prawns and clams, as well as anchovies to tease the tongue; and with a chilled glass of soave, it was indeed superb. While eating, we also drew up a plan for the following day. Sandy wanted to go to the beach for a couple days, so we thought we could go to Ostia, which could be reached by subway train. Ostia was the old port city of Rome, only forty minutes away from the Termini station. As Sandy packed the beach bag, she wanted to know whether I had some sun cream, which I said we could buy from a seaside boutique in Ostia. I told her that we wanted to leave before the mercury rose, meaning before ten. Thus, we decided to go to bed at 11.00 p.m.

As we changed our outfits to prepare ourselves for bed, she asked me to turn the light off for a while so that she could put on her new lingerie that she had bought a few hours prior. When I turned the light off and then turned it on after a while, I sighed in awe and said, 'You look beautiful and sexy.' She looked sensuous, sexy, and gorgeous. She was, indeed, seductive. With a height of five feet four inches and a rather slender body, her sex appeal couldn't be denied. Her stiff and slightly protruding bosom and rounded buttocks were visible through the silky layers of the lingerie. It was quite inviting, but I tried to resist with a deep breath. But to my surprise, she wanted me to massage her legs, and she laid herself face down in the bed.

I couldn't control my manly desires and approached her to offer my services. Meanwhile, my testosterone was waking me up, but I needed to keep calm, and with a gentle touch and a stroke, I slid my palms over her legs and buttocks. As she turned around, I saw that she was aroused, and she jumped forward to kiss me. As we stripped off and threw our clothes, we could feel the sensation of bodily heat, and we were like beastly animals exploring each other's flesh with exploding passion. When I asked whether she was still a virgin, she said, 'Sort of.' I realized that she was fully ready to explore a whole new world, and our pleasure-filled encounter lasted almost an hour. What a wonderful experience. Minutes later, half lying over my body while sipping on a glass of San Pellegrino, she said, 'That was the most enjoyable experience in my life, and it will be the most memorable too.'

After a tireless but enjoyable night, we woke up rather late but managed to leave home by nine in the morning to catch the train to Ostia. Luckily, this was a nice day with a tolerable temperature. In fact, this was the first time that I went to the beach for sunbathing in Italy. Sunbathing might be the last thing that someone like me, with tan skin, would consider doing. But I couldn't refuse to go with Sandy. When we reached Ostia, we first got some sun cream for Sandy and then headed to an isolated corner on the beach. The sun's rays were not intense, and there was a pleasant breeze while we sat on the beach, lying over the towel we had carried with. I helped Sandy rub the sun cream gently on her body, and as she sunbathed, I went to the water to keep myself cool.

Most of the time, I remained reading a book in the shelter under the parasol which we had hired at the beach shop. We didn't wish to spend the whole afternoon at the beach and thus decided to leave at half past two in the afternoon when the sun started to show its power. On the way back, we got off at the next station and explored some of the Roman ruins left in Ostia Antica. It was already six in the evening when we finally reached home, and we enjoyed a scoop of gelato in town after getting off the train.

At home, we took it easy, as we were planning to dine out the next day in Trastevere. I wanted to cook pasta for dinner with cremini mushrooms which I had bought a few days before. Cremini mushrooms are often referred to as brown or Italian mushrooms. The mature version of the common button mushroom looks slightly larger, but smaller than the older brother, the portobello mushroom. Italian people use cremini mushrooms in soups, pasta, and several other types of dishes. I wanted to cook a simple pasta dish by tossing cooked fettucine in heated olive oil with garlic and herbs sautéed with sliced cremini mushrooms. A dash of hot pepper and grated Parmesan sprinkled over the dish would enhance the flavour. As we were hungry, I went to prepare the pasta, and Sandy watched while I cooked. Soon, we got ready for dinner. It was a delicious but simple dinner with a glass of Frascati.

Soon after eating dinner, Sandy took a shower while I ended up having a cup of coffee. With my body sticky from the seawater and hot sun, I was also prompted to shower before heading to bed. As we were both ready to head to bed, I knew that it was going to be another enjoyable but long night. I didn't need to exaggerate the fact that I was rather mesmerized by Sandy's curvy body and voluptuous bosoms. When I turned off my light, Sandy approached and started to kiss me passionately while still standing. As I slowly stripped off her lingerie while trying to get rid of my pyjamas, I caressed her rear gently. While the foreplay continued passionately for some time, she became aroused as I touched her breasts and kissed her nipples. In no time, we both were in the bed, and one can only imagine the burst of excitement and joy of making love on that hot and steamy night.

After a restful night of sleep, we both woke up before eight while sunlight sneaking through the curtain made us more energetic. Sandy wanted to go to the beach again, and we opted to get some Italian breakfast on the way to the station. We quickly had a cup of coffee while preparing to leave after the morning rituals were over. This time, we managed to get to Ostia before ten, and we had plenty of time to soak ourselves in the sun until half past two in the afternoon. Since we had planned to dine out in the evening in Trastevere, we wanted to get back four or five in the early evening. I was planning to take Sandy to a traditional Jewish restaurant in the ghetto, near Trastevere. As we didn't have any reservations, we wanted to leave home as early as possible.

After a quick shower, Sandy and I were ready and headed to the bus stop. We managed to get to Trastevere by half past seven. Even at eight in the evening in midsummer, it seemed a bit early to dine in for an average Italian. Thus, we decided to reach the restaurant and reserve a table so that we could get there by nine for dinner. But to our surprise, there were a few tables already occupied, and we didn't want to risk losing the chance to eat at this restaurant. We decided to stay in and start with an aperitivo, a pre-meal drink, with some bites. Sandy ordered some red vermouth, and I wanted Cinzano. We were served the drinks along with pastrami-wrapped breadsticks. It took a while for us to consume the aperitivo, as the waiter continued to serve some traditional antipasti, including the Jewish-style chicken liver pâté. In Rome, we would be served a plate of pasta before the main dish, but we opted out and ordered a main dish of the classic Ashkenazi beef brisket, which was rather subtle and sweet and sour. Cooking low and slow to break down the brisket resulted in tender meat. Although potatoes and vegetables were traditionally served during Jewish holidays, it was not unusual to see these dishes served throughout the year in restaurants in the ghetto.

The delicious and flavourful brisket was easily consumable and the melted in the mouth. The brisket was served on a bed of vegetables and mashed potatoes made with olive oil, garlic, and rosemary. We were also served Jewish bread and kosher wine to go along with the brisket. It was indeed a wonderful meal, and I was happy that Sandy liked it. When we finished the meal, Sandy wanted some desserts and chose chocolate matzo, a layered cake, and halva made from sesame seed paste. It was already 10.30 p.m. when we got up to leave. On the way back, we walked for a while and then took a bus. It was really a long and tiring day, and we went to bed early after arriving at home.

The next day, when we woke up in the late morning, we realized that it was Friday and Sandy was scheduled to fly back to Texas on Saturday night. Therefore, we started to pack Sandy's luggage after a cornetto and coffee. I knew it was going to be a difficult job, given the amount of shopping she had done and the goods she had collected. It took a while, but we managed to pack all of her items in one suitcase. The other luggage she had left with me before she went on the European tour needed to be cleansed and arranged in an orderly manner. By separating out the goods that Sandy could stuff in her hand luggage, we managed to pack everything into two suitcases. The time was already 2.30 p.m. when we thought of preparing something for lunch. It didn't have to be an elaborate lunch; a simple pasta dish would do. For dinner, we could go out and have some pizza from the nearby takeaway.

In the late afternoon, we sat on the couch and relaxed with a glass of iced coffee. We just chatted about the good times we'd had in Rome and, for her, the entire European experience. She became a bit emotional and moved closer to me as we continued to chat. We were still in our night attire, which allowed us to be comfortable during the steamy, hot summer. With a close hug, we suddenly started exploring each other's bodies in a tender manner. I was conscious about the open window which needed to be shut, but Sandy shouted, 'Who cares?' I don't need to exaggerate, but we were simply immersed in a different world. We took advantage of every minute, and it was indeed a memorable experience.

Later in the evening, we dressed up after a shower and went for a stroll. We were not keen on dining out but decided to take a long walk to the city. It was a nice and cool evening after the hot and humid day. Villa Giulia was not far from where we were, and we passed through the park. We held each other's hands while chatting about the unexpected nature of the events we would encounter. Sandy used to say that her life had changed since she came to Rome, which she meant in every sense. She was slightly anxious about facing a boring life when returning home.

Who would know the final outcome. I cautioned that it all could end up as if it were just a dream. I should have said that the same applied to me.

As for me, it was a kind of dolce vita which I wouldn't have expected when I stepped on Italian soil a year before. But, unlike Sandy, I was destined to live in Rome for at least a few years, and the change in me was real and did not seem to return. We had a wonderful conversation not only about life in general but also about the hedonistic philosophy and approach to life that we tended to adopt during the post–dolce vita era. Some would even argue that it was the beginning of the breakdown of traditional and conservative approaches to life, as well as our family values in general, that we cherished.

On Saturday night, I accompanied Sandy to the airport and bade her farewell. This was rather difficult for both of us. We both promised each other to meet sometime in the future, but neither of us had ambitious plans. I could see tears coming down from her eyes as she became emotional, but it was c'est la vie, as the French say. She couldn't take her eyes off me as she entered the departure gate, and finally Sandy was gone from my sight. Back in my room, I felt lonely and sad, but I reassured myself that I would be all right in a few days.

18

THE FALL SEMESTER
1980: NESSUN DORMA

As September began, it was business as usual at the American College
of Rome, and we were heading for a fall semester which was scheduled
to begin soon. I had a call from Michael and Barbara to meet during
the coming week. After the Texans left Rome, the house that the college
had leased was empty, and I was to be heading back to Lucille soon. But
to my surprise, Barbara extended the lease and wanted me to stay as
warden. She expected few visitors from the United States. Since I didn't
have to care for any students during the fall semester, I made arrangement to stay with Lucille most of the time, but to look after the house
and amenities whenever required.

Now I was free and single; I thought I should make a visit to Susan's
before the coming week. We were supposed to return to the college by
midweek to meet Michael and Barbara in order to plan and discuss the
staffing requirements of the reception desk and other administrative
matters. On Monday, I made a surprise visit to Susan's, and she was
happy to see me. We had a long chat about each other's summer holidays. Susan was keen to hear about my experience with Sandy. As if she
were a jealous rival, she wanted to know whether I was serious about my
relationship with Sandy. When I expressed my sincere opinion about
my relationship with Sandy and the final outcomes, she seemed quite

comfortable with me, and we were back on track, like old buddies. Later in the day, we went for lunch at a nearby trattoria and took a stroll after enjoying the usual gossip while walking along the riverbank. When I asked about her mother and sister, she said they had been pleased with their visit and safely returned to England a couple of weeks ago.

On Wednesday, we were back in the college, and after a half-day meeting with Michael and Barbara, we were finally ready to welcome the students from Monday. As usual, Susan and I, along with another new recruit, Pat, would take care of the reception desk and phone calls. Existing students as well as new and potential students would start coming to the college to visit from now on. Barbara was confident that we could get at least forty new students for the fall semester. Michael showed us a new application form and course brochure. In addition, the college launched a paid advertisement in the English daily in Rome, which, it was hoped, would catch the attention of any potential international students who were new to Rome. Since the college offered the same courses and no new courses were on the agenda for the new semester, I didn't have much to worry about, as I was quite familiar with everything now. However, Michael often came up with a few new elective modules, which we were expected to familiarize ourselves with.

Meanwhile, I was back at home with Lucille, and things were no different, except Peakeo. Lucille gave away Peakeo to one of her dear friends who lived in the countryside outside Rome. In some ways, I was relieved, but I missed Peakeo very much. Lucille promised me to visit her friend to see Peakeo, as she also missed him so much. Lucille was secretive about her friend, an American citizen living in Italy. I was able to guess that he was involved in gathering foreign intelligence. She wouldn't elaborate on anything. In Italy, this was during the Red Brigades period, when political assassinations were common. As Lucille pointed out, it was considered a revolutionary movement aligned politically with the left.

The Brigate Rosse, or Red Brigades, was an armed far-left guerrilla group with Marxist philosophy operating in Italy in the seventies and the eighties. This period was sometimes referred to as the Years of Lead. During this time, social turmoil and political violence were common in

Italy. This started back in the late sixties, when the Italians were waking up to the difficult-to-sustain lifestyle followed by the post–dolce vita lifestyle of the 1950s and early1960s.

The Red Brigades wanted to establish a revolutionary state using an armed struggle that supported a Marxist philosophy and work ethic. It also wanted to detach Italy from the North Atlantic Treaty Organization (NATO). Its actions were considered political terrorism as the group went on to kidnap and murder prominent politicians, as well as industrialists and bankers. Its stance against NATO also made Americans brand it an international threat. One of the prominent people to be kidnapped and murdered was the former prime minister of Italy, Aldo Moro, in 1978. According to some estimates, the group could have been responsible for killing at least fifty people between 1974 and 1988.

The Red Brigades had become active in big cities such as Rome since the mid-seventies, and its criminal pursuits had continued by extending to attacks on public institutions, including the police and magistrates. It became antiestablishment as well as anti-communist, which prevented political parties from forming coalition governments with minority parties, such as the Communist Party. After Moro's death, it began to lose sympathy and support. Italian law enforcement and security forces responded firmly, the police made thousands of arrests, and several thousand were detained in the 1980s. In fact, the murder of Guido Rossa, a trade union organizer and Communist Party member, was the turning point. However, the influence and activities of the Red Brigade persisted until the late 1990s.

It was already mid-September, and we were facing a busy week at the college. My working day on Monday began early in the morning. Although Peakeo was no longer there, waiting for me to take him out for walks, I wanted to get up by seven in the morning so that I could get to the college before half past eight. By eight, I'd had coffee and toast, and I quickly left the house. When I reached the college, Michael and Barbara were already in, and Susan, too, was just at the door. Barbara had arranged for a quick breakfast so that we could have a meeting over coffee. Michael had already prepared the timetable for the semester and was ready to accept the new students for enrolment. In fact, we expected a rush of new and existing students throughout the week. After the meeting, which lasted an hour, Michael and I sat together to discuss academic advising for existing students.

By ten in the morning, as expected, there was an influx of students, mainly new prospects seeking admission to the college. This time, there were not many candidates from the Middle East, but from around the world. Most of them arrived with their parents, mainly mothers. They were the sons and daughters of executives and managers of international companies or multilateral organizations stationed in Rome. The announcement in the English daily was a winner, and most of the students even carried a copy of the newspaper in their hands. I took responsibility for handling these potential students, and Susan took over the issues of existing students. Most new students were not familiar with the American system of higher education, how the colleges and universities operated, or what courses they could offer for freshmen students. While I saw the students and their accompanying parents, Michael did the enrolment if anyone decided to join the college. Since they could pay for their tuition by instalment, a contract would also be signed with the director of the college, Barbra.

We were told that the college was open for enrolment of new students even during the first couple of weeks after the classes started. When we took stock of all our new admissions on Friday before the start week, we found that we had thirty or more new students who had already paid their initial instalment and registration fees. Barbara expected this number to go up to forty during the next two weeks. The college offered two courses, one in BS economics and business studies, and the other in humanities and liberal studies as majors. Almost 80 per cent of the new enrolment was for business studies, and the students were much younger, in their late teens or early twenties. Irrespective of the chosen field, every new student was required to take the same four modules during the freshman year.

On Friday, Susan and I were happy to see our continuing students, particularly our buddies, including Flavio, Daniel, Mona, and Lisa.

The group wanted to go for dinner at Mario just to chat and catch up with each other. When we met at the restaurant about half past seven, the usual gossip was still well and alive, and the dinner table offered the opportunity to crack jokes and laugh. As usual, Daniel was keen to know about girls among new students. Susan told him about an attractive forty-year-old Brazilian lady, but Daniel jumped at her, saying he was not interested in older women. In any case, Daniel was still pursuing Mona, although she had told him several times that she had an American boyfriend. Daniel wouldn't believe her until he met her boyfriend in person. As we finished the dinner and got up to leave, Flavio suggested going for a gelato, but most of us wanted to leave that idea for the next week.

Before we left, Susan reminded me of Monday-morning classes. Michael had scheduled classes for freshers on Mondays and Tuesdays, and this required us to be in the college early in the morning the following week. On Monday, Susan and I and others, along with Michael and Barbara, got to the college by eight in the morning, and we were ready to handle the situation when the students arrived to enter the classrooms. Almost all of them came to classes on time, and some came with their parents to ensure their attendance. By the end of the day, everything seemed to have gone smoothly, and, as expected, we had another three students enrolled in the course on Monday. When we had time to relax and chat in the evening, Susan pointed out one thing that was different. We did not have any exchange students from Texas. However, we had a study tour to Pompeii and Naples planned for new students, which would take place in early November.

I was shuttling back and forth between Lucille and the house which the college had leased. For the time being, I was alone at the house, which made me consider inviting a few friends and having fun. However, I was conscious about my responsibilities and how I should behave without causing disturbances to trigger complaints by the neighbours. Before any American visitors moved in, I wanted to arrange a get-together. Susan was the ideal person to organize any events involving friends, so I passed this message to her. The next day, Susan and I decided to host a party and invite only close friends and partners, including a few Iranians.

This would be a total of fewer than twenty so that I could manage to cook some lasagne and a salad for everyone. The guests would bring the drinks. Approaching Saturday seemed to fit this plan.

Between weeks, there was quite a lot happening in the college. We had our first class on Friday with an Italian professor, who was also the one of the executives of the state-owned oil and petroleum enterprise. All my buddies, including Susan, were enrolled in his class on strategic management. Professor Mogni had a pleasant but forceful personality. He sounded amusing with his typical Italian accent. Although I enjoyed his first lecture on large organizations, most of my friends didn't have a clue. Daniel and Flavio were just chatting, making unnecessary remarks on the girls in the class—particularly on the South Asian sisters who were busy throwing question after question at Professor Mogni. Once, the boyfriend of one of the girls who was also in the class got annoyed with Daniel and lost his temper. After all, it was fun, and we enjoyed it. In any case, these lot were not invited to our party on Saturday.

Mona and Lisa, as well as Mona's fiancé, were in early on for the party. Susan and I were just preparing the sauce for lasagne before placing it in the oven, but we were ready to welcome the guests otherwise. It was about half past eight when Flavio arrived with a girl I did not know. She was introduced to us as Sara, and she seemed charming and well dressed. Susan whispered to me, saying Sara was too good for Flavio. 'Poor Flavio,' I said. Lisa was staring at Sara with a strange look as if she were kind of jealous. Then, within a few minutes, there came Daniel, the loudmouth. He almost exploded when he saw Flavio and Sara holding hands. To add to the vibe, Mona introduced her fiancé to Daniel, which almost made his heard swirl. He jokingly said, 'Never mind, Lisa will still be single.' Then came Roy and his girlfriend, followed by David and Katherine. Susan's sister Ruby and her boyfriend came much later, as they had gone outside Rome to meet up with a friend. Finally, we had a couple of Iranian friends, Raji and Karve, who came soon after Anne and Louis. The only people missing from the party were Sayed, Susan's boyfriend; and Flavio's brother, Alex.

As we approached nine o'clock, we felt that it was already party time. With a glass of wine and something to nibble on, which we had in plenty, everyone was in a joyful mood. A few, like Daniel and Anne, along with Mona and her partner, were engaged in deep conversation. Susan and I were still busy preparing food and other necessities for the guests, but we found a few minutes-long gaps to mingle with the crowd. By ten o'clock, we had managed to get the lasagne and salad ready on the table, and voilà. I made three large trays of lasagne and a large bowl of mixed salad. Everyone loved the food and enjoyed the meal while chatting and gossiping. A few, including Flavio and Sara, took time to eat but kept themselves busy kissing and dancing to soft music in the background. This was later followed by other couples, but singles like Daniel and me targeted eligible girls for dance. Lisa was happily dancing with Daniel for some time, and I found Susan as well as Anne's friend Louise to cling on to. At some point in time, it seemed like the party was reaching a climax, with almost everyone having a wonderful time. Suddenly I felt that I was missing Sandy and remembered all the good things we enjoyed while she was in Rome. Three weeks ago, Sandy left Rome, but she still seemed to hang around in my mind.

We partied late into the night, and most of the guests left by around two in the morning, except for Flavio and Sara. Even Susan managed to leave with Anne and Louise. But I had two guys who stayed there as my company. Our Iranian friends Raji and Karve were drunk and lay over the sofa. Flavio and Sara were into each other and wanted to stay over, as they knew that I could arrange a vacant room in the house for a night. When Flavio approached me discreetly, I said I would be happy to situate them in the room. But he wanted me to keep this secret; Daniel was not to know. Fortunately, Daniel had left much earlier than expected, soon after the Molinari sisters left. It was almost three in the morning when I headed to bed.

The next day being a Sunday was godsent, as I didn't have to rush through to get up early in the morning. But I knew that I had a lot of cleaning up to do, and I was thinking that I should get Raji and Karve to help me with the clean-up. Of course, they woke up at the same time. I knew that offering a good breakfast when they got up would do the trick. I had some bread and antipasti from the party leftovers, which would make the breakfast table more attractive.

In the afternoon, Flavio and Sara kept knocking at the door, and I woke up to open it. Raji and Karve were still sleeping but Flavio made them get up. Luckily, we had a team now to help me clean up and start breakfast. As Flavio and Sara went to make eggs and prepare breakfast tables, I went to have a shower after my quick coffee. Meanwhile, Raji seemed a bit ashamed of himself after having been found drunk last night, but nothing seemed to bother Karve. For whatever reason, Karve had spent his past two years in the US and decided to leave for Rome to join the college. He said that he had gone through bad times while living in New York City. He had undergone a few sessions of rehabilitation therapy for drug addiction. He seemed very passive and drug-free but had a strange obsession with women and sex. He always showed an expression of innocence on his face and remained well behaved all the time.

In the late evening, when everyone had gone, I took a walk down to Lucille, hoping that Olga would prepare me a good plate of spaghetti. There weren't much left to do at the college in the coming week as far as student admission or enrolment was concerned, so I could take it easy and arrive for work leisurely. Lucille also seemed relaxed and restful as the day ended, and we sat to chat and catch up with our stories over a *spaghetti al-vongole*. She was curious about the party last night. She was also curious to know whether I had found another girlfriend after Sandy, who had left Rome a couple weeks ago. But I maintained my silence and said no. She bluntly said, 'Don't count on these American girls,' referring to my affairs with Sandy.

Back at the college, Michael and Barbara were happy to see more than thirty new students joining this semester, which would obviously bring in consistent cash flow. Michael had already planned to take the new students on a study tour to Pompeii the following month, and I would be expected to join him. In the meantime, he had already taken them around Rome several times. Although these study tours would help students learn more about the Greek and Roman arts, it was not mandatory to visit the sites with the tutor. My experience, however, showed that site visits would help us write our assignments. It was also fun to be part of the group and enjoy the travel and benefit from greater cultural awareness. I already had a meeting with Michael, and I was told that there were about twenty students who had already signed up for the Pompeii tour during the first week of November. But I did not expect any of my friends, including Susan, to join us this time, as we had already visited these sites with a great deal of joy. For me, however, a visit to this historic archaeological site was always exciting, and I learned some new things every time I visited. This was a site where digging was ongoing and had been in progress for almost three hundred years.

Throughout the fall semester, the business at college was as smooth as possible. As expected, a few American visitors arrived in November and stayed with me at the college residence for a couple of weeks. They were in an adult exchange programme in West Virginia. The four individuals—two gentlemen and two ladies in their mid-forties—also joined us to visit Pompeii. I was asked to look after them with city visits to Rome. Our visit to Pompeii lasted for two days, with one overnight stay in Pompeii itself in a nearby pensione. We also visited another site, Herculaneum, the next day, and took a tour to Naples Bay for a pizza in the early evening hours before returning to Rome. Although both of these ancient cities were victims of the eruption of Mount Vesuvius two thousand years ago, Herculaneum was buried under huge amounts of volcanic ash—almost five times that of Pompeii. This led to the discovery of this small city of Herculaneum much later than Pompeii. Both sites were still being excavated, but a visitor could easily cover Herculaneum in just half a day. After our pizzeria visit, we returned to Rome; by the time we reached home, it was midnight.

Meanwhile, October was almost coming to an end, but the weather in Rome was fantastic, with no signs of winter gloom on the horizon, and I should say that September and October remained the most beautiful time in Rome, with mild temperatures and very little rain, if any. In the evening, one could feel a bit of chill, and it was the best time to show one's outfits and accessories without any winter coat covering them. I always loved to go out, well dressed in casual clothing, and take a leisurely walk along the tree-fringed avenues while holding the hand of a female companion during the autumn in Rome. The Indian summer in Rome can last until mid-November. Suddenly there would come the arrival of Christmas—another good reason to be in Rome in December. Speaking of Christmas, this time Barbara had plans for celebration at the college. She was keen to organize a grand potluck dinner in early December before everyone split for the Christmas break.

Thinking about Christmas, I could not get away from the memories of the previous year's events and experiences. However, every Christmas event is different, and in Rome, Christmas always remained a unique celebration when everyone forgot their worries and family and friends got together during these once-a-year festivities. This year, a new friend of Debbie, Marinela, who had joined one of the special diploma courses in semiotics, invited me to join her parents in Padua. Marinela was a graduate of the University of Rome with a degree in cultural anthropology and a student of Dr Tomassini, who was the course leader for this diploma course at the American College of Rome. Some of our students also enrolled in his class as an elective. A fresher from France, Debbie, was carried away with this new course, and she had enrolled in the module. Common interest in the subject pulled us together in in-depth discussions and debates. We often discussed religion and the philosophy and interpretation of religious symbols. Debbie used to tell me that semiotics as a subject was very interesting, as it dealt with the study of symbols and rituals. It helps us understand how and why people create symbols and signs, as well as how we can interpret them. It further focuses on understanding human behaviour through symbols and signs that we associate with. Marinela and I came to know each other through Debbie, and I attended the semiotics class with her a few times. I wished Dr Tomassini was fluent in English, but he managed to communicate fairly well with the students in English.

As for Christmas in Padua, Marinela seemed excited to host me. Strangely enough, she had invited Debbie as well, and thus we planned to travel to Padua together. Debbie had a rather strange background, as her mother was a French Catholic but her father was an American Jew, and she grew up to become an atheist. However, we celebrated everything, whether it was Christmas, Hanukkah, or Eid. Debbie's French high school background gave her a leading edge on her knowledge and interests regarding philosophy. Whether it was about Camus, Descartes, Jung, or Karl Marx, she knew it inside and out, and I had a great deal to learn from her. She was just twenty-one but seemed incredibly mature for her age. Although Annie didn't show any romantic inclinations to anybody, she did have a sex appeal, with a slightly plump body that Renaissance painters such as Rafael or Michelangelo would have adored. Interestingly, she also liked cooking, which was another bond between her and me. Although Debbie didn't particularly mingle with our group or the Iranian group, Raji did desire to get closer.

In the meantime, as the days passed by, we were getting closer to the potluck dinner which Barbara had planned to host at the college. It was late November, and the last Saturday of the month was when we were to host the Christmas party. We'd already had a meeting or two which Barbara had called to discuss and plan for the party. We expected that at least fifty to seventy students and friends would show up, but how many would contribute by bringing a potluck dish? This was the major question we wanted to answer. Barbara had agreed to supply the drinks, both alcoholic and non-alcoholic, as well as one whole roast lamb and salads, along with fresh bread. Susan and I took the responsibility to invite and persuade as many as fifty students to bring some dishes. It could be most likely an occasion to show off ethnic food from several countries prepared by representative students at the college. Obviously, Susan and I planned to make native dishes. Surprisingly, when we announced the potluck dinner, both on the notice board and in person, we had a very good response, and almost everyone we contacted seemed excited and agreed to bring some food.

As we approached late November, teaching had almost ended, and everyone seemed busy preparing their coursework assignments. Some modules had in-class tests, including short answers and Multiple-Choice Questions. The college would stay closed from December second week onwards, and the reopening was expected to be around early January. In the meantime, we were ready for the potluck dinner party on Saturday. The party was to be held in the reception hall downstairs in the same building where the college was located. Decoration and other necessary arrangements had already been done, and the hall had a small kitchenet as well as toilet facilities. Susan and I also had done our errands so that we could start cooking our dishes on time.

On Saturday mornings, I began preparing for cooking. I wanted to make something innovative based on the Indian culinary tradition, but fused with European cuisine. It was a dish of aubergine and fried plantains, which I had tried out once on another similar occasion at Sally's but with potatoes instead of plantains. I called this curry moussaka or Indian moussaka. Once cooked, it was topped up with béchamel sauce and grated mozzarella, to be oven-baked. For the previous potluck, I topped it with mashed potatoes. Susan also decided to cook the same dish that she had for the previous potluck. She wanted to cook Persian lamb stew using the recipe she borrowed from the famous *Fesenjān*, or pomegranate chicken. This flavoured lamb dish contained diced lamb cooked in butter or olive oil with onion, garlic, and spices, such as turmeric, cinnamon, and cumin. The specific ingredients were pomegranate molasses and ground walnuts. Honey, dried cranberries, and orange peels were also added, and all was garnished with mint, parsley, and pomegranate seeds. At this time, our recipes were innovative and challenging.

It was a beautiful autumn evening, and as dusk fell, we slowly reached the party hall. Barbara and Michael, along with their son John and a few other family friends, were the first to arrive, and they had already prepared the antipasti and the drinks tables. The roast lamb was cut and placed on large warm plates on top of an electric food warmer. It was to be served by a caterer hired by Barbara. By eight o'clock, almost everyone was present and had brought their potluck dishes. A few of the dishes were native specialities, but most guests had brought common foods, and some of them appeared to be takeaway food from restaurants. Some of our Italian friends, including the Molinari sisters, had brought well-known dishes such as osso bucco, lasagne, and chicken cacciatore.

My curry moussaka and Susan's lamb stew stood out on the list. In addition, satay chicken was brought by an Indonesian student. She explained that it took more than just peanut butter to make good satay chicken; ginger, garlic, lemon zest, lime juice, honey, and soya sauce, along with some curry powder, were the key ingredients to make it flavourfully delicious. One Brazilian student who reminded me of Fernanda, whom I had dated in Paris, brought ceviche, a typical South American starter consisting of marinated diced white fish or shellfish with lemon juice and seasoning.

After all, it was a wonderful and joyous gathering, and the students were extremely delighted to attend the party. There was plenty of food and drinks to consume, and the crowd was not bad, with some sixty guests mingling with each other and chatting and nibbling on the food. The roast lamb was a hit. So were my moussaka, the lamb stew, and the satay chicken. The Italian dishes were delicious, and they were very different from the usual restaurant-cooked dishes. The homemade food definitely made a difference, which was the highlight of a potluck dinner. To make it interesting and entertaining, Barbara organized a raffle to give away several prizes. There was even a musical chairs contest, which Flavio won. Before the party came to a close after a brief speech by Barbara, most of the guests slipped away. The leftovers were carried back home by the guests, and by eleven o'clock, a small group of us got together to clean up the place. We left the party hall before midnight, with everyone saying, '*Buon Natale.*'

I always liked to attend parties on Saturday nights rather than Sundays, as doing so gave me plenty of time to sleep and rest on the following day. So, on Sunday, I slept until two in the afternoon. After a relaxing shower followed by a large plate of spaghetti with traditional tuna sauce, I took a walk to Lucille's in the evening. Olga was happy to see me and was about to cook some steaks and potatoes for dinner. We both had to wait for Lucille to come after a live opera she had gone to see with her friend Nancy, who was also joining us for dinner. It was after ten o'clock that they arrived, and during dinner we engaged in an elaborate conversation about Luciano Pavarotti's performance. It was

'Nessun Dorma' that Lucille and Nancy chatted about. Although I was not an opera fan, I went for an opera with Lucille once. Anyhow, I had nothing much to contribute to conversation. 'What a great tenor he is, and how beautifully he sang "Nessun Dorma"!' Nancy exclaimed. In English, 'Nessun Dorma' means 'let no one sleep'. This is an aria from the final act of Puccini's opera *Turandot*. It was a staple and favourite of operatic recitals, and Pavarotti was to make it popular worldwide. Luciano Pavarotti, who was born in Modena, Northern Italy, spent his early years in small opera houses until he made his debut at La Scala in Milan in the mid-sixties with *La Bohème*, produced by Franco Zeffirelli. By being there at the dinner table, I learned a bit more about opera. Immediately after Nancy left, I went to bed after a brief chat with Lucille, whom I had not seen for a while.

The next couple of weeks consisted of hectic, time-consuming coursework and writing, and I was approached by some students seeking help with their coursework. Susan and Flavio also wanted me to help them with coursework assignment for the International Business module. Debbie wanted me to stay with her in her apartment during the last weekend while completing the assignments. Although I didn't have any devious intentions, I had to say yes to her, as I enjoyed her company. We had already planned to visit Marinela for Christmas.

19

CHRISTMAS IN PADUA

By mid-December, we were all happy as the semester ended smoothly, and we were looking forward to enjoying a long holiday. As Christmas approached, only a handful of students were left in Rome. Susan had already gone abroad. So had Daniel, but Flavio and David had to stay in Rome. Within a few days, Debbie and I were to leave for Padua. Until then, Debbie wanted me to stay with her, as she liked my company. I thought that was the best option rather than being alone or staying with Lucille, as this also gave us an opportunity to enjoy good conversation and dining out or dining in, which we did from time to time. So I agreed to go home with Debbie. As we planned to relax and rest at night, I moved to the sofa, which was reasonably comfortable sleeping.

The following night, she passed a hint by saying I could join her in her bed. Although it seemed surprising, I just ignored it as if I hadn't heard anything. As with anybody else her age, she likely had the urge to make love, although she showed no signs of emotion or expression of desire. Later, while she was lying on her bed and chatting, she had the courage to call me loudly and say, 'Don't you want to have some fun? Come over here.' I thought she only meant 'some fun' and nothing more. And I said to myself, 'Never mind.' In the end, I jumped into her bed, and it was not a bad experience; it was a night of pure pleasure.

Fortunately, the unexpected sexual encounter with Debbie did not seem to lead to any long-term romantic relationship. Our friendship was solid, although it might have seemed strange to onlookers. Even Susan and Flavio, as well as Daniel, knew that Debbie and I were to visit Marinela for Christmas together. However, nobody dared open his or her mouth to crack jokes. As we planned to spend around a week with Marinela during the Christmas and New Year holidays, we booked our train for 23 December, hoping to return on the second of January

On the night of 23 December, we arrived in Padua, and Marinela was waiting to pick us up. She came with her brother Carlo, who drove a Volkswagen Beetle. Carlo worked as an engineer for the state electricity board and lived with his wife and child a mile away from Marinela's parents. Her dad was a retired school headmaster who had managed to build a large, cosy house with four bedrooms on the outskirts of Padua. We were provided separate bedrooms, and the house was warm and comfortable. Normally, they hosted Christmas lunch and the entire family got together to celebrate the event. It was a pity that our Italian was not good enough to converse fluently with her parents. Her dad, Rafaelo, spoke English adequately, but her mum, Laura, could not speak any English. Laura served us a plate of risotto with mushrooms and cheese in white sauce. This was delicious and fulfilling. After having a long chat with Marinela over an espresso, we headed to bed at midnight.

On the day of Christmas Eve, we woke up late in the morning, and the breakfast table was waiting for us. The breakfast was simple everywhere in Italy, but Laura had made some northern biscotti called *frollini*, which were made of flour, butter, sugar, and eggs. Many kinds of biscuit varieties could be found in Italy, but their shapes and sizes differed regionally. Laura also had some abbracci, or cream-flavoured circular biscuits, on the table, which went very well with either coffee or cappuccino. Once we finished, we took to the street by bus along with Marinela for a sightseeing tour of the city.

Padua, a city older than Rome, made me curious about why it was not so popular among tourists. For many visitors, it remained an intriguing city. The northern Italian region of Veneto offered several well-known cities to enthusiastic tourists, and Venice remained the most popular destination for many. However, only a few international visitors had even heard of Padua in the first place. This meant that you would not see large crowds of tourists roaming the streets, or coaches unloading tourists here and there. However, anyone familiar with historic universities may have heard about this magnificent city. The University of Padua is one of the oldest universities in Europe and had produced famous scientists, such as Galileo. I would say Padua was the birthplace of science in Europe. The University of Padua reminded me of one of the BBC documentaries I had watched about Christians conquering Islamic Spain in the late 1400s, during which time an enormous collection of books in Arabic were burnt, but a select few were shipped to Padua and Sorbonne in Paris after translation to Latin with the help of Jews, who were also persecuted along with Muslims. It should be noted that in the absence of a direct link between Greeks and Latin Europe in the realm of science and philosophy or even mathematics, the Arabs of Spain were the conduit.

Padua was an off-the-beaten-track city for me; I thought it could be a wonderful place for a day trip if one happened to live in Northern Italy. The fourteenth-century frescoes and the oldest academic botanical garden, or *Orto Botanico*, of the university cannot be missed by any discerning visitor. Debbie and I had a great time together visiting several fascinating places and attractions which we had never heard of before.

In the city centre, Marinela took us to the historic centre first. From there, we walked around Piazza dei Signori, Piazza delle Erbe, and Piazza della Frutta. We also visited Via Altinate, famous for its fashion and accessories. Boutiques were open until the early evening, even on Christmas Eve. However, we didn't spend time shopping, which we thought we could do another day after Christmas. Padua was not only a city of Roman ruins and the Renaissance, but also the centre of science and religion from the medieval era to the Renaissance. It was the home of Galileo, architect Palladio, and sculptor Donatello. The city also boasted a number of excellent museums. We went through fourteenth-century frescoes at the Scrovegni Chapel next to the Eremitani Civic Museum, which was closed on the day. Later, we also saw the medieval town hall called Palazzo della Ragione, where one could see traditional bakeries, butchers, and fishmongers. We then lingered into Pratto della Valle, said to be the largest square in Italy, which was built around an oval canal with seventy-eight statues of famous people standing to welcome visitors.

I was interested in seeing the University of Padua because of its historical significance. Being Italy's second oldest university, and one of the oldest in the world, the university has remained the centre of scientific research since medieval times. It was founded in 1222 and is considered the birthplace of modern medicine. The first anatomical theatre is said to have been installed there in the sixteenth century. We visited the historic seat of the university, Palazzo Bo, and wanted to take a guided tour of the facilities, including Galileo's podium, after Christmas. The university's botanical garden is considered the oldest academic botanical garden. The Basilica of St Anthony of Padua, a Roman Catholic Church dedicated to the cult of St Anthony, contains important relics of many Catholic saints, including St Anthony of Padua, who was buried in a chapel. The architecture and art of the chapel are worth mentioning; we saw frescoed ceilings as well as Donatello's bronzes for the high altar. The Abbey of Santa Giustina, a basilica dedicated to patroness St Giustina of Padua, stood next to the botanical garden and the country's largest square, Prato Della Valle. It contains several important relics and works of art. We didn't have time to see the baptistery museum or the diocesan museum, which stood next to the Padua dome.

Italians normally do not make much effort to cook a Christmas Eve dinner. However, Laura had something specially cooked for us. It remained a tradition in Italy to serve seafood for dinner on Christmas Eve. A large whole salmon that had been baked with diced potatoes, onions, and carrots was on a platter on the dinner table when we arrived after the city tour. Of course, we were late to arrive, as Debbie and Marinela had wanted to try out some gelato and coffee when we finished our site visits. The fish was served with spaghetti in tuna sauce as the primo.

On Christmas Day, everyone was up early, and Laura was busy cooking in the kitchen while Marinela stood by her side. Debbie was still in the shower while I was having my coffee and cornetto. Carlo and his family were already in the house, and Carlo's wife seemed to be assisting the mother-in-law with lunch preparations. Laura's sister Daniella and husband, Gino, had also arrived for the great occasion. Carlo had a sweet little boy, Armando, who was just six years old and was expecting Santa Claus to come and shower him with presents. Rafaelo seemed very affectionate with the little grandson, and they played and chatted together from the moment he arrived. When Debbie dressed up and came down, she couldn't resist hugging and embracing the little chap. Everyone at home was in a celebratory mood while sipping coffee and nibbling biscuits. Unfortunately, not all of them could converse in English, but we managed to chat and understand each other. We were not told what was going to be served for the Christmas lunch, but we could sense what was to come. The Christmas lunch usually consists of a traditional meal and nothing new or particularly special apart from the quality of the cooking and the food.

The Christmas Day lunch, or *Natale* meal, usually lasts for hours. In addition, any formal four-course dinner lasts for at least five to six hours in Italy. Unlike the meal we'd had the night before, Christmas lunches typically consisted of meat-based dishes. Laura had made a number of platters full of a variety of classic antipasti consisting of fine cheeses; salumi; cured meats, such as pastrami; olives; and marinated artichokes. We started to nibble on antipasti after half past one, and our first course was *lasagne Bolognese*. As we waited for our primo, or main meal, Daniela and Gino were curious about us and wanted to know more about me and Debbie. What brought us to Italy, how we had liked it so far, and whether we were engaged were some of the items we were asked about. The middle-aged couple thought that we should get married. This conversation also triggered queries about Marinela, who had passed marriageable age. Rafaelo then came to her rescue and said that she was to get married soon after her health problems were resolved. Marinela had a cyst in her breast which the doctors believed should be removed, although it seemed benign.

While we were busy chatting, we were served our main dish, roasted veal garnished with rosemary, garlic, and other Mediterranean herbs. We also had braised beef and roasted potatoes. There was plenty of food to consume. The diners joined to praise God, led by Laura and Rafaelo, for his mercy upon us and the great occasion to share the abundance with family and friends. Soon Rafaelo reached for a stock of select wines lying on the coffee table to the side of the dinner table. He uncorked a few bottles and poured samples into our glasses for tasting, after which we could choose the preferred one. Although we did not have any seafood to be accompanied by white wine, Rafaelo uncorked a bottle of Soave in case anyone preferred white. I tried to start with Soave, which is famous for its dry fruity flavour. Rafaelo had two popular red wines on the table: Amarone della Valpolicella and Bardolino, from the lake district. Debbie and I enjoyed trying both. The former was said to have a reputation for being among the most prestigious and expensive wines.

The sheer indulgence of eating and drinking continued, and even at four in the afternoon, we were still nibbling on cheese. Laura was waiting to bring us the dessert trays. My question was whether I could eat more. "Perhaps I can do a bit more," I said to myself. On the table, there were already many *dolce*, or desserts, to try out, including the traditional panettone and *pandoro*, as well as a range of biscuits. After a while, Laura brought a well-known cake called *Torta Pedrocchi*, made locally by the historic pastry shop Caffè Pedrocchi, in Padua. This had layers of coffee and chocolate sponge cakes sandwiching green mint cream. It was a rich and refreshing cake. The pastry shop itself had been a famous venue from the nineteenth century, and it was a historically significant place. Daniela baked a traditional Veneto cake called *Torta Sabbiosa*, or sandy cake, a traditional Italian cake originating from Veneto. Daniella explained that it is made with a combination of flour, butter, sugar, eggs, potato starch, baking powder, lemon zest, and salt. The butter and sugar were beaten until fluffy and then mixed with the egg yolks and the rest to obtain the correct texture.

Meanwhile, Carlo's wife had made some *Fregolotta*, which was a traditional crumb cake from the region. In addition to the usual ingredients of flour, butter, and sugar with lemon zest, it had chopped almonds. Laura did not miss the famous Italian dessert originating from Venice, tiramisu, which consists of layers of coffee-soaked ladyfinger biscuits with a mixture of mascarpone, eggs, and sugar. Finally, I should say that the dessert was made complete with dessert wine. Rafaelo had a stock of a few dessert wines. I preferred the famous wine from the region called Recioto della Valpolicella, which is made from a blend of a few air-dried local grapes. Of course, the big lunch was not complete, or as the Italian would say, 'Not perfect,' without a class of grappa and an espresso.

On the day after Christmas, Natale festivities continued, and friends and distant relatives were often invited for lunch. It could be an important meal, and it consisted mainly of seafood. If the household was to enjoy the meal without any outsiders, it was customary to finish the leftovers from the previous day. Although not as indulgent as Christmas lunch, Saint Stephen's Day lunch tends to be less elaborate. Some may even try new creative recipes. Generally, on this day, most dine out, and restaurants are fully booked as everyone tries to escape from the hectic few days in the kitchen. This is exactly what happened on Saint Stephen's Day. Rafaelo had already booked for lunch at a local restaurant, but it was just five of us with another retired friend, Silvio. The restaurant served a special seafood menu consisting of calamari and grilled vegetables for the starter, and traditional Tuscan saltfish, *Baccalà alla Livornese*, with creamy polenta as the main dish. Baccalà should be soaked overnight and desalinated thoroughly before cooking. This recipe consisted of cut and fried salted cod, potato cubes, and tomato passata cooked in olive oil, with garlic or onion. The food was delicious, and we spent a wonderful time on Saint Stephen's Day. After the meal, we took a stroll in the park before visiting Carlo for coffee.

The next day, we took a thirty-minute train ride to Verona, a city as good as Padua in terms of artistic heritage and culture. However, this medieval town had more to offer, making it more popular than Padua. Marinela accompanied us and took us through the historic sites. The story of Romeo and Juliet had made Verona a popular city worldwide since Shakespeare's writings. It had been a city of culture, galleries, opera, and Romanesque and Gothic architecture since medieval times. From the collection of paintings and sculptures in city museums, such as Museo di Catelvecchio, we can see evidence that it was a centre for artists during the Renaissance period. The first-century amphitheatre and other historic remnants also reminded us of the early origin of the city as well as the Roman footprint. Between our sites, we managed to have a visit to the Casa di Giulietta, or Juliet's House, and stood for a photo shot on the narrow balcony. Our visit to Verona would have been incomplete if we had not seen the Verona Arena, a huge Roman amphitheatre built in the first century. The arena currently hosted concerts and opera performances and remained a venue for summer festivities.

This ancient city appeared to have more Roman ruins than any other Italian city, and it remained a testament to its past popularity as a thriving Roman city. It was popular in the medieval era as well as during the Renaissance period. Verona boasted several remarkable monuments which remained intact. We visited a few key heritage attractions, such as the Basilica of San Zeno, a magnificent Romanesque building with beautiful frescoes and a collection of intriguing marble statues. The fourth-century complex, which contained the remains of a basilica, cathedral, and duomo, as well as the baptistry and canons' cloister, were worthy of a visit. Having seen these, we wanted to see the mysterious tombs outside the Church of Santa Maria Antica, which was surrounded by a wrought-iron fence.

After arriving at the Piazza delle Erbe, we passed through the charming and picturesque bank of the second largest river in the country, the Adige River, which meandered through the city. We could not afford to miss another beautiful piazza, Piazza dei Signori, which was surrounded by delightful historic buildings and the tallest tower in the city, Torre dei Lamberti, which attracted everyone's attention. This stunning eighty-four-metre tower, which was built in the 1100s, remained a unique meeting place, apart from being a tourist attraction. A statue of the poet and philosopher Dante Alighieri was right at the centre. Before we called it a day, we went to the market square, without which a trip to Verona wouldn't be complete. Piazza Bra was not only a popular market square among tourists, but it was also a vibrant square in the heart of Verona, where the huge Roman amphitheatre was located. As we got ready to return, Marinela wondered about the plans for the next few days. Verona was not far from the famous lake district, and Lake Garda was a stone's throw away from here. We decided to take a day trip to the lakeside within the next couple of days. Marinela said that a train from Verona to Desenzano del Garda, a town on the southern shore, would take less than thirty minutes. She noted that there were many opportunities for walking or even biking on the path along the river shore, not to mention the beautiful and historic villages around the lake and the famous botanical gardens.

Back in Padua, Debbie and I wanted to relax and take it easy, so we decided to stay close, exploring the natural beauty of the city and its surroundings. In the morning, we left home after breakfast and walked around the city independently. First, we kept walking leisurely, revisiting some of the sites, including those we could not visit before, such as the baptistery and the diocesan museum near the dome. We spent some time strolling in the famous botanical garden, where we enjoyed chatting about philosophy and religion while sitting on a bench. The overall ambiance was serene and quiet, as Padua in general was not a place where we would encounter herds of tourists. We picked up a panini from the food stall on the piazza and kept walking along the riverbank. After all, the winter sun was shining, and the weather was pleasant, with the usual chill of the season. When we returned home, Marinela seemed anxious about our return and was waiting to offer a cup of coffee and Christmas biscuits which Laura had made. She told us that she had already made arrangements to visit Lake Garda in the morning and that Laura would prepare us a packed lunch in the morning.

We were not fussy about dinner, although Laura was adamant that we should eat at least some pasta. We did not hesitate to have a plate of penne tossed with chopped asparagus and truffles in butter and cream sauce. As we discussed the morning trip over coffee with Marinela, she pointed out that Carlo had agreed to come with us in his car along with Armando. This would help us drive along the lakeshore, village-hopping. Although three key towns were popular among visitors from Europe, we would head to Desenzano first, rather than Sirmione or Peschiera, Marinela said. Desenzano, being a holiday destination in Sothern Europe, often attracted a large number of tourists from around the Alps regions during the summer, and the city hosted three popular beaches. Desenzano beach, Spiagga d'Oro, and Porto Rivoltella were popular among tourists. It was a relief that we had Carlo to drive around the lakeshores, and we were all excited to get going in the morning. We bade a good night and went to bed soon after coffee.

The next morning, we got up early, and Carlo and Armando were already waiting for us at half past nine in the morning. The winter weather was exceptionally good but felt rather chilly. It would take a good hour to get to the lakeshore. Since we had decided to have a good seafood lunch in a lakeside town, we asked Laura to skip the packed lunch, but a small panini seemed ideal to eat on the way. In the end, we managed to leave home at approximately ten. It was a very pleasant ride through the picturesque road, meandering through the hilltops and vineyards to reach the southern shore of Lake Garda. When we first saw the lake from an elevated position, it looked gorgeous, with a stunning vista. In some places, the view was still obscured by mist and fog, while the winter sunshine was dimly reflected by the waters. As we reached the famous city of Desenzano, it was almost midday, and we were reminded by Armando about the panini. While admiring the beauty of the sight, we sat on a bench along the roadside and ate the sandwich, hoping to find a cafe for a cappuccino.

We first wanted to prioritize what we wanted to see and later dine out in one of the medieval towns that were scattered around the southern shores. The city was ideal for promenades along the lakeshores and offered a picturesque old town and harbour. As we walked through the old town to the hilltop, we approached our first attraction, the Castello di Desenzano, which was a stone castle built some thousand years ago as a refuge from the barbarian invasion. It remained a defence against several invaders later and was subject to numerous battles over the centuries that contributed to its decay, leaving only the outer wall and the tower to be seen. The sight from the castle was a beautiful and unforgettable view that would remain with us forever. As we walked down from the castle, we made a brief visit to the antiquarium, where artefacts from the excavated Roman villa were displayed. We also visited the archaeological museum that contained artefacts from the Palaeolithic period to the Bronze Age. Since we did not plan to go on a lake cruise at the Sirmione Peninsula or a wine-tasting tour, we took a stroll on the lakeshores before we headed for our late lunch.

Among the several medieval villages featuring cobblestoned alleys and stone houses with courtyards, as well as trattorias and Christmas markets, we were forced to choose one particular town for our meal. Several medieval villages and towns were on offer. Limone del Garda, famous for its lemon gardens; Tremosine, a coastal town with a number of mountain Hamlets; Cassone, a medieval town with the shortest river; and Canale di Tenno, a picturesque village with medieval stone houses, cobblestone walkways and a Christmas market were considered. However, most of these historic towns were far away from Desenzano, and we had to choose one nearby town that was easy to reach before the restaurants stopped serving lunch. Considering our time constraints, we decided to try out a little-known trattoria along the southern shores, which was a thirty-minute drive from where we were. We chose Peschiera del Garda. Carlo noted that this trattoria had served fresh fish, and he had visited the place before. Long before the winter sunset, we were able to reach this small family run restaurant located just along the shore. They were still receiving guests, and I was so mesmerized by its location in a beautiful setting. Carlo suggested that we could visit a colourful medieval town called Borghetto sul Mincio on our way home which was not far from here but was located in the interior of the lake.

At the trattoria, as an antipasto, we were served with *Cisam*, a traditional dish made of a small freshwater fish called *Alborelle* on bruschetta with a dash of olive oil. The recipe called for pan-fried cleaned fish coated with a layer of flour in olive oil, garlic, onion, and bay leaf, and then soaked in brine before refrigeration. Cisam can also be served as the main meal. Armando was seen as a bit sleepy but managed to eat some frites. For the main meal, we had fresh butter-fried trout from the lake served with fresh French beans and sautéed potatoes. The glass of white house wine was a plus. We wouldn't consider the lunch being complete without a cup of espresso although we decided to skip the dessert as the time was running out and a short visit to *Borghetto sul Mincio* was on our agenda.

When we reached Borghetto sul Mincio, we were already in the province of Verona, and it was part of the town called Valeggio in the Valley of Rivero Mincio. We passed over the Visconteo Bridge, which had a fortified dam that was built in the late fourteenth century by Visconti. Marinela noted that several battles had been fought in this village involving Venetians, Lombards, Napoleon's army, and Austrians. As an ancient mill village, it has retained its charm. The stone houses along the river contain artisanal workshops, cafes, and restaurants. The restaurants still serve traditional handmade tortellini. The village also offers one of the most beautiful gardens, Park Sigurta. Unfortunately, it was already dark, and we could not fully enjoy the village visit. As we left the village, Armando was already asleep. After an hour's drive, we were home. It had indeed been an enjoyable day, but we felt tired. We thanked Carlo for accompanying us, and at night, we wanted to sleep earlier than usual. Debbie and I had a slice of panettone and coffee before hitting the shower room.

In the morning, we were late to wake up, and so was Marinela. For lunch, we found some leftovers to nibble on and stayed at home. Carlo and his wife, Stefania, invited the whole family to dinner, and Stefania and Armando were excited to host us. After lunch, Debbie and I took a walk through the nearby park adjacent to the woods. It was rather cold, and we were wrapped up with scarves and coats. At times, we were holding hands and chatting about the beauty of nature and life in general—topics more philosophical than the average young adult of our age would discuss. Debbie explained about her teen years of growing up with her mum, without a father next to her. However, she did not regret much, as she had the affection of her dad and love of her mother. She felt that she was free and independent—liberated, in a way. Suddenly we realized that we had to get home and prepare to visit Carlo's, so we returned home before dusk fell.

Marinela and her parents were dressed up and waiting for us to return, and we joined them to go to Carlo's. Debbie and I picked up some toys for Armando and flowers for Stefania early in the afternoon, while the family had other gifts with them. As we headed towards Carlo's, Marinela suggested that we should visit Venice the next morning, the thirtieth day of December, as we would not have another day before we returned to Rome on the second of January. 'On the day of the New Year's Eve, I wanted you to celebrate the evening and spend the night with one of my high school friends, Gabriela,' said Marinela. 'She promised to invite a few more friends.' We believed that this was the right thing to do. Meanwhile, at Carlo's, Stefania and Armanda were eagerly waiting for us, and we had a warm welcome. There was a cosy and warm ambience in the hall, with a Christmas Tree in the corner and colourful ornaments hanging about. Stefania had lit traditional firewood, and Debbie and I sat on the floor near the fireplace. We each had a glass of special warm wine, akin to mulled wine. Armando brought all his gifts to show us, and when we presented ours, he was extremely delighted and at once went to open the pack. It was strictly a family event, if not for Stefania's mother, who was seated to the side. Her father had died a few years prior because of heart disease.

The dinner was to be served on time, allowing us to get home early so that our trip to Venice the next morning could be made much easier with an early wake-up call. The dinner was then ready, and we all took our seats. We used ravioli with ragu sauce as the primo and venison with juniper sauce as the main dish. Stefania roasted the meat with seasoning and then covered it with juniper sauce, which she had made from red wine, garlic, thyme, and juniper berries. The venison was roasted to medium, leaving it tender and slightly sweet. Laura was proud of her daughter-in-law's culinary skills, and we all complimented her with praise. Stefania's rice pudding was also liked by all. We were served with a cup of coffee and a panettone before leaving. At home, we three sat to sort out the itinerary and decided to get up early as we had to take a short train drive to Venice. Marinela wanted us to leave before nine in morning so that we could cover most of the key attractions, although we wouldn't be able to spend time visiting museums and art galleries. In any case, as a study tour, Michael would take some of us with the visiting exchange students to Venice during the summer, and I would be able to join then if I wished.

Fortunately, it was a bright and pleasant day, and the train ride to Venice was smooth. It was just ten in the morning when we arrived at the Santa Lucia train station. We then took a ten-minute bus drive to Venice proper and got off at Piazzella Roma. Venice as a whole, being a lagoon city, consists of more than one hundred smaller islands. Since all major visitor attractions were located within walking distance, it was easier to hop around by foot, although some would prefer to use water taxis, ferry boats, or even gondolas. We decided to walk leisurely, and within minutes we reached our first attraction on our list, the famous St. Mark's Square. As I sighted the piazza first, I heaved a big sigh and paused for a while, and Debbie was almost speechless. This magnificent square seemed to radiate with St. Mark's Basilica, St. Mark's Bell Tower, and the Doge's Palace surrounding it. For the Venetians, it was the only piazza; the other small piazzas were called *campos*.

In fact, the bell tower was a lighthouse and watchtower. At ninety-nine feet tall, it served very well as a lighthouse when Venice was the hub of maritime activities as the centre of trade and commerce. We climbed the tower to enjoy the best view of the city. We also managed to take a peep inside St Mark's Basilica. Before we stopped at one of the several cafes lined up on the square, we looked at the magnificent gothic palace the next door. Doge's Palace stands as evidence of the Venetian Republic's dominance, which lasted for over a thousand years, and it has remained the seat of the republic for centuries. The openwork facades and delicate but imposing architecture essentially represent the Venetian gothic style. No visitor to the palace was not impressed by the monumental doors and majestic reception halls with frescoes and stuccos, or the imposing staircases. Who else could have been behind these artistic masterpieces, if not for masters like Tintoretto, Tiziano, Veronese, and Tiepolo? Doge's Palace is said to hide the tales of Venice, its myths, and even the most secret spots of the city. Casanova is said to have been imprisoned in one of the cells underneath the palace. Giacomo Casanova, who lived in the late 1700s, is one of the most famous Venetians, known for his being a great seducer and his amorous adventures. He is also the only person to escape the notorious prison at Doge's Palace.

Our next stop on the trail was the Libreria Aqua Alta, or the Library of High Water, and it was just a ten-minute walk from St. Mark's Square. It was hidden inside a bookstore where books were held in traditional boats or gondolas. The tradition was to protect books from soaking when the water level rose.

When we finished with the bookstore and library, it was almost half past one, and we thought a quick lunch wouldn't do any harm. Marinela suggested that we should get some Venetian *cicchetti* and a glass of wine, as locals would do. Therefore, we looked for a *bàcaro*, or osteria-type bar, so that we could have some cicchetti. We walked up to the Rialto Bridge looking for an old bàcaro called *Do Spade*, which was located behind the Rialto Market Sestiere San Polo. Do Spade offered a variety of traditional cicchetti in a cosy but packed atmosphere. Most of the items on offer on the table were seafood-based, and we enjoyed the finger food with a glass of local wine while sitting on a stool instead of taking time for a traditional meal.

Within half an hour, we were out at the Rialto Bridge, another top attraction of Venice. It was an ideal setting in which to watch the Venetians going about their daily business, mingling and doing errands while admiring a spectacular view of the Grand Canal as gondolas transporting couples crisscrossed each other's paths. We also took the opportunity to take a peep at the Rialto Fish Market. It was rather entertaining to watch the fish vendors vying for customers while showing off their daily catches. Passing through the narrow streets and alleyways, we headed towards the Jewish Ghetto, which dated back to 1516. The oldest in the world, the ghetto has retained its old character. The ghetto has two parts: an old side, Ghetto Vecchio, and the new Ghetto Nuovo. Jews continued to live in these ghettos up to the present day. In the end, we walked back to the Rialto Bridge, and Debbie and I took a gondola ride to St Mark's Square while Marinela walked to the piazza to meet with us when we disembarked. Before we took the train home, we spent time shopping along the narrow streets around the piazza. We spent some time browsing the shop windows, but there was nothing much to buy other than a couple of Murano glass vases as souvenirs. A visit to the island to see the Murano artwork was something we missed owing to time constraints. Anyway, it was a fantastic day out, and back home, we did not want to do anything more than feed ourselves a large plate of spaghetti that Laura had made for us, before going to bed after a quick shower.

The next day, when we got up, it was a fresh and relaxed day, and we were looking forward to attending the New Year's Eve party at Gabriela's. However, Gabriela warned that she expected this to be a get-together rather than a party. In the late afternoon, we all went to the town looking for something to grab, such as a bottle of bubbly Asti Spumante for the party. As everyone arrived at Gabriela's after dinner, Marinela was wanting us to have dinner by at least 9.00 p.m. We were told that Laura was preparing saltfish by using a traditional recipe. It was a pleasant walk on our way back in the cold and crisp evening air. We had enough time to enjoy our dinner leisurely and to get ready for the night out. However, Rafaelo warned us that it could snow that night.

Before we left for Gabriela's, Debbie and I wrapped up in warm clothes and even carried winter caps with us. It was approximately a kilometre away, so we decided to walk. As we arrived at the party, it was just after half past ten, and a few of the guests had already gathered. Almost everyone else arrived soon after we came. Marinela seemed so excited to see a number of old friends who were high school buddies. Some of the friends were married and had come with their spouses. Gabriela and Marinela, along with another friend, Laura, appeared to be single. Altogether, there were eleven students, excluding both of us. I do not remember their names except for a few, including a journalist friend of Marinela, Ana, and her husband, Franco. The host had prepared some finger food and antipasti, and there was plenty of wine and bubbly for the night. Everyone seemed bubbly and cheerful, sipping wine and chatting. Some of the attendees had not seen each other for years. Debbie and I tried not to be left isolated, and thus we mingled with the crowd, as most of them spoke good English.

As the New Year bell chimed, we exchanged greetings with kisses and a toast. We then gathered around and sang Serenata di Capodanno and welcomed the New Year with a bang. Gabriela also baked a cake, which we gathered around to cut and share our joy. The year 1981 was born, and we were entering this new and exciting year with new resolutions. Every one of us had different aims to achieve, and therefore we all had different issues in our minds. I was thinking about the college and my future, but that was something we all seemed to experience year after year, and nothing significant could materialize when the year came to an end. Debbie and I had a deep conversation about this while others were stretching their memories back to their high school years. Just before 3.00 a.m., we managed to slip away and get home.

There was nothing much we could do the next day but prepare for our journey back to Rome. We enjoyed sipping coffee and having panettones while chatting about almost everything we could think of. The next morning, Rafaelo took us to the station, and Marinela accompanied us to bid us arrivederci. Our journey was smooth and swift, and we arrived in Rome before noon with many unforgettable memories. Although Debbie seemed interested in dragging me home with her, I decided to depart and go to Lucille. I suggested that we meet each other before the college opened the next week. Michael and Barbara reminded me before the Christmas break that they expected me to be at the college on the fifth of January, the first Monday of the year. Susan was expected to be present from the week after.

Section Five

THE CULTURE
TRAIL 1981

The study tours continue in 1981, and a tour of Pompeii illustrating the decadent lifestyle of the inhabitants of an ancient Roman city buried by the ash of an erupting volcano and the discovery of fascinating artefacts remains a highlight. The accompanying leisure excursion to the beautiful Amalfi Coast of Naples, with a visit to the captivating island of Capri, is a plus. A trip to Tuscany to explore the birthplace of the Renaissance and the accompanying culinary expedition sum up the second half of the summer.

20

POMPEII: THE
DECADENT CITY OF
LOVE AND SEX

The spring semester of 1981 at the American College of Rome was
to start on Monday, 26 January, and I believed Michael and Barbara
had been busy preparing for the new semester throughout the holiday
season. They were dedicated and hardly seemed to take a break during
these holidays. I remembered them visiting relatives in New York the
previous year, but this time, they wanted to take just a few days off, rest-
ing at home. In any case, I made sure to get to the college on Monday.
Surprisingly, they arrived late, but they did come before noon. After the
initial meeting, we went through the forthcoming admission agenda of
the new students. Barbara was confident that we would receive enough
students to start a new freshman class. A minimum of fifteen students
would be required to make it cost-effective. Michael and I were proactive
and prepared to face such a scenario.

In the meantime, timetables for the second semester as well as for
the rest of the classes were to be in place, and Michael and I had our
plan ready before the enrolment of students starting from the second
week. Michael and Barbara had already approached the required tutors,
although their availability as per the timetable had not been confirmed

yet. As we started the day, nobody showed up, and there was no need to receive any visitors, but there were a few telephone calls to be answered. They consisted of queries from a few potential students who had seen our ad in the *Daily News*, the only English daily.

During the week, we had a few more calls and visits from potential students, and we were cautiously optimistic that we might hit the threshold number of students for a new class. As usual, the difficult job was for Michael, who had to finalize the timetable, and the allocation of classrooms remained the real logistical problem. Except for the freshmen classes, the sizes of the other classes did not exceed twenty. An average of three classes was offered to every cohort of students. Technically, a minimum of four classes would be delivered on a typical day from Monday to Friday, with junior and senior classes falling mostly on Thursdays and Fridays. Normally, Michael would end up teaching at least one class per day. Barbara taught one or two classes a week. There were a few dedicated part-time tutors from the corporate sector who taught a couple of classes regularly every semester. The college also employed a few Italian professors from the university to deliver a few classes whenever they were available to do so. In the second week, I expected Susan to show up, but she didn't arrive from abroad. But we had a phone call from England on Monday saying she would arrive on Tuesday and expected to be at the college on Wednesday.

However, I was ready to receive students who sought admission or information. I even had another colleague, Kate, from the office to assist me. Since I was familiar with the course offerings and modules, I was able to manage myself, but all new enrolments needed to be handled by Michael and Barbara. Wednesday I was told that everything seemed to be moving smoothly with the timetable and that it should be ready for distribution by the end of the week. Luckily, Susan also had arrived as expected, and now I had some breathing space to manoeuvre as she would attend to all the phone calls, and I could handle the visitors as well as some enrolment of the current students.

By the end of the week, on Friday, Barbara wanted to pick up a few exchange students from the airport, but she later informed me that they

wouldn't come before the first week of May. That was a big relief. I was
pleased to see Susan after a while, and I wanted to go for a walk with
her on Friday after the college was closed, but she had some other plans
with Sayed. So we decided to meet Saturday evening.

In the evening, I went to see Lucille, and Olga was about to cook
some pasta and veal slices, for which I was welcome to join. Olga normally sautéed the lightly breaded veal slices in butter and served them
with chips. After dinner, I decided to stay at Lucille's. I met up with
Susan in the early evening of the next day and spent some time chatting
over some homemade sweets from her mother. I fancied the light-green
baklava, made of pistachios. Persian sweets were less sweet than their
Turkish counterparts. Susan also brewed some loose-leaf tea to go with
the sweets. She seemed very delighted to have visited England, as her
father had arrived in the UK after a long struggle with the authorities
following the Islamic revolution in Iran in 1979. When I asked how he
was, she hinted that he was frail both physically and emotionally, requir-
ing constant support and care from family members.

Although I had heard about the Islamic revolution, which had
brought Iranian students to the American College during the past couple of years, I was not aware that it adversely affected the life of the
average citizen in Iran. Susan explained to me how the revolution had
badly affected them and many more people of the upper social class who
had supported the previous regime of Shah Mohammad Reza Pahlavi.
According to her account, many of them were indiscriminately imprisoned and tortured by revolutionaries led by Ayatollah Khomeini. Shah
Pahlavi ruled Iran for thirty-eight years, from 1941 until he was ousted
in 1979. And with his pro-Western alignment, he had fostered economic
development. Khomeini was a high-ranking Shia cleric with authority
who had been in exile for fifteen years in France. He overthrew Shah
Pahlavi's regime to establish an Islamic republic. The revolution resulted
in a huge exodus of affluent Iranians to Europe and the USA. Susan's
mother, who was a high-ranking officer in the Shah's Civil Protection
Unit, also managed to flee to the UK, leaving behind her husband in
Iran. Since Susan had been living in England while attending boarding

school, she had not had a chance to see him for a long time. She was extremely happy to see him during her visit.

When we were ready to go for a quick dinner in one of the local trattorias in Trastevere, Sally walked in at the door with a friend. The Piazza Santa Maria was as busy and hectic as it always was on Saturdays, with diners and tourists flocking around, looking for a place to eat. We passed through the alleyway to reach our trattoria, where we could try out a local but authentic pizza. We had to wait for nearly ten minutes to grab a seat, as the place was packed. The restaurant also served traditional dishes, but we wanted to try out the pizza, which usually would come with an egg over the toppings, and we ordered a seafood marinade pizza, while Susan wanted a vegetarian pizza. During our conversation over dinner, I was able to hear something new that hinted that trouble might be brewing in her relationship with Sayed. Although she was open and transparent with me even in personal matters, I thought I should not dig too much to find out more. I knew she would reveal it when the time was right, and I kept quiet. However, I wondered whether Flavio knew anything about it. After dinner, I accompanied Susan home and walked to catch the bus.

As the semester started in late January, Barbara warned me that the fresher class would begin a week later, as she wanted to see a few more students join the course. Only ten new students were enrolled, but another five had been admitted. All of the other classes started on time, and I thought I had only one module to attend this semester. It was a module that addressed global business challenges. Michael also wanted me to enrol in another module called American Political Tradition, which would start in February, as Michael was expecting a visiting professor from the United States to teach. Most of our buddies had been enrolled in the same modules, and life at the American College was set to continue as usual. We had some new students joining the college from several countries, and they were mainly sons and daughters of the diplomats assigned in Rome. A few South Americans from Argentina and Peru, as well as a couple of Malaysian students, were among the freshers who started the course. Since Texan students were expected to arrive in

May, Michael decided to start the summer session in late May so that he could continue until early July. This would help him cover both the Pompeii study tour and the Tuscany trip during the semester.

As the term progressed, in mid-February, just before Valentine's Day, I was reminded of Sandy. In fact, Sandy sent me a postcard from San Antonio a week prior saying that she had not forgotten the good old days in Rome. I had nobody this year as a Valentine date, although Debbie seemed to linger around. I resisted calling her for a Valentine date, even though we had already had a couple of dinner outings. Instead I suggested to Susan that we should go on a dinner date, as she seemed to have split with Sayed. In any case, I did not have any ulterior motive except friendship. She agreed, and we had a very pleasant experience, although in the eyes of onlookers, we were a Valentine couple. Lucille was a bit suspicious, but I had to explain the nature of our friendship. In the meantime, Flavio and Catherine were deeply in *amore*, while Daniel was making a move on Mona, and they did go out on a Valentine date. Believe it or not, Debbie went on a date with one of the Iranian students, Raji, who had been chasing her for some time. Suddenly, in the middle of the semester, a story began circulating about Nasrin and Benjamin, who were to get married while still at the college. Nasrin, one of the two Bengali sisters who had revolted against her parents' wish to marry a cousin back home, seemed adamant to marry Benjamin. In addition, marrying a non-Muslim was considered sacrilege by her parents' family members in Bangladesh. James, the son of a diplomat, seemed to be deeply in love with the girl.

Another pleasant news item was the wedding of Kenney, a mature Armenian student from Iran, and Becky, from the United States. Michael even hinted by saying that the college had become a dating agency. Susan and I thought there would be a few more marriages to take place in the near future. As time rolled on, in late April on a Friday, Michael and Barbara were preparing for the arrival of the Texan exchange students, and I was briefed that we should be making the house ready. The following day, later in the evening, the group was picked up by Barbara and brought to the house to stay with me. They were a total of eight in number, with three middle-aged couples, one single young man, and a single girl. Both singles were to spend time in the college during the entire autumn semester, while the couples would return in August. Mike and Debora, Dan and Phyllis, and Raymond and Lucy were the couples. The first two couples were retired, and Raymond and Lucy were in their forties and not married but living together. Tony and Dana, both singles, were in their late twenties. Both were mature students in San Antonio and intended to spend a semester with us after summer. Tony was a real southern lad with a penchant for travelling. Dana had been married but recently got divorced and wanted to pursue her higher studies. Her dad, a medical doctor, helped her with tuition expenses and travel.

As expected, I was assigned a job to look after their needs. Dana enjoyed a single room in the house, but I had to share a room with Tony. After their first visit to the college in the morning for induction with Michael, I had to introduce them to the famous city of Rome. The Texan group seemed friendly and jovial, with a southern sense of humour. They had read about Rome and Italian history, and a few had already visited the city some years prior. Mike, Debora, and Dan were retired academics, but Raymond was a self-employed mechanic. Tony was a builder-cum-carpenter. Dana, who had been married to her high school lover, did not seem to have worked. I took the group around the most popular tourist sites, and by the end of the day, it was time for dinner. As expected, I took them to Mario for their first dinners in Rome.

As Mario was like our home, we were able to sit and relax over a glass of wine. Chef Mario was aware of the newcomers' curiosity and anxiety, and he brought some homemade antipasti, which was unusual, as he had never served this to us before. While enjoying the starters, I briefly explained Italian food culture and tradition. The main menu item of the day was a braised fillet of sole in tomato and garlic sauce, served on a plate of penne arrabbiata. They were all happy and well-fed, and they looked forward to hitting the bed after a long day.

The next day at the college, Michael and I were busy preparing the itinerary for the Naples-Pompeii visit. He was planning a two-night stay around Naples as a visit to the Amalfi Coast, and a trip to Capri, a beautiful small island along the cost of Amalfi, was included in the itinerary. After counting the visiting Texans, there were only fifteen seats left if anyone else wanted to join us. Since most of the students had already seen Pompeii, we did not expect this number to be more than twenty-five in total. I was a sort of tired of Pompeii now, as were the members of our group which Susan led. However, Amalfi and Capri were places of interest we could not resist. I was expected to join the tour as part of my job. As we wanted to travel during the last weekend of May, I had to publicize the event, which I did immediately, and my first audience was our group and a few students who had joined the course in the previous semester.

By the third week, my list was already full, and as expected, Susan, Flavio, and Daniel had signed up to go, along with a few Iranian students, including Raji, Debbie, and Karve. Also attending would be the Molinari sisters and the eight Texas visitors. In fact, the total number had exceeded twenty-five, which would require a large coach. But it didn't matter, as the college charged the students for accommodation and food. This meant that we could recruit more students. Kenny and Becky wanted to join too. In the meantime, I ensured that money was collected from the students and the itinerary was distributed. We planned to leave Friday morning and return on Sunday evening. By the end of the week, I confirmed the number of participants to Michael, which was thirty in total. This time, it was only Michael and I from the college, and even Susan had to pay like any other student. When we departed Rome on Friday, 29 May, it was a chilly morning at seven thirty. We were able to reach our destination, Pompeii, in the late morning. It was a pleasant day, and as Michael started his usual onsite lecture introducing Pompeii, many of the old students slowly broke away, leaving the Texan group and a few following the study tour. I decided to stick with them for courtesy's sake, although I had seen the ruins a few times. As planned, we were to meet for lunch at one of the local restaurants with rural but charming character located immediately next to the local rail station.

We were warned that the lunch would be ready at half past one.

After lunch, Michael wanted to take a tour to Herculaneum, the sister city of Pompeii, which was buried by the ash and lava from Vesuvius when it erupted in the year AD 79. After an exhausting site tour, we arrived at the restaurant on time, while the rest of the group was seated and anxiously waiting for food to be served. We could order a plate of spaghetti with freshly made tomato sauce with wild mushroom and garlic as the primo, and either rabbit or chicken as the main dish. We had to choose either wild rabbit cooked in white wine, green olives, and capers using a Sicilian recipe, called *Cunnighiu a Portuisa*, or hunters' chicken, called *pollo cacciatore*, as the main dish. Most of us ordered the former, but some of the Texans wanted the chicken cacciatore because it sounded new to them. We also served some common antipasti and a green salad, as well as a glass of house wine. Some ordered disserts and coffee after lunch.

While enjoying lunch, my attention turned to a curious, charming young woman with a long black hair seated just opposite me. She kept staring at me as if she wanted to converse with me. Later, after we got up, Tony, with whom I shared a room in the house, came to me and said, 'Did you notice that girl who was staring at you?'

'Yes, Tony I even wondered why,' I replied.

He pushed me to go and chat with her. Outside the dining room, a few of us, including Susan, sat on the terrace of the restaurant cafe, which also partly served as the platform of the rail station. We enjoyed fine weather over a cup of espresso while gazing at passengers waiting to catch the oncoming train to Naples. Then came this curious young lady who boldly approached me and said hi to me. I asked her to sit next to me and started to converse. Kirstin was an American metrological student spending time in a German university in Hamburg doing some research as part of her doctoral studies. She looked as if she were in her late twenties. When I asked about her plan for the rest of the day, she said planned to spend time in Naples and hinted that she would stay overnight. I managed to give her the address of our hotel, which was located in Pompeii itself, before bidding her goodbye. That was the end of the story.

After lunch, Michael and the Texans left for Herculaneum, but I stayed with our group. We spent time strolling along the town centre and nearby parks. Some even went to visit Naples, which was a thirty-minute ride from Pompeii. I remember Michael reminding us that the hotel check-in would take place after 5.00 p.m. But I thought we should be able to check in at Hotel del Sole before five. In fact, I was the one who would be helping colleagues sort out their rooms according to the list that Michael and I had prepared. The dinner was to be served at nine, soon after the sunset. Susan and the group had a wonderful time playing cards and throwing Frisbees in the park, and just before five in the evening, we all gathered at the hotel. The guys at the reception desk were expecting us, and with Susan's help, I managed to arrange the rooms for whoever was already at the hotel. I had to wait for Michael and the rest of the crowd for thirty or more minutes. When it was done, I went up to our room, which Tony was already in. Ours was a comfortable room with twin beds. Some rooms had multiple beds, and four students had to share them.

The Hotel del Sole was popular with European and American visitors and welcomed foreigners through the Neapolitan charm. The hotel had a large dining hall with an excellent food service tradition. Susan and Flavio were already talking about going to a disco in town after dinner, and Tony and Dana also wanted to join us just for fun. After a quick shower, I came down to see the dinner arrangement at the dining hall. Michael and the Texan visitors were already seated and waiting for the rest of us to join them. They were sipping an aperitivo with some typical antipasti.

Tony and I, along with Susan and the group, sat at the corner, and the Iranian students were next to us. After the house pasta dish, we ordered either a seafood dish or mutton cooked in a Neapolitan style, with fresh tomato cubes and aubergine. We could order marinated or grilled jumbo shrimp or cod cooked in cream sauce. Plenty of green salad on the side, as well as fresh fruits and a gateau slice as a dessert, were served to complete the course. When we had finished the dinner and were sipping on the coffee along with our gateau, a surprise visitor suddenly appeared in the dining hall. Tony was shouting at me, saying, 'There she comes!' It was no one but Kirstin, who rushed through to see me. Tony got up and gave her the seat next to me, and Susan and everyone else were gazing at me as if they hadn't seen anything like this before.

Kirstin had returned all the way from Naples, leaving her friend there in the pensione. Susan and Flavio, along with Daniel and the Molinari sisters, were preparing to go to the disco, and Tony wondered whether I would join them or stay put with Kirstin. Being an understanding adult, Tony even hinted that I could have the entire room for tonight. Kirstin and I stayed in the dining room after the others left. The server even brought a slice of gateau and coffee for Kirstin, and we stayed chatting while the dining hall staff bussed the tables and cleaned the hall. We were not that keen to go to the disco or even spend the time at the bar, but we went for a stroll outside, holding hands and sharing an occasional kiss. This was like an infatuation on her part.

Being half Native American, Kirstin may have found me similar to someone among her relatives, or perhaps I rekindled her memory of someone from a previous encounter. For me, it was like a dream come true, and I thought there was a real chemistry between us that pulled us to each other like magnets. Indeed, this was a dolce vita experience. I was sure that this would boost my playboy image. Kirstin fluently spoke German, which was something unusual for an American woman of her age. Her dad was an engineer working for a Boeing contractor, and her mother was half Native American. Kirstin had South Asian features with beautiful long hair and a charming face. Her tall, slender body with long legs made everyone wonder where she was from.

Finally, we made our way to the room, and I was sure that Tony wouldn't disturb us before one o'clock in the morning, so we were free to enjoy a fantastic time together. However, I knew that it was going to be a one-night stand. Soon, I turned off the light as she began stripping off her clothes, and then she pulled me in and took my clothes off while both of us were still standing. She sort of tantalized me when I tried to get to her nipples, but she kept on engaging in kissing me passionately. I got the impression that she was a master in these matters. She hinted at taking it easy and going slowly. As I moved down to her breast after a strenuous sensuous massage, we pulled ourselves to the bed. I sensed that this was an exciting moment for her. After a while, she wanted to change our position, as if she wanted to take the lead. We engaged in further foreplay, leading her to reach out to me mischievously. What excitement and pleasure life has to offer! I thought I needed to reciprocate this act of love. I should concede that when it came to making love, she seemed to be very mature, and the entire experience provided an opportunity to learn from an adult, although she was of the same age as me. When the first part of the show was finished, it was just after midnight, and we still had time before we would be interrupted by Tony.

We both got out of the bed, and I reached out for a glass of water from the bottle left on the desk. Every room had a large bottle of mineral water and glass provided by the hotel. As both of us were unclothed, I wanted to ensure that the window curtain was closed before turning on the light. We paused for a good thirty minutes while caressing each other. We kept chatting and got to know more. Kirstin was in an exchange programme between American and German universities, and she would spend time until December in Hamburg this year. She planned to tour Italy during the summer with her German friend Astrid. She hinted that she would love to spend a few days with me in Rome in July before returning to Hamburg. After a pause, I suddenly got up to turn the light off, but Kirstin pulled me back and asked me to leave it on. I didn't object to that and sat back when she started to kiss me again. The ritual continued for a while before we really got down to business. It felt to me as if someone was watching us make love in broad daylight.

After an exhausted workout, we fell asleep, and I didn't hear Tony's arrival, which I had been told would be around half past two in the morning. We managed to have a few hours of good sleep and woke up at seven in the morning so that we could shower before Tony got up. Later, we headed to the dining hall for breakfast when there were only a few students there. Luckily, Susan and the crowd were missing, and I was able to comfortably bid goodbye to Kirstin.

In the morning, as per our itinerary, we would be heading to the

Amalfi Coast and later taking a boat ride from Sorento to the beautiful island of Capri. As planned, we left the hotel before nine and headed towards Salerno rather than Sorento along the cost. Technically, the Amalfi Coast is described as the southern coast of the Salerno Peninsula from Vietri sul Mare to Punta Campanella on the southern edge of the Sorrentine Peninsula. The famous coastline consists of thirteen towns and villages, such as Positano, Amalfi, Minori, Conca dei Marini, Ravello, and Praiano. While Amalfi itself is considered the centre of the coastline, Positano remained the most visited and admired town. Some towns and villages boasted stretches of beautiful golden beaches, while others were located on clifftops over the ocean. Our plan was to spend the entire morning viewing the marvellous coastline, hopping in and out of the coach before taking the boat to Capri from Sorento. We entered the coast from Salerno and came down to Vietri sul Mare, which was considered the gateway to the Amalfi Coast.

After passing through a long stretch of hilltop and beachside roads, we arrived at our first stop, Minori, next to Maiori. Minori was famous for its underground ruins and handmade pasta. After refreshing ourselves, we headed to Ravello, which did not take much time. Ravello was a famous town among some historic figures, such as JFK, and boasted some spectacular views along the Amalfi Coast. Ravello was not far from Amalfi itself which was considered the heart of the Amalfi Coast. We took a stroll on the narrow streets and visited the cathedral in Amalfi. Michael told us to resist taking a coffee break until we reached Positano, which was the most impressive town of the Amalfi Coast. It was a picture-postcard town with beaches, sun, and beautiful landscapes. Most agreed that it was better than Amalfi. Its restaurants, cafes, shops, and scenic views offered the best experience for a discerning visitor. At Michael's suggestion, Susan and I had a delicious soft pastry served with a lemon-flavoured cream called *Delizie al Limone*, a regional specialty, at a cafe. Finally, we stopped in one of the most beautiful towns along the coastline. Some would even call it the most romantic town on the Amalfi Coast, with stunning views. Praiano is situated along the coast of the Bay of Positano. We could see the Torre a Mare, or the Tower in the Sea, from this enchanted town, and the island of Capri was in sight too.

We hurried to catch the boat to Capri from Sorrento so that we could arrive there to have lunch at one of the island's restaurants before they closed for lunch. Capri was a short boat ride from Sorrento for which Michael had already bought tickets. We were able to reach Capri just after 1.00 p.m. It was a short walk to the restaurant from the port, and I was impressed to see the staff waiting to welcome us and seat us. I didn't know that Michael had lunch reservations. Some of us sat at a long dining table with benches on both sides, under grapevines hanging over us. There were a few more tables for the rest of us, and the waiters immediately brought us platters of starters filled with grilled vegetables and some deli meats, as well as marinated anchovies and artichokes. Jars of red and white house wines were already on the table along with freshly baked local bread. We were served a plate of fettuccini in olive oil with anchovies and mushrooms seasoned with garlic and red-hot peppers. For the main dish, we were offered either *frutti di mare*, fresh tuna, or *tonno fresco* cooked in olive oil with fresh tomato, garlic, and herbs. I had tuna, but I grabbed some of Susan's frutti di mare. We were pressed for time, as we had to see Capri and get back to Sorrento so that we could stick to the plan and return to Rome by night.

Capri had two sections: the Town of Capri, with the majority of the population, and the Commune of Anacapri, on the eastern hills. Many were attracted to this island because of its sheer beauty. Similar to all Italian towns and cities, Capri has a rich history. This ten-square-kilometre limestone island had been a resort town for Roman Emperors, and in the nineteenth century, it was occupied by the French and then the British. After lunch, we strolled along the streets of Capri and visited the Grand Port, Marina Grande, and Piazza Umberto, which were popular places to spend time. Some of us wanted to visit Anacapri, but it could only be reached from the sea via a flight of eight hundred stairs called Scala Fenicia. We also observed ruins of the two castles and St. Costanzo, a tenth-century church that is among the oldest in the country.

Michael wanted us to spend some time in Sorrento before darkness fell. Therefore, we returned to the boat soon after half past five in the evening. In Sorrento, we took a stroll around after checking in to the hotel located in the town itself. We were warned that dinner would be served by nine o'clock, so we had a good couple of hours to take a walk in the town centre and window shop, as the stores were still open. Susan and our gang were already planning to go to a nightclub after dinner, and I thought it would be a good idea, as we were not pressured to get up on a Sunday early in the morning. After a smooth check-in, some of us left the hotel to explore the town centre. However, some decided to stay up and attend to their personal needs. We were told that we would be taken to the Sunday market after breakfast late in the morning. But I decided to walk instead of shower.

Sorrento, a coastal resort town facing the Bay of Naples in south-western Italy, attracted visitors from several European countries during summer. The Sorrentine Peninsula, which consisted of several fishing villages and resort towns, was not different from the Amalfi Coast, and many often chose Sorrento as the centre for their visits to Amalfi and Capri. Sorrento, on the clifftop, remained separated from the busy marinas: the beach and the ocean were captivating to the naked eye, with azure-blue waters with a greenish tone. The town was famous for cafe-lined squares, such as Piazza Tasso. There was a web of narrow alleys in the historic centre that included a fourteenth-century church, Chiesa di San Francesco. In fact, I was with some other students, and we spent time browsing the narrow alleys while enjoying fresh ice cream and watching the sunset. At nine thirty, we all got together for the dinner, and as usual, we had all the varieties, from antipasti to an array of sea-food dishes to be served. In fact, the table was full of starters, and I opted to have fried calamari, squid, and prawns that were served with chips. In any case, I didn't want to miss the famous Sorrentine dessert *Delizia al Limone*, which I had already tasted in Positano. The lemon delight was delicate and full of fresh lemon flavour, consisting of a soft sponge cake covered with delicious whipped cream. This authentic dessert was said to take several stages to prepare: flavouring and aromatizing the cream, making the sponge dome, and preparing the custard and lemon cream. This dessert was something that would linger in my mind for a long time.

The dinner was quick, as everyone wanted to attend the nightclub. Half of the crowd was already heading towards the disco. The night life in the late spring and summer did not begin until late in the night, and by the time we got to the disco, it was almost eleven o'clock. I had the company of all our group members, including Mona and Lisa, as well as Flavio. However, all of us were singles except Daniel and Mona, who informally dated for a while. There were several new students who had joined the trip, and finding a dance partner was not an issue for many of us. The music was loud, and everyone jumped and moved to the beat. In fact, one did not need a dance partner. Anyone could dance with anybody on the floor, as nobody was attached to anyone. For me, it was really loud, and I found it difficult to make conversation. Some of us took to the upper deck, on which they had tables and seats to enjoy a drink. There was a Bee-Gees album that was very popular during that time. To my surprise, I even saw Michael watching us dance from the upper deck. He puffed on a cigar and chatted with visiting students from Texas. Tony and Dana were dancing with us, and I was able to swing a few minutes with Dana. Daniel and Mona clung together and danced for a long time, while Flavio from time to time went to disturb them. I saw Tony having a good time with Lisa. In the early morning, everyone slowly found their way to the hotel. Susan and I left at half past one, and the hotel was just a few hundred metres away from the disco.

The next morning, some were keen to visit the Sunday market with Michael, and I joined the group just out of curiosity. It was a flea market and a farmers' market. To be honest, I didn't find anything interesting about it, but I did pick up some seasonal cherries, which I loved so much, knowing I could eat them on the way back to Rome. At the hotel, Michael was pressing us to get ready to leave, as we had to get to Naples for lunch. However, before lunch, we would spend time visiting the famous national museum, which I had seen several times. I also remember Michael telling us about the pizza lunch; the plan was to get there at 2.00

p.m. Finally, we managed to depart from Sorrento before midday and arrived in Naples on time to visit the museum. The Texans and Michael were keen to get to the museum, and we stayed back, taking a walk in the neighbourhood around the piazza. Some stayed in the coach while listening to music. Iranian students, along with Debbie, ventured out to visit the town, but I warned them to be back before half past one in the afternoon.

A famous pizzeria was located in the hills overlooking the Bay of Naples, with a beautiful view. This old-time pizzeria served a variety of pizzas, and the last time I was there, I tried their seafood pizza with squid, tuna, and anchovies. Neapolitan pizza was considered to be the best in the world, perhaps because of the flavour imparted by Mediterranean herbs and olive oil. In addition, real mozzarella cheese and tomato sauce are unique components. As expected, Michael and the group came out at half past one, and luckily everyone managed to gather on time so that we could get to the pizzeria before 2.00 p.m. The restaurant was located on a historic and colourful street, but parking was a problem for the coach driver. We were unloaded at the site, and the coach was drawn away. We had an entire lounge for us, and we decided to get a buffet deal where we could eat as much as we could and choose whatever we wanted. We simply had to pile up our plates with pizza slices and enjoy them with a glass of house wine. Of course, we were told we were to have only one glass of wine each, but we sneaked in for another glass. We stacked our plates with slices and moved to the terrace, where we could enjoy the beautiful day outside. It was, in fact, a gorgeous day, and we had a wonderful pizza lunch with a glass of Neapolitan wine. Not at all bad. As the free lunch on the college account did not include coffee or desserts, some were tempted to test the local sweets, but a few of us decided to have just a cup of coffee.

With full stomachs, everyone seemed nippy, and the driver was kind enough to bring the bus to the nearby road as prepared to leave Naples. It was half past four in the afternoon when we departed. We knew that the driver would stop for a break after a few hours of driving, but most of us fell asleep on the way back. In Rome, I had to wake up a few students when we reached the college site. I made sure that everyone got out safely with their belongings before I headed home with the Texan visitors. Susan and Flavio went with Daniel, and the Molinari sisters took a cab home. The Iranians and others split off while Raji walked home with Debbie.

21

THE SUMMER 1981: THE JOY OF SEEING TUSCANY

The summer had not yet started, but we were already experiencing early summer heat. It was quite a busy time at the college, and everyone seemed contemplating their coursework assignments. I myself had a few assignments to do, and the submission deadline was fast approaching. Of course, Susan and Flavio wanted my help with their writing assignments. The Iranian students were clueless and struggled with their homework even before the end of the semester. For a couple of nights, I spent time with Susan and Flavio, guiding them on their writing, and I needed to spend a few hours penning my own assignments. Michael was busy taking the Texans around, and the final study tour for the exchange visitors was scheduled for mid-July. This would be a fascinating trip to Tuscany but was not meant for regular students, although anyone lingering around after the semester ended was free to join.

By the end of the month, I heard that Marinela wanted to meet with me and Debbie over coffee, as she had made an important announcement. I tried my best to get hold of Debbie, but she was never around. Luckily, Raji happened to pass by, but when I queried, he replied with some anger that they had split up and he had no idea about her whereabouts. With the help of Susan, we finally came to know that Raji had made her pregnant and she had left for France to seek help in order to abort her pregnancy. After all, she was just twenty-one years old, and she wouldn't have liked the idea of becoming a mother while pursuing her studies. There was quite a lot of smoke in the air, and the rumour circulating among the Iranian group alleged that Raji wanted to marry her so that he could apply for an American passport. Obviously, Debbie refused to marry him, but nobody knew why or how she had let him make her pregnant.

In the meantime, I met with Marinela over coffee and heard all she had to tell us about her recent breast screening, which had given her a clean bill of health. She also announced the good news of her recent engagement with the man she used to date. When I asked whether she had any plans to tie the knot soon, she chuckled and said, 'Not this year.' I hugged her and said, 'Congratulations.' It made me marvel that in a very short time, so many things could happen, and I was curious to find out whether everything was okay with Debbie. But I was confident that she wouldn't miss the end-of-semester assessments. Marinela had the same feeling, and we both wondered whether we could be of any help. As we both walked to the college, I ran into Susan, who brought us good news, saying that Debbie had called the college to let us know that she would return on Monday. What a relief. Marinela and I sighed with joy. As Marinela hurriedly headed to her class, Susan and I ended up chatting at the reception desk until late in the evening.

During the last weekend in May, as promised, I spent time with Susan and Flavio, helping them complete their coursework assignments. There was another friend of Susan, Sana, who begged to join us, and it was like a tutorial session as I helped them do the assignments. I didn't mind, as I was getting all the attention, and it was gratifying, too. I told them that it was all about learning a logical approach to planning and writing. A lack of facts about a specific subject and terminology would play a part when they found it difficult to write, and communication skills were not so much an issue with them. But Sana seemed to have some problems with her written language skills, although she could converse well in English. We started in the early afternoon and finished by eight in the evening. Susan's landlady, Sally, was away, but she could be returning soon. In the meantime, Susan brought pizza slices from the takeaway joint at the piazza. When we finish eating, Sally showed up with a friend. Sally wanted us to join them for a glass of Asti Spumante or bubbly, as her friend had just won a court case back in the US. It was not a bad Saturday evening. Flavio took me home, and Sana wanted to walk, as she lived somewhere nearby.

On Monday, Debbie didn't show up as expected, but she came on Tuesday. She still had a few days to complete her assignments, and she was fully capable of doing so on time. She didn't appear to be emotional or weak, but she wanted to have a chat with me. In the evening, I invited her to have a pasta dinner and chat over a glass of Chianti. Neither Michael nor Barbara knew what had really happened, but everyone among the group, as well as the Iranians, was anxious to know more after seeing Debbie around, who appeared to be as normal as ever. But gossip and rumours could still make her uneasy. Strangely enough, however, Raji was missing, and we didn't see him around the college for some days.

At home, we chatted while preparing the pasta for an early dinner. I heard that Raji had kept pushing her to the edge by emotionally torturing her to get her to marry him. All he wanted was to get an American residency permit. Debbie thought he was mad and refused to accept the fact that she didn't want to live in the US. She sort of hated the American ego and mindset. Although she had both American and French citizenship, she didn't feel as if she were American. Moreover, at this young age, she was unprepared to marry anyone. When I asked whether they loved each other, she asked whether I was joking. This was a brief fling and nothing more. Debbie knew that everyone might have heard the news that Raji had made her pregnant, but she wasn't too shy or embarrassed to tell me the truth. She thought it was her mistake that she had not protected herself during the sexual encounters. She didn't put the blame on Raji, but she seemed convinced that their relationship had reached an endpoint. After dinner, I accompanied her home and wished her luck with her coursework assignments as I bade her goodnight.

Michael and I met midweek for an hour to plan the trip to Tuscany, which would involve visiting key places of artistic and cultural importance, including Florence and Sienna, as well as Pisa and Luca. While all the exchange visitors were expected to participate in the trip, Michael expected another ten to fifteen students and others to join us. Our estimate included thirty-five participants, plus or minus three. This meant that a standard coach of forty seats would be fine. The tour would take three overnight stays. The ideal dates for the tour appeared to be during the first or second week of July, as we would have been through with all assessments and grading by the end of June. In addition, after mid-July, it would become difficult to cope with the increasing number of tourists, and finding accommodation would be difficult in Tuscany. After Rome, Florence remained the second-most-visited city in Italy, along with Venice. Luckily, we didn't have to plan the trip on a weekend, as there was no regular teaching scheduled for July. This prompted me to make an announcement on the notice boards and publicize the trip before students left the campus for summer holidays.

By midweek in June, we were already in summer, and the final grade and results were posted on the board. Most of the students had already left the campus after the submission of their coursework, and they would not bother seeing the results before the next semester in autumn. In the meantime, Michael delivered a few seminars to exchange visitors from Texas during the break so that the building was often frequented by them and a few other students who were eager to see their results. Susan and I were scheduled to be at the college throughout June and July, and I would be joining the Tuscany tour. We already had some students sign up for the trip, and by the end of the week, I would know the exact numbers so that Michael could do the hotel booking.

During the remaining weeks of June, Flavio and Daniel, as well as a few Iranian students, popped up to the college, which kept us busy chatting and gossiping. Occasionally, we went dining out, and Mario remained our hub. Unexpectedly, one day, Raji showed up from out of nowhere. He seemed kind of lost and obviously had not submitted any of his assignments. Fallout with Debbie was definitely one of the causes of his current predicament. Susan and I tried to console him and invited him to join us on the trip, but he seemed set on the idea of settling in America. Another friend had already succeeded in doing so by getting married to an American friend. We took him over to Mario for dinner, and surprisingly, even Daniel showed up with another friend. In the end, while at Mario, Raji got drunk to the point that he found it difficult to stand. We shouldn't have let him drink so much in the first place. Somehow, we managed to take him home, with Daniel's assistance.

The remaining few days in June passed quickly, and we were ready for the Tuscan trip earlier than we'd thought we would be. On the second day of July, we left Rome early in the morning with thirty-four people on board a comfortable air-conditioned coach. The crew consisted of two experienced drivers. It was a few hours of arduous journey to Siena, and we arrived at a half past one. Since we all had some form of packed lunch, Michael insisted on doing the hotel check-in first, before looking for something to eat. We were reminded that the Palio event took place at seven-thirty sharp in the evening, and we were to head to grab a good spot around the perimeter at the Piazza del Campo to witness this colourful and spectacular horse race. Some decided to shower after check-in, but most of us were ready to soak in the pre-Palio excitement at the piazza. Our hotel was not far from the piazza, but a few of us decided to take a stroll and explore the medieval streets and piazzas of Siena, for which the city had a reputation, owing to its structured town planning traditions. Tony and I, with Dana, visited the Siena Cathedral and stopped to admire the Fonte Gala fountain before climbing the Torre del Mangia to enjoy the breathtaking view. I sighted Michael along with the rest of the exchange visitors and a few other students passing through the Cathedral Square and looking for something to eat.

Siena, being a beautiful city dating back to medieval times that had been rejuvenated during the Renaissance, had plenty of things to offer to the discerning visitor, both architecturally and culturally. The Palio was considered a big cultural event in Europe; it took place on the second day of July and sixteenth day of August every year. Michael had deliberately planned this trip to coincide with the Palio, although he'd had to dish out a premium price tag for the hotel. He even thought of searching for accommodation outside Siena, but finding a suitable hotel for thirty-six people in a small town, such as Pienza, was not an easy job. After a few hours of sightseeing in the city, we finally arrived at the Piazza del Campo, well in time before the race.

We grabbed a panini and a drink from a cafe and found an excellent spot, but there was still an hour's wait before we immersed ourselves in the vibrant and colourful atmosphere of the pleasant summer evening. However, time flew by quickly as we kept watching the crowd eagerly waiting for the event to occur. Suddenly we saw the procession of pageantry with colourful costumes representing various *contrades*, or city wards, including a marching band. I thought this was a sign of the forthcoming Palio race. As anticipated, at seven-thirty, we witnessed adrenalin-driven thundering horses dashing through the human-made streets around the piazza. There was great excitement when the energetic crowd cheered for the winning jockey. The winning horse came from the Tartuca Contrade. Ten horses participated in the race, representing ten of the seventeen contrades of the city. The city authorities employed a lottery system to select participants, and the remaining seven contrades were automatically included in the next year's list. There was a huge overnight celebration after the winning horse was paraded by the jockey to the cathedral. The previous night, we had also been told that the city celebrated with a communal dinner served on long wooden tables in the largest piazza of every contrada.

It is worth mentioning what we heard of the Palio race from Michael while we were travelling towards Tuscany a few hours prior. The Palio was a Sienese tradition that evolved from combative games, such as boxing and bullfights, organized by the contrades during medieval times. In recent years, public races were said to have run across the entire city. When bullfighting was outlawed by the Grand Duke of Tuscany in the late 1500s, the contrades took them to the Piazza del Campo. When they replaced buffalos and donkeys with horses in the sixteenth century, the race took the name 'Palio'. The race was preceded by a colourful pageant, or *Corteo*, as part of the Palio march. Alfieri and flag wavers in medieval costumes were included in this process. The Palio was a short three-lap race run on the perimeter of the campo, which was covered by several inches of dirt. The city authorities painstakingly prepared a track every year for the event. The selected ten horses were ridden bareback by jockeys who wore contrade costumes. Often, a few jockeys were thrown away, and the respective horses would finish the race without their riders. In the Palio, the winner was always a horse, not a rider.

Soon after witnessing the Palio celebrations for a couple of hours, we all returned to the hotel, where the servers were waiting to see us seated for dinner. It was nearly ten when we had dinner. Although the city offered a range of restaurants in which authentic regional cuisine could be enjoyed, we ended up dining in the hotel's restaurant, as our accommodation expenses included dinner and breakfast. Most of us were not keen on the food but were tempted to go out to be part of the Palio celebration, which would continue overnight. In fact, we left after eating hastily. One of the specialities of Siena was a homemade pasta called *pici pasta*, which resembled thick spaghetti. I tried it with *cacio e pepe* sauce, or simply ground pepper and local pecorino cheese from Pienza, a picturesque medieval town not far from Siena. Another speciality I was able to taste was *melanzane parmigiana*, a simple baked dish of sliced aubergine layered with pasta sauce and grated Parmesan cheese. Michael and the crowd tried wild boar stew. A local wine, Brunello di Montalcino, was a pleasant addition to meals.

The next morning, soon after breakfast, we left the hotel and drove through the scenic rolling hills of the Val d'Orcia to Pienza, which was famous for its medieval heritage, renaissance architecture, and pecorino cheese. After walking around the town and appreciating its beauty and cultural heritage, we visited a local winery, La Foce, and toured the vineyards with a guided tour on winemaking while engaging in tasting their prized Brunello wines. In the early afternoon, it was necessary to take a lunch break before we headed to Florence, which was around a one-hour drive. Most of us got away with a panini and drink, but some preferred a good meal. A gelato and an espresso were a plus. You should not miss ice cream in Pienza; it was a Tuscany delight.

In the early evening, we arrived in Florence, and our hotel was not far from Piazza della Signorina. The hotel check-in was smooth, and afterwards, I managed to take a leisure walk along the Arno River and explored the vibrant Piazza della Signorina with a few colleagues. One thing is for sure: I realized that the city was already crowded with tourists as we returned to the hotel.

Florence remained the Cradle of the Renaissance, and exploring the city fully would require at least two whole days, but we had at least one whole day to do so. For now, we were ready to enjoy a wonderful Florentine dinner at the hotel. As we entered the dining hall, we could see the long side table full of antipasti, both Florentine specialities and regular items, such as olives and cheeses. We were free to pick, choose, and indulge as much as possible. The one which caught my attention was the traditional Florentine antipasto *crostini di fegato*. This popular item consists of croutons covered with chicken or goose liver mixed with finely chopped anchovies, onions, and capers. Other antipasti offered were cured meats, such as salami Toscano and prosciutto, as well as pecorino cheese, along with the famous bruschetta. The most preferred item was crostini with a glass of white wine. When we finished eating the antipasti, we were served a plate of pasta with wild boar ragu sauce, a Tuscan version of Bolognese, and ravioli stuffed with porcini and truffles. I preferred the latter. Some even preferred *ribolita*, a traditional Florentine peasant soup made of cabbage, beans, and stale bread.

While Tuscan cuisine featured a variety of entrées, the most famous secondo was Florentine steak, or *bistecca alla Fiorentina*. The tenderized T-bone steak could normally weigh one kilogramme and would be charred on both sides but extremely rare on the edge and inside. Tony and I wanted to try this out. It was not normally included in the tourist package prices because of the cost, but I was prepared to dish out a few extra lire. It was served with roasted potatoes and beans. It took some time to finish eating. Most students opted for Tuscan-style chicken with artichoke hearts and porcini mushrooms. The hotel had a stock of choice Tuscan wines, but the most popular among them was Chianti. They even served us a glass of Chianti Classico along with the main dish. Apart from Chianti, there were other popular wines on the display at the restaurant bar for discerning guests. They included the iconic Sassicaia and Nobile di Montepulciano, as well as Brunello di Montalcino. This is not to mention the good white wines, such as the earthy, dry Vernaccia di San Gimignano and Bianco di Pitigliano.

For dessert, we were told to pick up anything from the table, which included the classical Italian dolce, such as tiramisu, as well as local specialities, such as *torta della nonna* and panna cotta. Seasonal fruits were also abundant. I tried out almost everything but liked my favourite, tiramisu. A glass of *vino Santo* to go with the dolce and an authentic cup of espresso were the final menu items. The Torta della Nonna, or grandmother's cake, was not bad either. It was similar to vanilla custard pudding, but with many eggs and whole milk, making the filling rich, smooth, and creamy. The pastry was tender and crispy. Panna cotta was another creamy pastry with vanilla flavour which was easy to make. After dinner, some went out for a night out, but I went to bed early so that I could have a fresh morning, as Michael wanted us to be ready soon after breakfast at half past seven.

In the morning, as expected, everyone was at the dining hall for breakfast on time, and the full-day exploration of Florence started with an on-site lecture at the site of the duomo. As we gathered around at the piazza, Michael briefed about Florence and the Cradle of the Renaissance. The role of the Medici family was well emphasized in this regard, and the famous renaissance masters, such as Michelangelo, Raffaello, and Brunelleschi, were credited as pioneers. The Renaissance was not any particular movement but an artistic and philosophical concept emerging from a collection of creative endeavours directed towards the expression of art and architecture over a period of time between the mid-1400s and mid-1500s. Initially a wealthy and influential banker, Giovanni de Medici, as a patron of art, provided the base to kick-start the process, which was later to be energized and facilitated by his son,

Cosimo de Medici, after his death. Therefore, the Medici tradition continued to make history.

Florence was not only the birthplace of the Renaissance but also an important trading hub even before the 1400s. The city saw its influence coming from the European wool trade centred around it and the political power held by wealthy merchants. They were also generous enough to spend their wealth building cathedrals, towers, and art galleries, fostering creativity in art, architecture, and intellectual development. This also prompted competition among rich merchants, thereby rekindling the city's rebirth. The Renaissance in Florence was also a social and cultural revolution that would spread all over Italy and Europe. In my opinion, it was also a sort of good life, or dolce vita, in some sense. However, instead of decadence creeping in, as during the time of dolce vita, the Renaissance provided the base for social upliftment and lasted over a hundred years.

After Michael's speech, we went to see the marvels of Brunelleschi's majestic duomo. The Cathedral of Santa Maria del Fiore, on which the dome sat, was the largest cathedral in Europe until St Peter's in Vatican City was constructed in the early 1700s. The history of the duomo is fascinating, including how Brunelleschi managed to get a job to do from the commission. It was indeed a marvellous feat in engineering and architecture, not to mention the sheer size of the dome, which was the largest dome at the time of its construction. The duomo was also famous for the works of masters like Michelangelo, Donatello, and Giotto, and a visit to the Grande Museo del Duomo was a must. Michael spent a few minutes explaining the significance of the sculptured entry door in the north, Porta della Mandorla, before we wanted to climb the steps up the dome. Some of us climbed inside the dome using the narrow steps to get a glimpse of the panoramic view. It was not possible for everyone to climb the steps.

Our next stop was to the Academia Gallery, where a vast array of paintings and sculptures was displayed. The Gallery of the Academy of Florence was best known as the home of Michelangelo's iconic sculpture, *David*. The gallery's collection of Michelangelo included some unfinished works of the master, such as the sculpture *Saint Matthew*. It also hosted other sculptures by the master and a large collection of paintings by Renaissance artists, along with Florentine paintings from other periods. It remained the main art museum in Florence, although smaller than its rival, Uffizi, which was the most visited museum in the country. Other valuable works on display were Florentine paintings covering the late thirteenth to sixteenth centuries, including those of Botticelli, Sarto, Sandro, Uccello, and Giambologna. Famous paintings, such as *The Rape of the Sabine Women, Venus and Cupid*, Dal Ponte's *Coronation of the Virgin, Annunciation and Saints*, and *The Descent from the Cross* were some of the works on display.

The Academia Gallery should have led us to the next famous museum, the Uffizi Gallery, named after the offices of Cosimo de Medici's administration. However, some wanted to have a coffee break, so we paused for a while at Piazza della Signoria. Michael told us that it took four years to build Uffizi after Cosimo commissioned the architect Giorgio Vasari in 1560. It remained a public office for the Medici family until 1584, when it was converted to an art gallery.

The Uffizi Gallery displayed the work of all the well-known masters of the time. Da Vinci's *Adoration of the Magi*; Raphael's *Madonna of the Goldfinch*; Michelangelo's *Tondo Doni*; Caravaggio's *Medusa*; Titian's *The Venus of Urbino*; Giotto's *Ognissanti Madonna*; and, finally, *The Allegory of Spring*, or *Primavera*, and *Birth of Venus* by Botticelli were the most popular paintings that no visitor would miss. Undoubtedly, Botticelli's two works were among the most famous artworks in the Uffizi Gallery. There were many more, and we spent time gazing and admiring in the gallery until lunchtime. We still had to visit the famous old bridge Ponte Vecchio, Santa Croce Church, and Piazza Santa Maria Novella. Michael tried to take us to a trattoria for a quick lunch, but it seemed difficult to find a place that would fit all of us. Ultimately, we ended up having a panini or quick bite at a cafe.

After lunch, we headed towards the famous old bridge over the Arno River. Ponte Vecchio, as the name indicates, dates back to Roman times. This is a stone-arch bridge that houses the famous goldsmith and jewellery shops, or bottegas, from 1593, with the blessing of the Grand Duke of Tuscany. Some of our female students spent time browsing jewellery items, and others took photographs, but quickly we all gathered to head towards the Santa Croce Church, which was a huge complex covering ten thousand square metres of space. Any art lover would not miss this church, which displayed some four thousand works of art in their original form. The complex consisted of a basilica, sacristy, Novitiate Chapel, Medici Chapel, Pazzi Chapel, cloisters, and former refectory. This is not to mention the monasteries of Franciscan friars and a historical archive. Historians would call this a living heritage, as it continued to function as a church from the Renaissance period, with the works displayed in their original setting. The works included those of Renaissance masters, such as artists Brunelleschi and Donatello. Visiting the Pazzi Chapel, designed by Brunelleschi, took us back to real Renaissance times. Meanwhile, the works of Donatello showed versatility in handling various materials to represent varying artistic genius over various periods in his career: the metal statue *Saint Louis of Toulouse*, wooden *Crucifix*, and a relief of the annunciation in serena stone and terracotta were his masterpieces.

As the evening approached, but still under the gaze of bright sun, we became immersed in exploring Piazza Santa Maria Novella. Although the main attraction in the piazza could be the basilica, most flocked there to enjoy the stunning view of the vibrant square. The enlarged facade of the basilica dates back to the renaissance period. At this time, it was the oldest church facade remaining in Florence without any alteration. Visitors were also keen to see the architecture of the church and the artistic works of Masaccio, Ghirlandaio, and Giotto. The building opposite the church and its architecture, as well as the relief works of the former San Paolo Hospital, now the Novecento Museum of Contemporary Arts, were also key attractions to visitors. The day of our visit was the food fair in the piazza, which offered delicious pastries, including artisan chocolates. When we finished the day, we returned to Piazza Della Signorina to witness a gorgeous sunset over Ponte Vecchio. Afterwards, some went to have an authentic

Tuscan meal in the city, skipping the dinner at the hotel, but the rest headed to the hotel as it was time for dinner. As it was a tiring day, I decided to have dinner before taking a shower. The dinner was nothing extraordinary, but we were able to eat something that was different from what we'd had the previous night. By the end of the day, Michael reminded us that we should be ready to leave the next day, soon after breakfast at 8.00 a.m.

On our last day in Tuscany, we were all propped up to bid a farewell to Florence and head to Pisa and Luca. When we reached Pisa, it was late morning and seemed like a pleasant day to enjoy visiting the lean tower. This iconic Tower of Pisa, which could be seen along with the Roman Colosseum in every Italian tourist brochure, was indeed a miracle in some sense. As we gathered at Piazza dei Miracoli, where the tower stood, Michael briefed us about Pisa and the tower. After the Crusades in the eleventh century, the charming coastal city of Pisa prospered along with Genova as a trading hub. Being a port city in the thirteenth century was commercially advantageous. As with most of the Tuscan cities of the era, there was no shortage of wealthy merchants in Pisa who were prepared to spend their money building churches and palaces to show off their wealth and glory. During this period, they built cathedrals, baptistries, and towers, decorated with sculptures by famous artists such as Guglielmo Pisano and Nicola Pisano.

The leaning tower is one such icon. Built as a bell tower during medieval times, it retained the final structure of the cathedral complex. This white marble structure was designed to stand fifty-six metres tall, with eight storeys. Soon, the engineers noticed the structure to be leaning slightly, owing to uneven settling of the foundation on the soft side of the ground, when only three stories had been erected. When construction stopped because of war between states, it helped the foundation settle, which may have prevented it from an early collapse. However, the lean did not stop even with a slightly changed design and structure when Giovanni di Simone began to rebuild it almost one hundred years after the pause. This interrupted the construction, but in the fourteenth century, they managed to finish the upper stories, including the bell chamber, and over the centuries, bells were installed gradually. The engineers believed that the tower continued to lean.

As we were free to stroll around the cathedral complex or even the city for some time, some of us ventured to climb the tower, while others spent their time taking a few obligatory pictures. Of course, a photo in front of the leaning tower would be fun to send to family members and friends. We didn't pause to take a lunch break, as it seemed too early, and Michael suggested that we drive to Luca first and find a suitable place for a bite. As we drove through the beautiful countryside with stunning views of the shining summer sun, it was indeed a wonderful experience.

Luca was a wonderful small city, a hidden gem of Tuscany not far from Pisa. As we were unloaded from the coach before finding a parking place, everyone was looking for something to eat. We headed to the city centre, walking through the narrow streets, and ended up in a local eatery for a quick lunch. Since the lunch was on us, we were free to choose where to eat, and some chose to seek a good trattoria. I chose to have some local pasta served with seafood-based white sauce at the eatery.

After lunch, Tony and I, along with a few other students, ventured to take a stroll through the maze of rather narrow cobblestoned streets inside the renaissance walls. Later, we spent some time at Piazza dell'Anfiteatro and climbed the Guinigi Tower to enjoy a breathtaking view. It was unusual to observe tall oak trees at the top of the tower. On a pleasant afternoon, leisurely walking was what the doctor had ordered, and I wondered what could be better than walking on the top of the ancient wall. We also visited the house of a great opera composer, Casa di Puccini, before returning to the coach park. It was 5.00 p.m. when everyone found their way to the coach, and we left for Rome immediately. In less than five hours, I returned home with the visitors from Texas.

The next day, I visited the college and joined Susan to describe the highlights of the Tuscan trip. She regretted not having joined us. In the afternoon, Michael suggested that we should go for a drink in the evening with the exchange visitors before they departed Rome to go on a European tour. But Michael noted that Tony and Dana would come back to spend time at the college studying as exchange students for a semester. Therefore, we all got together at six in the evening for a happy-hour get-together. Even Barbara joined us and suggested that we should have arranged for a dinner outing. We thought it was too late, but some did go for dinner along with Barbara and Michael. Susan and I returned home leisurely, picking up a slice of pizza on the way. As we were supposed to continue working at the college until the last week of July, we hoped to see each other almost every day. The college was scheduled to be shut for a few weeks from the last week of July to mid-August.

Section Six

A DREAM COMES TRUE: FALL 1982

With graduation on the horizon, Zain seems excited as his mission is accomplished, at least partially. But life after graduation continues with finding and choosing a viable option and an alternative direction for the future. With his hope of securing an American study visa fading, Zain finds an opportunity to continue his postgraduate studies in Paris, France.

22

MISSION
ACCOMPLISHED

The summer joys soon dissipated, and most of the time, I was with Lucille. Susan was outside the country for a while, visiting her family in England. Flavio and Daniel all had taken monthlong holidays, and finally, everyone was back in Rome with a fresh air of hope and enthusiasm. Since Olga was out visiting her relatives most of the time during summer, Lucille was alone, and my company was very much appreciated. In fact, we spent a week at a nearby beach resort called Fregene, which was north of Rome. Lucille's friend Margarita rented out a holiday cottage near a pine forest in Fregene that was not far from Rome.

The beach at Fregene is long and wide, with white sand lying in the summer sun. It was only thirty kilometres from Rome. This small coastal town was full of character and historic charm, including a fishermen's village that was located in the most beautiful part of the beach. A meal at the fishermen's village was a must, and we visited a few times, as we both enjoyed the catch-of-the-day menu that changed every day. *Fritto de mare*, or *fritture*, including fried anchovies and spaghetti with freshly made clam sauce, and mussels with pesto were my favourites. The pine forest where we stayed had a history of more than four hundred years. It was believed that a pope wanted to plant pine trees to drain and dry the wet soil in the seventeenth century, and some of the trees in the forest could be among the oldest in Europe. Interestingly, some of the shooting of Fellini's famous film La Dolce Vita was done in the Fregene pinewood in 1960. This resulted in worldwide exposure of the Fregene pinewood through the film.

Back in Rome, the summer was still alive, with hordes of tourists flocking to the honeypot attractions, while we were back at the college by mid-August. During the semester, I would continue to stay with Tony and Dana independently in single rooms, as there were no exchange visitors except two girls on the exchange student programme from Charleston, West Virginia. This semester remained the last term for at least twelve senior students, including me, because of my advanced standing and credits from summer courses. Susan, Flavio, and Daniel were expected to join the list, but only time would tell. Barbara was hopeful that we could recruit between thirty and forty new students for the incoming semester, and the newspaper advertisement in the English daily was already in place. Courses were scheduled to commence on 21 September, and we had just over a month to recruit, plan, and schedule. So Michael was busy preparing the academic calendar, and he wanted me to work with him in this regard during the first week in the college.

As we drew up the plan and prepared for the next semester, both potential and existing students began to arrive at college. Susan and I were busy dealing with admission inquiries and enrolment from late August. As usual, while Michael and I handled the enrolment, Barbara tended to the tuition payments because most of our students were on instalment plans. In the meantime, Tony and I had to pick up new exchange students arriving in the USA. Tony was also on the college payroll, as he enjoyed a partial bursary from the college. Lisa and Becky were two sophomore-year students travelling out of the country for the first time. They seemed very curious and naive and lacked basic knowledge about Italy or Rome. Thanks be to God, their pocket guidebook kept them confident and happy. I reckoned that Tony and Dana were not bad when they arrived in Rome the previous year. We showed Becky and Lisa a free room upstairs, and they seemed happy to stay with us.

In the meantime, Michael had completed the semester timetable, and the senior-year graduating students had to enrol in a few elective modules, such as American Political Tradition and International Relations. There were no study tours except for a few excursions in Rome. The new exchange students were supposed to travel around on their own if they wished to complement their knowledge of Roman or Greco arts and culture or Renaissance art and architecture. As far as the semester results were concerned, most of the senior students had managed to pass their modules so that they could progress to the final semester except Daniel, who had two incomplete grades, and Ruby, who hadn't passed any modules. Daniel would be happy to repeat the semester, as he could join Mona and Lisa along with David.

As time passed, Barbara counted the number of new recruits, which stood at twenty-five by mid-September. However, she was hopeful that by the next week, the enrolment would go up to thirty-five. Meanwhile, she was pressing me to chase unpaid students before the classes began. I did my best to catch them when they came for enrolment as well as by contacting them if they were late to show up for enrolment. The outcome was better than expected, as some had never thought of an instalment payment plan before. Many Italian parents were not aware of this arrangement, as they usually paid in full for the entire semester when their sons and daughters were enrolled.

When the teaching started on twenty-seventh of September, we enrolled more than thirty new students, but it was a few less than the target of forty. There were no new Iranian students except for a fled colonel from the Iranian Army and his twenty-one-year-old daughter Samira. The colonel wanted to follow classes to enrich himself, and Samira was enrolled in the degree programme. As usual, Michael and I spent the first day on induction sessions for the new students, and Susan and Tony had arranged a snack lunch for everyone. In the end, the first few weeks passed smoothly, and I was assigned the responsibility of attending to the needs of the two new exchange students who were staying with me. As expected, all senior students were enrolled except Daniel and Ruby, who would stay with junior-year students. I was also happy to see

Debbie, who submitted all her assignments and successfully completed the semester so that she could enrol in the new semester.

Raji had been away for some time, and nobody knew his whereabouts. His friend Karve dropped out of the course, and we heard from fellow Iranians that he had left the country, perhaps to Germany. One day while a few of us were dining at Mario, to our surprise, Raji showed up from out of nowhere. He came with another Iranian student, Shahed. In our group, we were five: Susan, Tony, Dana, Anne, and me. This is the first time Raji and Shahed were destined to meet Dana and Tony. In fact, Raji and Shahed came looking for Susan and me, and by chance, they found us at Mario. We also came to know that this was Raji's birthday.

As they both joined us for dinner, I introduced them to Tony and Dana, and I immediately sensed an impulse flashing through Shahed's eyes when Dana, who sat next him, was introduced. Shahed, being a tall, attractive man with a gentle voice who spoke reasonably good English, caught Dana's attention. While we were gossiping about day-to-day affairs at the college, Shahed and Dana were deeply immersed in their own conversations. Raji was drunk, as usual, and Anne had to drive him home after dinner. Unfortunately, Shahed had to go with him, leaving Dana with us. Susan also went home with them as we three walked home.

As we progressed through the semester, everything seemed to move as smoothly as could be expected. The assessment week was on the way in two weeks. Meanwhile, Barbara was already planning for a Christmas gathering at the reception hall on the lower floor before the students left the campus on break. The graduating students, who numbered around twelve, seemed nervous but confidently worked hard to achieve satisfactory grades. Michael had scheduled the graduation event for the second or third week of January; the exact date was to be decided before the Christmas break. And I was told that Tony and I would be occupied with helping Michael and Barbara in the preparation of both events—the Christmas party and the graduation ceremony. However, there was a good chance that Tony would return home in January, but luckily after the graduation ceremony.

By early December, the students had almost completed their coursework assignments and were ready for submission. Christmas dinner was planned for 12 December, and Barbara had contracted an outside caterer to prepare and serve food. I was as busy as usual writing my assignments while helping a few others do their writing. Susan and Flavio seemed to be determined to graduate. The college was scheduled to close for the Christmas and New Year holidays on 18 December, to reopen on 4 January. Michael had also announced the date for the graduation event as 15 January; it would be held in the evening in the elegant restaurant of a historic hotel. Since the number of graduating students was less than fifteen, the total number of guests expected would be less than thirty. It seemed Michael had reserved a private dining hall in the restaurant that could accommodate approximately forty to fifty guests.

On 12 December, Susan and Tony decorated the party hall with Christmas ornaments, including a decorated tree. In addition, all other necessary arrangements were made for guests to gather and relax while enjoying a wonderful traditional meal. Although all students were invited, many had already left Rome, and the final count indicated that about one hundred students and their guests would come to the party. Unlike the previous year, it was not a potluck dinner but was catered by an external contractor. Obviously, it was to be a traditional Christmas dinner with an American twist, and roast turkey with gravy and roast potatoes and carrots were to be served. To make it Italian, guests were to be served Christmas lasagne and tiramisu. Of course, a selection of red and white wine would also be available.

As a winter evening, we gathered at about half past seven, and the guests started to arrive soon after 8.00 p.m. The caterer was already busy readying the tables with all the goodies to stuff our plates, along with a glass of Orvieto or Frascati. Some guests wore Christmas hats and blew horns, which were annoying at times. As the meal was served as a buffet, guests were free to roam around and mingle with each other with their food in their hands, or they could sit around a table and enjoy their food. Some students were even accompanied by their families, which I thought was a great opportunity for them to go around and chat with other students or the staff of the college, including Barbara and Michael. Of course, the Iranian students were upbeat and seemed to have a great time. The talk of the town was about Dana and Shahed, as well as Becky and Kenny. Even Michael could not take his eyes off of the couples' intimacy as they expressed their passion with occasional kisses. Rumours were floating around, and these two couples were about to tie the knot very soon. Unfortunately, Raji pursued the wrong person for a partner, and Debbie refused to offer the young Iranian a chance to dream of setting foot in the USA. Debbie did show up at the party, but not Raji. The party ended before midnight.

The weekend was a time for a bit of relaxation, and I had peaceful sleep on both days. I still had to go to college for another week, beginning Monday. Susan was planning to take off to England, so I would be alone. Lucille wanted me to stay with her over holidays. Strangely enough, this year, Olga also wanted to spend time in Rome during Christmas and the New Year. At the end of the week, when the college was shut for a couple of weeks, I packed my bag and headed to Lucille's. Tony flew home to Texas. Dana, too, was away from Rome, with Shahed, perhaps travelling in Italy. Back at Lucille's, I was very comfortable, and thanks to Olga, I did not have to do household chores or cooking.

On Christmas day, we all got together and made a fantastic lunch with roast lamb as the main dish. Of course, we also had seasonal vegetables and roast potatoes with rosemary and olive oil, ravioli in pesto sauce, and a *Struccolo de Pomi*, a traditional dessert from Trieste, Olga's hometown in the far eastern part of Italy. The lamb, cooked to medium, was full of flavour and delicious. Olga had marinated the lamb leg overnight with garlic and herbs and ground pepper and pine nuts in olive oil. The apple strudel, or Struccolo de Pomi, may have a Turkish origin as a modified version of baklava, which was popularized by the Ottoman Empire. Trieste lay on the coast of former Yugoslavia but remained a part of Udine in Italy after unification. Olga wanted me to visit Trieste with her. She had an elder brother and family living in Trieste. In the afternoon, we took it easy and enjoyed a quiet day.

From early this year, Lucille had been living in a wonderful part of Rome called the EUR, a suburban part of the city that had been newly developed under the dictator Mussolini. Owing to the rural environment, the surrounding areas were silent and peaceful. During the post-Christmas week, we went to the park or drove a few miles away from the countryside and visited a few friends of Lucille. For New Year's Eve, we had been invited to join one of Lucille's American friends who lived in the countryside not far from Rome.

On 31 December, Lucille and I went and got an artisan panettone and a bottle of bubbly. In the evening, we had a simple pasta meal and got ready to visit Lucille's friend Rosemary, who lived in the outskirts of Rome, about a thirty-minute drive away. Rosemary wanted us to be there before 10.00 p.m., but we managed to get there only by half past ten. It was a brand-new housing estate, and our host had a wonderfully fitted three-bed apartment. She lived with her husband, Eric, and teenage son, Ben. She also invited a few friends: one middle-aged Italian couple, Pietro and Laura, and another retired American lady, Phyllis. When we reached there, Ben was waiting to be picked up by his friends for a New Year's Eve night out. I was left out with a much older generation celebrating the New Year. It was good for a change after all, and I had two wonderful New Years in Italy. The first was at a nightclub in Rome, and the last year was in Padua with Debbie and Marinela.

In any case, Rosemary prepared plenty of food to put on the table to nibble, and I tried out some of the items while watching the Italian state TV channel that aired live shows before the clock struck midnight. Lucille and friends spent most of their time debating Italian politics. Olga was with me watching TV, and when the time was right, everyone else joined to witness the arrival of 1982. There were kisses first and then toasts of bubbly with traditional New Year's greetings. Rosemary was quick to serve some home-baked cake along with panettone and freshly brewed coffee. We chatted until one o'clock in the morning and returned home before 2.00 a.m. I knew it was going to be a long night of sleep, as was the case with others.

23

LIFE AFTER
GRADUATION

With the arrival of New Year's, another chapter in my life came to a close as we headed for graduation. After the college reopened on the fourth of January as planned, Michael and I worked relentlessly to organize the graduation ceremony, which had been scheduled to take place on 15 January. Sorting out the grades of graduating students, finalizing the results, coordinating with the press, printing certificates and transcripts, inviting external guests and speakers, and more remained to be done before we liaised with the restaurant at the Majestic Hotel. Collecting tuition dues and graduation fees was another matter to be addressed. Barbara needed the final list to work on the finances. We hoped to complete all these tasks by the end of the week, which would give us another week to finalize everything from our side. Luckily, Susan was back in the college, and she tended to the matters of the reception desk, but it was too early for student enrolment in the spring semester. Tony was also with us in case any other matters needed to be handled, and he worked with Barbara to fix any repairs or maintenance issues.

Finally, only ten senior-level students met the graduation requirements. I, Susan and Flavio, his brother Alex, and Anne and Raymond were included in the graduation list. The two South Asian sisters, the American boyfriend of Nasrin, and an Iranian friend of Susan, Sana, were other graduates. Michael had already given the go-ahead for graduation gowns to be couriered from Charleston by air. We also visited a historic hotel that seemed as if some investors had to rescue it. But the restaurant looked fine and seemed well attended on any occasion. Our guest list included thirty attendees, including most of the lecturers. Michael had invited an American professor attached to a French university as the chief guest. By now, the college seemed busy, even though the students were visiting to check their results and progress. When I conveyed the message of graduation to Flavio and his brother, as well as other friends, they all seemed thrilled and excited.

On the night of graduation ceremony, we met at the hotel about half past 8.00 p.m. Tony and I had already moved the gowns and caps, which had arrived on time a day before. As the graduating students and lecturers were gowned, we had to walk slowly to the restaurant hall, which had been decorated to suit our occasion. Professor Mullin was an art historian from California who was teaching in Paris. Michael had known him for well over five years, and he often visited Rome with his students. The theme of his speech was achievement, and he emphasized the fact that university education was just the beginning of the journey of lifelong learning. As the chief guest, he also handed over the diplomas to the graduating students, which were passed on by Barbara while Michael read the names. All ten graduates seemed very delighted, and they were proud of themselves, while some of the parents attending the ceremony were hopeful for uncompromising futures for their sons and daughters. Even Lucille, my guest, was full of joy. Soon after the award ceremony, we ran around to take obligatory photos. Unlike in a large ceremony, ten students could easily fit in and capture essential moments.

Soon after the photo session, we served the food in a four-course set meal, starting with antipasti and ending with desserts and coffee. Either melons with prosciutto or special toast with duck pâté were offered first, and then a choice of pasta with carbonara sauce served as the primo. Either grilled salmon or fillet of sole with hollandaise sauce came as the main dish, followed by some sautéed seasonal vegetables. Crème brûlée or tiramisu was served for dessert, followed by an espresso. The guests were offered plenty of house wines, both white and red. Some suggested that we toast with a glass of bubbly to celebrate the achievement, and unexpectedly, to our surprise, we were offered a few bottles of fine champagne to pop open by the waiter, which Barbara had secretly requested. It was a wonderful evening with a lot of excitement and self-gratification. Some even wanted to go out and enjoy a night out at a disco, but I decided to go home with Lucille.

Ten days after graduation, I returned to the reception desk along with Susan, welcoming new students. Since we had completed our studies, we had been working on a full-time basis. The Spring semester classes started on 25 January, and fifteen students were enrolled in the freshman semester classes. Most of the new arrivals were international students, including only one Iranian. Luckily for Michael, almost all of them chose economics and business studies as their major, and thus there would be no lengthy on-site art history classes this semester. Meanwhile, Daniel, David, and the Molinari sisters were present on the premises, but it was sad to see that our old gang was no longer at the college. However, Susan and I were confident that some of them would show up at the college from time to time.

With a sizeable number of Iranian students hanging around at the college, life was not as boring as it would seem, as they would organize some parties every now and then. One such event was a farewell party at Razi for Shahed and Dana, who had just been engaged to be married and were scheduled to depart for Texas. They had planned to marry as soon as they set their foot on US soil. After months of waiting, undergoing rigorous interviews, and dealing with red tape, Shahed managed to obtain a spouse visa, but Becky and Kenny were still waiting to hear from the American Embassy. We were making fun of Tony, hinting that he should have married an Iranian student and helped someone realize her dreams. Becky, unlike Dana, had not been married before and was only twenty-four, whereas Kenny was thirty years old, and no one knew about his background, except the fact that he was an Armenian from Iran. With all of these people in the party house, it was quite fun and entertaining. The Iranians, who normally wanted to be identified as

Persians, were very much entertainment-minded people with a great sense of sarcastic humour. They also tended to be good at demonstrating hospitality to their guests. Their delicious and mild Iranian food was also great, especially pilau rice cooked with saffron, nuts, and dried berries. Unlike Indian cuisine, Persian food is not spicy hot.

Back in college, life continued as usual, and we were soon approaching the semester's end in late May. Before the semester ended, Daniel and the Molinari sisters, Mona and Lisa, wanted to organize a leisure trip to Emilia-Romana, a province in central Italy, but to the east of Tuscany. This region, one of the most popular areas in Italy, includes cities such as Bologna, Ferrara, Modena, Piacenza, Ravenna, and the coastal town of Rimini. The independent state of San Marino was not far from the clusters of these cities. Susan and I thought it should be planned for early May, before the assessment week began. However, Flavio would not join us unless it was in June or July. Mona was willing to take up the challenge of planning and organizing the trip, and we expected the number to be about ten or eleven, including Flavio. Even though Tony had shown some interest in joining us, he would confirm this in a few days. To make everyone happy and flexible, we decided to go to late June. This would also make it easy for me and Susan to get a few days' leave from college during the slack period.

The end of the semester passed unnoticed, and in June we were excited about a forthcoming trip to Emilia-Romagna, a prosperous region in north-central Italy. Mona had painstakingly planned the trip with rail tickets from Rome to Bologna and put up an itinerary to visit a few cities, including the historic cities of Piacenza, Modena, Ravenna, and Rimini. A day trip to San Marino was also arranged, along with a beach day in Rimini. It was a four-night itinerary, with two nights in Bologna and two nights in Rimini. The region remained a cultural, economic, and touristic hub, not to mention the influence of the oldest university in the world, which continued to shine in the areas of scientific research and technological advances. The region's capital, Bologna, the seat of this famous university, plays an important role in the prosperity and popularity of the region. The region is famous worldwide for its culinary excellence and for some leading automobiles made in Modena. The area's Parma ham, Parmesan cheese, and balsamic vinegar are known worldwide, as are the automobile brands Ferrari, Lamborghini, Maserati, Pagani, and Ducati.

It was a Wednesday during the last week of June, and the group took a train in the afternoon. Tony could not join us, as he had to man the reception desk at the college. Flavio came with his girlfriend, and Susan came with Sana. Daniel and David and I stayed together, while others had their double-bed rooms in the hotel Mona had booked. Of course, the sisters stayed together, although Daniel was always behind Mona. As this was a leisure trip, we were not so much into the arts as we were the food. We arrived on time for an evening stroll in the city and enjoyed a good meal. Our pensione was cosy, small, and situated in a narrow lane close to the major piazza, Piazza Maggiore, and the Basilica of San Petronio. The piazza itself was a sprawling square lined with arched colonnades embedded with cafes and bars, as well as the Neptune Fountain, the basilica, and the city hall. In the late evening, we walked along the canals and went sightseeing. As we had almost a day to spend in Bologna the next day, we planned to see the medieval towers and the famous university then.

Meanwhile, we spotted a decent trattoria to explore simple but authentic local cuisine, and we were trying to avoid flashy expensive restaurants. At this local joint, the chef and owner cooked and served one specific menu each day. Here one would not encounter any tourists but just the locals. We were given a bowl of tripe-filled Tortellini broth, followed by a plate of tagliatelle with sliced mushrooms in butter sauce, sprinkled with a copious amount of grated Parmesan cheese. We expected him to serve us a plate of *tagliatelle al ragu* in Bologna, but it was so good that I wanted to ask for more. In the meantime, we had a choice of house wines to order. We first tried a glass of Pignoletto, a famous regional white wine, to start with. He also had local Lambrusco red wine, which we ordered for the main dish, and *Zucchine ripiene*, or stuffed courgette. Courgette in the region was a bit sweeter than usual and easy to hollow out so that it could be stuffed with such items as mortadella and Parmesan cheese. We were also served a cup of *torta di riso*, a local creamy rice pudding, to finish the dinner. The price tag was reasonable, but the wine was extra.

After dinner, we were looking for some entertainment, and with little effort, we found a local nighttime spot that catered to university students. It was a smoke-filled and packed place with a dance floor bombarded with loud music. Fortunately, the premises also had a separate hall for quiet drinkers, with most of them sipping imported beer rather than wine. As we spent time together gossiping and trying out local wines, Daniel wanted to go dancing with Mona. Flavio and Carla followed. I was left with Susan, Sana, Lisa, and David. A couple of times, we all went to the dance floor just to join the party and to witness our two couples having a fantastic time. At about one o'clock in the morning, we decided to take off, although Daniel was hesitant. At the pensione, Daniel tried to get Mona to spend the night with him, but as a decent Catholic girl, she refused to consent. Daniel was ready to pay for a separate room if Mona had consented to be with him.

The next day, our plan was to spend time in Bologna in the morning and head to Modena by train. With the understanding that we would meet at the station by midday to catch the train, a few of us left to see the university quarters, while others were free to do whatever they wished. Being a first-time visitor to Bologna, I was so impressed by its historic roots throughout the urban landscape, which was cluttered with architectural marvels: neoclassical, Renaissance, and baroque-style buildings, towers, and piazzas. The world's oldest university, the University of Bologna, founded in 1088, was itself impressive. With almost a thousand years of history behind it, it was still one of the most popular places of study in the world; we could not miss it. This university has produced some of the most famous names in history: Copernicus, who devised the theory that the earth was revolving around the sun and not vice versa; Marconi, who invented the radio; and scholar-poet Petrarch were some of the famous names that we knew.

Having read about the university's colourful past, we moved to Piazza Galvani in the heart of the city to see the permanent site of the university called the Archiginnasio, which was built in the mid-fifteenth century to bring all different places of learning into one place. The Archiginnasio itself was a stunning structure with a large porch and arches supported by carved sandstone columns. It used to be the centre of vibrant academic life. Having seen the university, we rushed to see the twin towers of Bologna before heading to the rail station. These structures were built during the early twelfth century and have remained the symbol of the city ever since, but today they are leaning, causing concerns for the city authorities. The names of the towers, Asinelli and Garisenda, were said to represent the two wealthy families that had financially contributed to their construction. The towers were located at an intersection leading to five gates on the old city wall. We did not have much time to explore more, and we rushed to the station to see whether our friends were already there. In fact, we were a bit late to arrive but had enough time before we jumped on to the train towards Modena.

It was a short train ride, and we passed through a beautiful valley of grapevines that were almost ready for harvesting. Flavio, Daniel, and David were obsessed with the idea of visiting the Ferrari automobile factory, and we agreed to do that as soon as we arrived in Modena. Daniel and Flavio were car enthusiasts, and they would go mad when they saw an impressive sports car. At a factory which looked almost like an artisanal workshop, unlike the modern-day automobile manufacturing plant, we were able to spend time watching and admiring craftsmen engaged in shaping the body of a 512 BB while the engineers fixed the engine components in the other corner. This mid-mounted flat-twelve engine (Bosch K-J fuel injection) road car designed by Leonardo Fioravanti at Pininfarina was one of the last in the BB (Berlinetta Boxer) series. This model was first shown at the Paris Motor Show in 1976. Later, in 1984, the model 512BB was replaced by the iconic Testarossa. Daniel was so pleased to see how his favourite car was made with his own eyes in person.

Immediately after the factory visit, we headed to the city for a quick lunch, as everyone was hungry. We found a cafe-bar where we could have a sandwich with a local flatbread called a *tigelle*. It was, in fact, an

Emilia-Romagna treasure ideal for a midday meal. This sandwich was called by the name of the bread itself and contained cheeses, vegetables, and toppings between the two layers of tigelle. Modena was a city that we could cover in half a day, and we visited a few places, such as the Ducal Palace, the cathedral, and the University of Modena, which was one of the oldest places of learning in Europe. A quick visit to the tower and Estense Library was our last attraction before we headed to Bologna for another night of relaxation. It should be noted that Modena is the birthplace of the famous tenor Luciano Pavarotti, not to mention the famous balsamic vinegar. As we walked to the station, Mona suggested that we should try our dinner here in Modena, as we still had the entire evening to spend. We all agreed and found an osteria.

We simply decided to go for the primo first and try out a main dish later instead of waiting for any antipasti to be served. At 6.00 p.m., we were also pressed for time, as we needed to catch one of the last trains at 10.00 p.m. Tagliatelle al ragu was served first for a few, but Flavio, Carla, and I had a tortellini broth. In and around Modena, there were three types: smaller ones, tortellini; medium-sized ones, tortelloni; and the large ones, tortellaci. For the main dish, Flavio chose boiled beef, which came with corned tongue, potato, and more, and Susan, Daniel, and I ordered cannelloni stuffed with minced meat that was coved by ragu sauce and topped with grated Parmesan cheese. This was sufficient for the meal. A few others tried out a regional version of lasagne made with lots of meat sauce and béchamel sauce. Of course, a couple of bottles of Lambrusco di Modena were consumed during the meal. To finish the meal, a classic and favourite dolce of Modena, *bensone*, served as a dessert. It is a small, dry, sweet cake-like stuff with a lemon flavour. As with most traditional Italian desserts, we were served espresso. As we finished, it was half past nine, and we rushed to catch the train at 10.00 p.m.

The next day, we packed our bags and headed to the station to catch the morning train to Rimini, the coastal resort in the Adriatic. As we had planned to stay two nights at the resort, we would check in to the hotel and make a daylong excursion to San Marino, a small independent city-state in the mountain. The state of San Marino, the oldest republic in the world, had a population of just twenty or twenty-five thousand in the early 1980s. This constitutional republic was founded by a Christian stonemason, San Marinus, from the Dalmatian island of Arbe, who fled from persecution from Romans in the year AD 103. The current constitution is said to have originated in the seventeenth century, and the republic is one of the oldest surviving democracies in the world. San Marino didn't join the Italian unification in 1862 but remained independent from the Republic of Italy although the republic surrounded the tiny state.

We were on time to explore San Marino, as it was just after midday when we arrived in Dogana, the largest city of the republic. Although there were no immigration formalities, I immediately took out my passport to get it stamped as a souvenir. However, uniformed border guards secured the entry gate to this small, independent republic. Then, with a traditional sandwich called *Piadina*, made of two layers of flatbread filled with local delights, and a can of cola, we moved to the capital city, also called San Marino, which sat on the slopes of Monte Titano. The old city is known for its medieval wall and narrow cobblestone streets, as well as the three towers on top of the three peaks. There we found three tower-citadels dating back to the eleventh century. We started from the heart of San Marino, the Liberty Square, which was the home of the striking Palazzo Pubblico, or the government building, with its neo-Gothic facade, and we were lucky enough to see a changing-of-the-guard ceremony.

Climbing the towers or the peaks themselves was a daunting task but remained an essential activity for all visitors to the city. The historic architecture, urban layout, public and urban spaces, and restored walls of the citadel contributed to the uniqueness of this picturesque capital city. We climbed the first two towers: Guaita and Cesta. Guaita was the oldest and most famous tower, built in the eleventh century, while Cesta, which was located on the highest peak of Monte Titano, housed the museum of weaponry. We visited this museum, which is also called the Museum of San Marino. The third and lowest peak was Montale, which dates back to the fourteenth century. We also had a quick peep at the State Museum of San Marino, which showcased artefacts and artworks related to the republic's past.

The republic itself was divided into nine *Castelli*, or municipalities, where each one was managed by a council that delivered public goods and services to citizens. The councils also had the duty to involve residents in the planning and organization of all cultural activities and events. San Marino never had a war since its inception, although every Italian state waged a war at least once before the union. The democratic nature of this small community, with effective judicial and institutional functions, further explains why the rest of the world could not learn from their model. San Marino's representative democracy rested on civic autonomy and self-governance. San Marino's model survived over seven hundred years and remained a testimony to a sustainable living cultural entity.

San Marino's cool and pleasant weather, even during the summer, made us very comfortable, but we all felt the effect of the arduous climb as we walked down the slopes. It was already in the early evening, and the bus ride to Rimini would take between thirty and forty minutes from Dogana. Therefore, we hurried to catch a bus to Dogana while feeding ourselves on another sandwich and snacks. Nobody was planning to spend time eating a long dinner, but we thought that a nice shower before hitting the bed would be ideal. In the meantime, Daniel was suggesting we go out partying in Rimini, but there wasn't much consent from other members of the group. A few ventured out drinking and entertaining themselves at the hotel.

Rimini, on the Adriatic shore, was a delightful but overcrowded beach resort. Even fellow Europeans from Germany, Austria, and Switzerland flocked to Rimini during the summer. Most of our gangs wanted to soak themselves in the sun and thus headed to the beach during the morning hours. Our hotel has its own secluded beach area. Guests could hire a parasol and beach chairs if they wished to spend time reading a book leisurely, but most of them seemed obsessed with getting their fair share of sun. Daniel was extremely happy to be with Mona, who was, along with Flavio and his girlfriend, spending time on the beach helping each other rub sun cream on their bodies while soaking in the sun. As the sun climbed higher in the afternoon, Daniel and his sisters made their way towards the glistening ocean and opted for a refreshing dip in the cool waters of the Adriatic. Flavio and Sara preferred to stay put underneath the parasol, reading a novel while listening to the rhythmic sound of the ocean waves that offered a soothing soundtrack to their pastime. Susan and I, along with Sana, left the hotel to explore the city after breakfast. However, we all agreed to meet at the hotel before 8.00 p.m. for a dinner outing.

The morning sun made a bright day diffusing into the cobbled streets of Rimini as Susan, Sana, and I, friends united by their passion for history and adventure, embarked on our exploration of the ancient city that was once popular with the Romans. Our first stop was a majestic monument that stood over the city for two millennia, the grandiose Arch of Augustus. Being a history buff, I regaled Susan and Sana with tales of Roman Emperors as they admired the intricate carvings which depicted battles and victories. Leaving the stories of the Roman era behind, we ambled through already bustling squares. The typical aroma of freshly baked bread and roasted coffee beans, as well as a strong smell of espresso, wafted from cafes in the streets. Susan and I, the resident foodies, couldn't resist the allure of a local *pasticceria*, and we soon found ourselves savouring fresh and flaky cornetto and sipping on bitterly delightful espresso.

After boosting our energy with sugar, we continued our journey, drawing on the imposing medieval fortress Castel Sismondo, which had witnessed numerous battles and sieges over centuries. Susan and I, the history enthusiasts, examined the ancient ramparts meticulously and marvelled at the architectural ingenuity of the time. From the very spot we stood at, I began to imagine knights crossing swords and archers firing arrows. For a moment, I was in a different world. As the majestic sun climbed higher just above us, casting long shadows across the historic city centre, our hunger pangs returned. While stumbling through the cobblestone streets, Susan spotted a charming trattoria tucked away in a narrow alleyway. The invigorating aroma of simmering Mediterranean sauces and the sounds of animated chatter lured us. We feasted on plates of steaming pasta and fresh seafood sauce, which took us to the heart of the Italian culinary tradition.

Having filled our bellies, and feeling satisfied and high-spirited, we strolled along the iconic Rimini Beach with our feet sinking in the golden sand. We could sense the soothing sounds of the gentle rhythm of the waves lapping against the sandy shore. The trio admired the vast expanse of the azure-blue Adriatic Sea, which stretched miles and miles before us. We reluctantly turned away from the beach as the sun began to descend on the opposite side of the planet, painting the sky in hues of grey and orange, and patches of rainbow colours, which seemed to be brimming with memories of the long day. Our final stop was a stunning Renaissance church, the magnificent Tempio Malatestiano, adorned with intricate marble carvings and frescoes. Susan, captivated by the artistry, was eager to point out the biblical scenes depicted on the walls, while I stood numb, admiring the architectural marvel in front of us. As the sun dipped below the horizon, casting an ethereal glow on the city's urban landscape, we reluctantly ended our exploration and returned to the hotel. We left the city carrying not just touristic souvenirs and photographs but also a deeper appreciation of history and local traditions.

Luckily, everyone had made it to the hotel before eight, and we were determined to find an authentic seafood restaurant; after all, we were still in Emilia-Romagna. Mona had already done research on the Rimini's culinary spots. Surprisingly, Moira's choice for dinner was nothing other than a trattoria, where we three had a plate of delicious pasta with fresh seafood sauce. As we didn't have time to explore the niceties during lunchtime, we all agreed to enjoy our dinner there. Apparently it was one of the popular seafood joints visited by the locals, and visitors were unaware of its existence. But it also served some traditional dishes of the region. In the summer, eight o'clock in the evening was not that late for Italian dinners, so we were on time to grab seats for all of us.

The menu at the small trattoria was not extensive but was rather limited to a few selected items that revolved over the week. The antipasti of the week included bluefin tuna, called *tonne carpaccio*, which consisted of thinly sliced pieces of fresh tuna served with olive oil, capers, lemons, and spices. After tasting this delicious starter, we had the primo, and we were given a choice of either seafood or ragu sauces to be served with one of the lesser-known pastas of the region called *Passatelli*. This hearty pasta, made from thick dough consisting of breadcrumbs, Parmigiano Reggiano cheese, eggs, and nutmeg surprised us. I opted for seafood sauce made of clams, prawns, and squid in tomato, garlic, and Mediterranean herbs. Traditionally, this pasta was served in a rich beef broth which some locals enjoyed. The main dish of the day was sea bass, which was a highly sought-after fish owing to its white and juicy flesh. On the Adriatic coast, it was often served grilled to retain its natural juiciness. The fish were charcoal grilled with olive oil and herbs, and served with fresh lemon juice. To accompany the meal, we were also served a plate of black risotto, a classic Adriatic dish containing onion, garlic, red wine, and cuttlefish.

The dinner was fulfilling and was a delicious meal accompanied by local Lambrusco wine. We were also offered a cup of rice pudding which was a local specialty and came free of charge. As we returned to the hotel, we were reminded by Mona about our train departure time at ten in the morning. That gave us plenty of time to sleep as well as for a leisurely breakfast. It was a pleasant summer evening which romantic couples could not resist taking advantage of, and they disappeared. The rest headed to the hotel. I badly needed a shower before hitting the bed at 11.00 p.m.

In the morning, it was good to see each of us enthusiastically having breakfast. Our luggage was packed, and we were ready to head to the station, which was not far from the hotel. As Mona settled the hotel bill after breakfast, I reminded everyone that we had to reimburse her for the shared expenses. Some of us had already paid her expenses, but a few of us still had to settle the payment.

When we arrived on the platform, the train to Bologna was ready to take passengers. It was a standard train, but from Bologna, we had to change to a fast train to Rome which departed at 11.00 a.m. The local train ride was rather short but stopped at several stations. As we arrived at Bologna, passengers were still waiting to board the train to Rome. Mona had booked seats for this train, as it would take some three hours to reach the destination. On this train, we could even enjoy a formal lunch or grab a panini from the restaurant car.

It was a comfortable journey with excellent services. We didn't bother moving away from our seats, and we were lucky enough to be served coffee and snacks, including paninis from a vending pushcart. Daniel and Flavio were lying down and snoring, which was a bit amusing and made us laugh. Lisa had a good sense of humour, and she cracked jokes which kept us awake throughout the journey. Even Susan could not keep her mouth closed. She narrated traditional Persian stories that stimulated our minds. The stories of Mulla Nasiruddin are considered intellectually stimulating in addition to being humorous. When the train arrived in Rome, it was necessary to wake Daniel and Flavio up. Both had brought their cars, which were parked in the vicinity of the Termini station in Rome. Susan and some others wanted a lift home from Daniel, but I walked to the bus stop.

Section Seven

1982–1983: FAREWELL DOLCE VITA

Zain gains admission to a French *Grand Ecole* and manages to get a French residence visa. While Zain and Susan bid farewell to Flavio, Daniel, and other close friends in the late spring, Zain sees his dreams comes true and says arrivederci to Lucille and Rome in September 1983.

24

THE LAST CHRISTMAS
IN ROME

The rest of the summer days in Rome passed in the blink of an eye. As the autumn began, in September, we were as busy as usual. Susan and I continued to be employed at the college, but now on a full-time basis. Tony was preparing to leave Italy, and he would continue to pursue his dreams at Texas Lutheran College. Again the college admitted some thirty new students that would keep Michael and Barbara happy and occupied, not to mention that they would also ensure the continuity of our jobs. Michael and I spent time preparing the semester timetable while Barbara was preparing the budget and finances for the next academic year. Most of the time, Susan and I staffed the reception desk and tended to the incoming students for admission and re-enrolment. Unfortunately, we wouldn't get to see our batch-mates this semester, except Daniel and David. But Flavio would show up from time to time whenever he had time, hoping to see both of us. The teaching began on 27 September for the new semester, and everything went smoothly. While there were no exchange students to join this semester, a few were expected to arrive in late November for a brief study visit.

Michael was to continue teaching with his arts history modules as well as other subjects under liberal studies. Barbara was assigned to teach two modules, including English. With the latest craze for information technology, Michael introduced an elective IT module, and he was lucky to find one Greek engineer to teach this, and I had signed up to audit it. On my home front, Lucille seemed happy to see me back to stay with her. The college had given back the rented house, as there were no long-term visitors expected this semester. Susan continued to live with Sally, and she thought she would leave for good by March or April of the following year to live in England since her sister Ruby was still in the college.

I didn't have many options but to stay in Rome until I found an opportunity to pursue my studies further elsewhere, as I was determined to finish my graduate studies. Luckily, I still had a home to live in, as long as Lucille was able to put up with me. Additionally, for the time being, I had a source of income from my job with the college. I had also been warned in a recent discussion that I had with Michael and Barbara about moving the college to different premises from January of the following year. Barbara thought that the current premises were expensive to lease and that the landlord wanted to vacate the building for restoration work.

As the semester progressed, we felt that things were not as they used to be, as there were all new faces except a few, such as Ruby and Daniel. But Susan and I always managed to have good time. Whenever someone like Flavio showed up, we considered going out for dinner. After breaking up with Sayed, Susan didn't see anyone else, but as good friends, we saw each other even on weekends. We liked each other's company, and we dined out and gossiped, as well as engaging in intellectually stimulating conversations. The Iranian students still seemed to hang around, but most of them lagged in their studies. Their motives appeared to be different, and some seemed as if they were lost in paradise. They enjoyed a European lifestyle, but almost everyone was hooked on the idea of migrating to America or Canada. A couple of families, in fact, had settled in Australia early this year. The two brothers Samir and Moshen, as well as Razi, had left Rome with their families to find a new life down under, in Australia.

A week before the college was to shut for Christmas, we heard that Kenney had received his US resident visa as the spouse of a US citizen. A farewell party for Kenney and Becky was to take place, and the Iranians had already arranged for the event on the coming Saturday. In fact, a newly married couple was prepared to foot the bill for the cover and drinks at a disco attached to a local restaurant. invitations were open to everyone who would pay for his or her dinner at the restaurant. Susan and I wanted to join them at the disco but not for dinner. Since we had not heard from Raji for a long time, we wondered whether he would show up at the party. Debbie and Marinela were still around, and their studies seemed to be ongoing. Debbie wanted to have a night out with me during the Christmas break, and I consented to it. This year, Susan and I were invited to Christmas lunch at Barbara's.

On Saturday, I met Susan in Trastevere for an early afternoon lunch so that we could spend time gossiping and then join the farewell party at the disco, which was located at Ostiense, not far from Trastevere. In our famous pizzeria, we were sort of nostalgic when recalling the memories of the past couple of years. A glass or two of chilled Frascati kept us chatty for over a couple of hours. I asked Susan, 'Have you been put off by the idea of getting tied up with someone?'

She crisply answered, 'No, not for now. But at the moment, I am free as a bird.' She wanted to spend some time with her mother and try to get to know more about her father, who had arrived in England after a very long isolation period In Iran. She then queried, 'What about you?'

'I do have this ambition to complete my master's degree first, but I am ready to consider it if someone right shows up in my life,' I said. I explained to Susan that I was in the process of applying for an MBA course at Southern Baptist University in Texas and had received an I-20 form from them, which was needed to apply for a student visa. The university wouldn't issue this certificate without proof of finances or academic achievements. Lucille and Mike from Texas, who had been with us the previous year as an exchange student, sponsored the application. Susan wished me all the luck in getting the visa, for which I had an appointment with the visa consulate at the US Embassy in January.

After lunch, we had another couple of hours to kill, so we strolled along the riverbank, sometimes stopping at a bench, making time for stimulating discussion. On one occasion, I wondered why Iranians were leaving their country and why they all wanted to settle in America. When I asked Susan for an explanation, her answer was clear. 'Anybody who enjoyed the Western lifestyle during the Shah's period wouldn't like to go through the hell of an Islamic regime,' she said.

'Why America?'

She replied, 'Because they have been brainwashed to believe that America is a paradise.' She pointed out that at least a third of the diaspora ended up in the UK, mainly in London and southeast England, and she was brought up in a boarding school in Eastbourne early on before the Islamic revolution in 1979. As we got up from the bench, we suddenly realized that the winter sun was already setting. As we had to get ready to attend Kenny's farewell party, we headed home, but we had plenty of time to join them at the disco before 10.00 p.m.

Almost all Iranians from the college joined the party. As we entered the disco, we were pleased to see Kenny's smiling face glued to Becky while receiving us with a warm hug. A server suddenly appeared from the dark with a tray filled with glasses of bubbly spumante. Kenny, who was in his thirties, seemed content, and he rushed to introduce his family members, whom we were meeting for the first time. His parents didn't speak much English, but his sister did. Their fellow Iranians bounced up and down to loud disco music. Surprisingly, even Raji was present at the party, and I had a long chat with him discussing his future plans. I had heard that he had been away from Rome for some time and was now counting on his luck to find an American companion to marry. As we approached the bar area, the bartender pointed out that the hosts offered a limited range of drinks free of charge. I wanted a glass of Soave, while Raji went for a bottle of Peroni, a popular Italian beer. I was cautious not to trigger his memories of Debbie but chatted about life in Iran at the moment in general. Because everyone was in a celebratory mood, we joined the crowd on the dance floor. The party went until one o'clock in the morning, but Susan and I left early. On the way back, the taxi driver was asked to drop Susan off before driving me home.

At the end of the following week, Kenney and Becky dropped by to see Barbara and Michael and to bid us farewell. Kenny seemed to be somewhat emotional. They planned to live in Houston, as Becky's parents had already made some arrangements. Kenny was determined to settle down with a job. He had already ditched the idea of pursuing higher education. On arrival just a few days before Christmas, Becky's family arranged to hold a wedding reception on a grand scale. Back in Rome, Susan and I were looking forward to enjoying the Christmas lunch at Barbara's. On the home front, Lucille was expected to fly to London for a brief visit, while Olga had already left Rome for Christmas. Debbie, meanwhile, visited her mother in Paris during Christmas, as her mother observed Christmas as a Catholic. She returned to Rome soon after Christmas to spend a few days with me.

Meanwhile, I was not successful with my US visa application. After a half-hour interview by the visa officer as if I were a criminal, he thought I would be a burden on public funds, as my sponsorship letter was not strong enough to grant a visa. Now I had to think of other alternatives, and one option I had in mind was to go to Paris to join a master's degree course in the International Hotel Administration jointly taught by a prestigious grand ecole in France and Cornell University in New York. I had already sent my preliminary application, and I was to proceed with the full application process, as they thought I was eligible to enrol based on my experience in Saudi Arabia and my newly acquired degree from the American College of Rome, awarded by the University of Charleston, West Virginia. Again, funding the studies would be an issue to be tackled later.

On Christmas Day, I woke up just before midday and got ready to attend lunch at Barbara's. I was supposed to meet Susan to accompany her for lunch, so I walked all the way to Trastevere, as there were no public transport services on Christmas day. The entire city was deserted, with no sight of any traffic or even humans on the road. Luckily, Susan was ready when I reached her home, and we took a leisurely walk, and it was as free as ever, without any interruptions on the streets. Christmas lunch at Barbara's was a family event with just the newly arrived visitors from Texas and two middle-aged ladies, Jacky and Pam. They were family friends of Barbara and Michael and would stay with them for a couple of weeks. We heard that they all had planned to travel around Southern Italy during the break, visiting Naples and Sicily in particular.

The Christmas meal was a normal traditional American-style lunch with stuffed turkey and roast potatoes, carrots, parsnips, and Brussels sprouts. Barbara did make a wonderful leeks and potatoes soup to start with and a rich Christmas pudding to end the meal with. The warm mulled wine was also appropriate for this season. Susan and I bought a bottle of mid-range Chianti red, and it went very well with the meal. After the meal, we spent some time with Michael and Barbara discussing the nitty-gritty of moving the college to a new location in Lago de Argentina, not far from the current site in Via Piemonte. Although the new premises were located in a convenient site, the space seemed tight with only three classrooms for teaching. We were also reminded that this move would take place on the ninth and tenth of January and that we were expected to be present, although it appeared to be a weekend.

Having had nothing much to do outside to kill the day, we stayed chatting with Pam and Jacky over coffee and biscuits. The ladies, typical southerners with investigative minds, didn't seem to be devoted to Christianity either but were much more interested in Italian art and culture. I thought they were a very good fit for Michael and Barbara. They both were curious about us, and when I said that I was from Ceylon, they had no idea where this strange country was.

We were bombarded with a barrage of questions. What brought us here to Rome, and what was our future plan? Fortunately, they had heard of the recent revolution in Iran, so it was much easier for Susan to explain what brought her to Europe. Pam was surprised to see that someone like Susan was from Iran, as she thought there were only dark-skinned people living in Iran. She looked at me, saying I looked Mexican a bit. Jacky wanted to know if we celebrated Christmas in our countries.

Susan replied by saying, 'Majority Muslims in my country don't celebrate Christmas.'

Then I said, 'Neither the Buddhists nor the Hindus or Muslims in my country celebrate Christmas.'

However, we both went on to explain that Christians in our countries celebrated Christmas. After a long chat, at four-thirty in the afternoon, we took off after saying arrivederci to the new acquaintances while
thanking the hosts. We thought that, after all, it was an enjoyable day.

I accompanied Susan to Trastevere and returned home. It was rather
a boring night, as I was alone at home, as Lucille was expected to arrive
only on the twenty-eighth. While Flavio and Sara were expected to join
us at Sally's for New Year's Eve, I would be spending a few days with
Debbie, who would arrive soon from Paris. The next day, Susan and I
wanted to browse a few Christmas markets that Romans were fond of
visiting on the day after Christmas.

I was glad to see Debbie back in Rome when she knocked at the door
in the late morning on the twenty-seventh, just a few days before the
New Year. She arrived early in the morning in Rome, although her flight
was expected to be delayed because of snow in Paris. At this time, her
eyes told me that she really wanted to have fun. We made some breakfast
and enjoyed chatting into the late morning hours. She started talking
about her mother, who was becoming almost difficult to live with, as
she seemed hysterical, screaming at everything and everyone she came
across. She wanted to live a good Christian life but protested that it was
impossible in this world that was full of vice and decadence. Debbie
thought that she knew why her father had left her mother. However, she
knew that her mother was worried about her being the only daughter.
Debbie thought she would be happy if her mother found a place in the
monastery. In any case, Debbie showed herself being mature for her age,
and she believed that life was for living and not for getting entangled in
all the issues around her.

There was a kind of intimacy between us at this moment as I
wrapped my arms around her and hugged her. The daylight sun was
struggling to appear bright from its shelter of clouds, and the afternoon
was already darkened even at 1.00 p.m. Suddenly, she began kissing me
with a passion that I haven't seen before. I knew it was an invitation to
land on a galloping horse to take a ride. In the next minute, we both
engaged in a vociferous act of sexual expression. We spent over an hour

in the bed, gulping a bit of juice or water during pauses. Around four in the afternoon, not long before the winter sunset, we both got out and had a shower, hoping to take a walk to the city centre. As Lucille was expected to be home the following day, Debbie and I would stay together in her place for a few days.

We walked down the road to reach the riverside and took a leisurely stroll along the bank, as it was well lit. We talked about the previous Christmas event with Marinela. Although we hadn't shown any intimacy between us in Padua, I detected an air of suspicion in Marinela's mind. In fact, we hadn't had such feelings between each other. Even now, we didn't seem to have any deep feelings between us, but just a romantic interlude triggered by sexual desire. We did not care much about relationships, but as humans, we seemed prone to emotion, and our relationship stood as a test of our strengths and weaknesses. We strolled for almost an hour and finally ended up in Piazza Navona. The weather was crisp and cold, and I felt chills in my spine. The time was right for a quick dinner and to head home for a long night of joy. Few restaurants were open during the festive season, but we found a family-run trattoria for a homely meal.

Back home, we chatted over a cup of coffee which Debbie had made from a special Columbian roast that she had brought from Paris. She seemed obsessed with her mum's pathetic situation, and I tried to console her occasionally. She shouted, 'Why can't she go and live with her fucking husband? They are not divorced, just separated, after all.' I had to reach out and embrace her. Suddenly, she laughed and said, 'Who cares what she does; let's enjoy life.' I was glad to see that she was back on track from this slight distraction of her mind. In a couple of minutes, we were all over one another. Although she was not sexually active, she seemed to have a hidden passion for sex. Our sinful partnership continued for some time before we got burned out.

A day later, I went to see Lucille in the evening along with Debbie. Lucille was happy to see us together. Lucille's visit to England had been rather short, but she thought it had been successful. She wondered whether I was going to join her for New Year's Eve tomorrow at her friend's house for what was to be just a family event like the party the previous year. However, I was supposed to join Susan at Sally's, and Debbie would be joining us too. Lucille wanted me to cook some lamb chops she had brought back home. I found some potatoes and broccoli, and Debbie and I had ended up preparing a wonderful dinner. Over the dinner table, Lucille chatted about her theatre visit to West End. The play she had seen was *Annie*. It was based on the comic *Little Orphan Annie* by Harold Grey. It played at the Adelphi Theatre in the Strand, Covent Garden, one of the famous areas for theatres in London's West End. Lucille seemed excited to regale us with the story of the play. It was one of the best-loved musicals. Annie, an orphan from the depression era who was abandoned on the doorstep of a New York city orphanage, was obsessed with the idea of finding her parents. Lucille thought that the villain, cruel Miss Hannigan, who ran the orphanage, was brilliant and funny. In the end, Annie managed to foil Miss Hannigan's evil schemes and was able to find a new family and home with a loveable grace by befriending the president of the United States, Franklin D. Roosevelt. We both enjoyed listening to Lucille as we were having the meal. We left Lucille at approximately 10.00 p.m., leaving her to have a peaceful night. But I knew Lucille wouldn't go to sleep before midnight.

The rest of the week was rather joyful; we spent quite a lot of time chatting, walking, visiting parks, cooking pasta, and dining out. For New Year's Eve, we made some pastries and chicken bites, as there would be plenty of food from other guests. As we were expected at Sally's after 9.00 p.m., we still had plenty of time to kill during the afternoon. In the meantime, we just took a walk down the road to pick up a bottle of bubbly. We also got a couple of paninis to keep our tummies filled until ten in the night. After arriving home, I went to have a shower, and Debbie had one afterwards. I liked Debbie's coffee, so we made a fresh cup of Columbian after the panini.

At Sally's, it was already bubbly and full of chatter when we reached there at ten. Susan was lively and cheerful as always, and Sally was delighted see us. It was not the first time Debbie met Sally, and I was glad to see her comfortable without being nervous in a crowd of middle-aged

Americans. The party was rolling on, with all of the attendees nibbling on things with glasses of mulled wine in their hands. As expected, there were plenty of things to eat, from cooked food to cold deli stuff with a variety of cheeses. The background music was essentially Natale, or Christmas, in tone, with Sally choosing one from Sinatra from time to time. It was an adult party at which eating and chatting remained themes. Sally's friend had baked a wonderful dish of Scottish salmon with potatoes, carrots and parsnips on the side. Susan had baked some quiches with plenty of cheese. There were a handful of bottles of fine wine on the table that could last overnight.

While Debbie went on to mingle with the crowd, I had a long chat with a couple from Cleveland, Ohio. As it was one of the major mining and steel-producing cities in America, I was keen to know what it looked like to live in a smoky, snow-covered city. Ben and Madi had been married for over ten years, and they both were in their early forties. Ben's dad used to work in the steel factory, and they came from an ordinary working-class family. Ben had managed to get a college education, and now he worked as management consultant for an Italo-American firm. Madi was a typical American housewife and had a wonderful eight-year-old boy who was with them at Sally's.

To answer my question, Ben was keen to point out Robert De *Niro's* movie *The Deer Hunter*, which had been filmed mainly in Cleveland. It was a movie about the Vietnam War and managed to grab a few awards although it was controversial in terms of wrongly depicting the reality of the American position and the status of the Vietcong guerrillas. However, the movie shed light on the people and lifestyles of Cleveland and other steel-making towns in Ohio. It was released in 1978, and I saw the film in 1981. I thought I had a good picture in my mind about Cleveland, Ohio. When I asked them if they wanted to go back to Cleveland, Ben said, 'Oh sure, as soon as our child grows up and goes to college.'

As we approached midnight, everyone was excited and started holding glasses filled with Asti Spumante. Debbie, Susan, and I stood together holding hands and wished *Bon Anno* with a kiss as the clock needle hit the midpoint. Another day and another year. We welcomed 1983 by walking out and greeting everyone in the hall. It took some time for everyone to leave. At two in the morning, we were still chatting and gossiping, while others had already left, including the host, Sally, who had gone to bed a long time ago. Susan thought we should stay over, and she prepared the two large sofas for us to lie down until morning.

The next morning, when we woke up, it was after midday, and Susan was just preparing the morning coffee. When we took to the street, there were no buses running, and the roads were empty, even at midday. We walked home slowly and went to sleep straight away when we reached home. We got up just before sunset and prepared pasta for dinner along with a simple salad. The first day of the year was rather short, and we went back to sleep earlier than usual. The next day, I headed to Lucille, who was celebrating new year with a longtime friend. She confessed that she'd had a wonderful time.

25

SPRING 1983:
FAREWELL PARTY

On the morning of 9 January, Susan and I arrived at Via Piemonte to lend a hand by helping with the relocation of the college. The new premises were located at Piazza della Pigna, just a block away from Largo di Argentina in the centre of the city. Barbara was happy to see us, and we immediately got to work moving the files and folders in boxes. The crew had already moved the chattels and office furniture to the new two-story building where Michael was directing the show. Because it was a central city location and often difficult to move around due to traffic and crowds, they chose a weekend to move. They had planned to complete everything on Saturday so that we could set up everything inside the building by arranging the furniture and chattels.

It was five in the evening when we managed to complete the moving. At two in the afternoon, Barbara arranged some paninis for a quick bite. The new premises had only three rooms for classrooms and another three rooms for office space. Fortunately, two bathrooms and two free-standing toilets could be used by students. The kitchen space was modest, and the spare room attached to the kitchen was a plus. For events or functions, we could hire a hall with all the facilities in the building attached next door. Although not as large as the facilities at Via Piemonte, it seemed modest and adequate—given the number of students, which seemed to be sliding. On Sunday morning, Susan and I came just before midday and spent the time helping Michael and Barbara sort out the files and folders so that we could be in business as usual on Monday. Barbara had already advertised in the English daily about the change of location and the new admission dates for the spring semester, which had been scheduled for next couple of weeks. The classes were to begin on the twenty-fifth of January.

The next couple of weeks were expected to be hectic for all of us, as the preparation for the new semester, including admission and student advising, would take up most of our time. While Susan would be attending to phone calls and drop-in enquiries, I was to help Michael with admissions and advising for enrolment. We expected at least twenty-five new admissions, but Barbara was not expecting students from Texas this semester, except for a few summer students in June. Susan had already given notice to the college saying she would be leaving Rome for good in April or May. Even I had indicated that I would have to leave by summer if my admission to the Cornell-ESSEC programme in Paris was to come through. Barbara and Michael were aware of these things and told us that they were making arrangements to replace us by May and wanted us to prop them up until mid-May. However, my departure was not 100 per cent guaranteed, as it depended on several factors beyond my control.

The semester turned out as expected, but Barbara was rather disappointed, as the new enrolment stood at just twenty students. Another few would join during the first three weeks, but how many would end up paying the full fee was the big question for Barbara. Meanwhile, the Iranian students, most of whom were lagging in their studies, were prompt with payments. We still had fourteen students hanging around. We even had an Iranian girl moving from Hamburg, Germany, to study at college this semester. I still helped Michael with his short excursions, and in fact, his students from the Art History module were taken to Pompeii only for a one-day tour. The study tours were not as exciting as they had been in the past.

As time moved on, Susan hinted that she would leave Rome before the last week of May, and she wanted to host a dinner for all her friends she had come to meet at the college. I thought it was a good opportunity for me to bid them goodbye as well, as they were my friends too. I suggested that we arrange a dinner at a restaurant and invite all those who would be available in Rome. It was already May, and the weather seemed pleasant to host a get-together at her home for a drink and then move to a restaurant in the vicinity of Trastevere. We agreed to host a farewell dinner on the seventh of May, which was a Saturday. Daniel and Flavio; Raymond and David; a few Iranian friends, including Sara; Ruby and her boyfriend, of course; Debbie, and Anne were available and showed interest in participating.

In the meantime, I had a letter from Paris to tell me that I had to appear for an interview before confirming my application to enrol in their programme. I wrote to inform them that I could not come to Paris just for an interview, as getting a visa remained a problem after France ended the visa-free travel for people from my country. But luckily, they responded by saying that they could arrange for me to see a lady who was the general manager at a luxury hotel in Rome. Immediately, I arranged to see her for an interview, which was scheduled for the end of the month. The lady manager was the alumnus of the School of Hotel Administration, Cornell University, New York. The course I was seeking admission was a joint programme between Cornell and a reputed French Grande Ecole.

On Saturday, Susan and I got together at her place and made the necessary arrangement for the evening get-together. Sally was also helpful by offering a hand as well as some drinks. Taken together, there were fifteen expected, including us. We booked a table for fifteen at a nearby restaurant for dinner to be served by eight-thirty to nine in the evening. The dinner consisted of a traditional three-course meal with a choice of a pasta dish as the primo and either rabbit or veal as the main dish, to be accompanied by house wine and a dessert. The menu prices were prearranged, and Susan and I split expenses.

In the early evening, with wonderful spring weather greeting us, we welcomed our fellow college mates, who had been very close to us all during the memorable three or more years. It seemed very difficult to think that the years had passed by so quickly. Flavio and Daniel showed a sense of bonded affinity towards us in their faces. I felt a special sort of pull towards Susan, who was a very special person among the group members. Indeed, it was a slice of dolce vita that these special friends had to offer us. They were friends in need and friends always.

There were two surprising guests. Daniel had managed to bring Mona and Lisa with him, although they wouldn't join us for dinner. I was really delighted to see them, and this was the first time I was able to meet them after the graduation ceremony. The evening gossip was mainly about our study tours to Sicily and Pompeii, romantic encounters, flirting, sexual adventurism with strangers, and the fantastic time we'd had during the trips, including the wonderful food we had, were the highlights. We all had something to share with each other, and the chatting over a glass of wine continued until we were ready to leave for dinner. In fact, the restaurant was just a few metres away, and it was like directing the guests to our own dining room.

As we moved out to enjoy the dinner, we found the weather was very pleasant, and I wondered if we could dine alfresco. The restaurant manager seemed happy to serve us on outside tables, as there were a couple of tables left free, and she asked the servers to bring out a few more chairs. Straight away, we began to order food, starting from the primo. As we were given the choice to pick from a few items, I wanted to try tagliatelle with porcini mushrooms in cream sauce. Most of the others chose ragu sauce, but Debbie and I opted for mushrooms. Chatters continued to gossip while Susan and I enjoyed the stories that Flavio and Daniel had to regale us with. For the main dish, we chose either *Spezzatino di coniglio alle acciughe* or braised veal. '*Coniglio*' means 'rabbit', and this special dish was prepared by gently frying the meat in olive oil with garlic and herbs, such as rosemary, thyme, and sage. The fried rabbit was then cooked with a small amount of vinegar and anchovies, along with the juice from the meat left in the frying pan.

We dined until midnight while continuing our gossip over an espresso and grappa. The end of the event very much felt sad, as we all said goodbye with kisses and hugs. Soon Susan would be gone to

England and I might have a chance to go to Paris. While I was saddened by the mere thought of leaving Rome for good, there was a sense of excitement and hope on the horizon. Susan, in the meantime, had no idea what would she do or where she was headed in her life. It was sad to think about her breakup with her boyfriend, although she managed to cope very well. Anne gave me and Debbie a ride home, and that was it. I thought that dolce vita had come to an end. 'But who knows,' I said to myself. 'The next destination could be even better.'

In the week ahead, Susan promised to come to the college to bid farewell to Barbara and Michael. They expected me to be there until the end of the month, which I did not have any problems with. The semester was also approaching its final days while the students were preparing for the assignments and tests. The atmosphere at the new premises was not as at Via Piemonte. Barbara had found someone to replace us, mainly to tend to the reception desk and phone calls. Daniella was expected to work from the next week. She had completed her high school at an overseas school in Rome. I had a chance to meet her once, and she seemed pleasant and well presented, with a good command of English.

By the end of the week, I realized that Lucille had been waiting to see me home with good news. Since I was busy with Debbie and Susan, I did not have a chance to visit Lucille. The Paris Grand Ecole had called home to let me know that I had been admitted to the postgraduate course in international hotel management and that I could even apply for a bank loan to pay my tuition fees, which came to nearly $5,000 US dollars for two years. What great news! I could only cry with joy and excitement. However, there was a hitch, and this time, it was the French visa and two-year French residence permit. I thought it was going to be easy, but time would prove otherwise. I had three months to plan and arrange everything before leaving Rome in early September. Based on this timeline, I wanted to see Barbara and let her know. The next day, I managed to negotiate an arrangement with Barbara to continue working at the college until the end of June. Michael suggested that I could train Daniella to help him with admissions. In addition, that would give me a chance to save a bit more cash before I took off to Paris. Lucille had already negotiated a deal with an oriental handicraft shopkeeper to work during the summer. The owner, a Pakistani gentleman, Naqvi, wanted an English-speaking person to attend to the visiting tourists during summer.

On the sixteenth of May, Susan left Rome. Daniel and I, along with Flavio, took her to the airport. Indeed, it was a very emotional goodbye. Ruby and Charles also showed up at the airport. We all promised to see each other sometime in the future, and she promised to visit me in France. By late evening, her flight had taken off to London as we returned home, and I could see tears running down Flavio's cheek during our chat in the car. Daniel reminded us that he and Ruby had completed their final semester at the college too, and Ruby would be leaving for England by midsummer. When we arrived at Rome, I suggested that we all visit Mario, our famous trattoria, for a simple dinner before heading home. All agreed, and even Ruby and Charles joined us at Mario. Obviously, I could not leave Debbie alone. After dinner, I went with her to spend the night. I should not be complaining much, as I had a good and compatible friend. Debbie's company was indeed a great consolation during my last few months in Rome.

26

ARRIVEDERCI A ROMA

The summer was already on the horizon, and staying around the college seemed a bit boring. I helped Daniella with a few things that she needed to be exposed to and showed her how to prepare for meeting the potential students seeking admission. Debbie wanted to go with her somewhere for a couple of weeks, but I was not keen on spending money. I had promised to work for Naqvi during the summer months. But for a few days adjacent to a weekend, I could consider taking off with Debbie. She also wanted to visit the summer Milan fashion week, and I thought that was not a bad idea.

In the meantime, I was shuttling back and forth between Lucille and Debbie. In July, I started my job with Naqvi. From time to time, Debbie would fly back to Paris to visit her mum, but she wanted to spend a good part of the summer in Rome, working on a semiotics project with Professor Tomassini. I continued to work for the college during June and helped Daniella with admission matters. She seemed smart enough to pick up skills quickly. The college was not what it used to be, and I realized that it was the time for me to bid farewell with all my good memories of the past three and a half years. It was very sad to see myself leaving Michael and Barbara, who had been extremely helpful in making me a very happy individual with the courage and knowledge to conquer the world. I would never forget them in my life. At the American College of Rome, mine was a real college experience with a family touch. It was really a part of dolce vita, not just education and the receipt of a piece of paper saying that I was a graduate. The friendships I made would last throughout my life. The life experience I gained would help me with my future adventures in France, the USA, and the UK.

In June, the summer heat made our life a bit harsh with unusual levels of humidity, which necessitated the installation of table fans. Lucille had already bought two of them, and Debbie wanted one for her room. Meanwhile, she felt nervous about seeing that her dad was visiting Rome, as she had not seen him for a while. Benjamin seemed like a typical American Jewish man from Brooklyn, New York.

As a Holocaust survivor who immigrated to America with his parents, Benjamin had managed to obtain a college education and earned a good living by working as a stockbroker. He wished his daughter would continue her studies in America, but she didn't like the idea of settling in there. When Debbie introduced me to Benjamin, I thought that he would not consider me anything more than just an acquaintance. But to my surprise, he seemed polite and courteous. He was a soft-spoken gentleman with a good sense of humour. Benjamin took us for a wonderful dinner at a fine restaurant near the Quirinal Palace. While dining, he went on to regale us with his own life stories after his divorce from Debbie's mother. He was apologetic to Debbie for having left her mother, but he gave us assurance that he would never abandon her. After dinner, I headed home while they both kept chatting.

In July, I began working for Naqvi. As the owner and manager of the business, he visited the store every day, but he never dealt with customers. Nino, a fifty-year-old Italian, looked after the shop, but his English fluency was very basic. Naqvi wanted me at the store almost every day if I could make it, mostly in the evenings, which was when foreign customers usually visited. Along with antiquities and handicrafts from Pakistan, the store traded in handwoven cloths and 'stich and things'. Local market traders, whom Nino looked after, often visited the shops. One day, Nino wanted to introduce me to Laura. She was a market trader during the day and a working girl at night. As a call girl, she had her own selection criteria, which Nino told me before she stepped in. Money was not a big issue, as she earned adequately as a day trader, and as a single woman, she enjoyed her life dating with a few select men. She was in her early thirties and attractive. Laura was not interested in a permanent partner or a boyfriend. Nino said she wanted to improve her English-speaking skills, so I had a good chance of being picked up. In fact, Nino was correct; Laura wanted to go out with me on a date, and she even offered to pay for a meal out. I could not help but take up the offer.

By late July, I received my enrolment papers from the ESSEC Business School, one of the prestigious Grande Ecoles in France. This prompted me to apply for a French visa as soon as I could, since I had to be in Cergy-Pontoise, a Parisian suburb, before mid-September. But I knew it was not going to be easy, as my residency status in Italy seemed a bit problematic since I did not have a resident permit per se but lived on a visitor visa with frequent renewals. Lucille tried to get me proper residence permits and even met with the chief of the Rome Police Authority, who dealt with immigration matters. But Dottore Bernadetti had patted my back and sent me home, saying I didn't need to worry as long as I didn't make any trouble. Years had passed since then, but I had lived in Rome and enjoyed dolce vita without a resident permit.

Unlike in the case of American visa applications, there were no interviews to tease the applicant's brain. It was a simple process of checking my documents and making sure I had the means to support myself. But the visa officer politely told me that I had to get my visa from back home, as I hadn't had Italian residency. I realized how difficult it was to overcome this hurdle in an official manner. My only hope was that Lucille could find a way. I was disappointed and waited until Lucille returned home. I didn't even want to see Debbie, as she wouldn't understand these tricky things that someone like me had to endure when it came to travelling abroad. However, one thing is certain: Even if I could travel visa-free as I had a couple of years prior, I would still need to apply for French residence once I got there, which could be cumbersome without a proper entry visa in the first place. Normally, visitor visas are not convertible after entering a country.

Meanwhile, I started preparing meals for both of us, as it was already after sunset, and Lucille would be on her way home. It was ten in the evening when she finally arrived, and before opening my mouth to let her know that I was cooking some dinner, she asked whether I could pull out a chicken breast from the fridge. I let her know that I had already done so and had them ready to cook. She was not aware that I had gone to the French Embassy for a visa; nor did I show any emotion or anger at the outcome until we were seated to dine. First, she was curious about Debbie and wondered whether I'd had an opportunity to meet her dad, and she even suggested inviting him to dinner. I ruled that out by saying that Benjamin had already left Rome.

I then came up with my topic, and I explained what the French visa officer had to say. She immediately consoled me and said, 'Don't worry, I know the chief consul general at the French Embassy.' When the consul had arrived in Rome, Lucille had helped her find the apartment in which she lived. Lucille promised to call her the next day. With her assurance, I regained my confidence. I thought I could go to bed with hope.

The next day, Lucille waited to call the consul general until she was home in the evening, and she phoned her after 7.00 p.m. She briefly explained that I had received admission papers to enrol in the Cornell-ESSEC master's programme and I wanted to get a visa. After a few questions related to my nationality and health certificate from an embassy-approved medical practitioner, as well as the attestation from the French cultural attachés, she made an appointment to see her next day. Thanks to Lucille, I thought this was the first step towards getting a visa. However, this was not yet the time for celebration. I had all the essential supporting documents, such as the health certificate and the letter confirming partial bursary and assistantship to cover maintenance expenses. In addition, Lucille provided a funding guarantee in addition to my eligibility to apply for a bank loan from a leading French bank. Banks do not fear lending to students for such a high-profile course as at an elite institution like ESSEC, regardless of where the students come from.

It was three in the afternoon when I saw the French consul general in her posh office. She was nice and polite, and she asked me to sit first as she browsed through my papers and directed at me a question: 'So what is the problem?'

I simply replied by asking her, 'Madame, how long will it take to get the visa?'

'Come tomorrow at this time and collect your passport from the counter,' she said. I did not mention my status in Italy, nor did she question it. Voilà! It was nearly time to celebrate, but I would not do so until tomorrow. Back home, I let Lucille know, and she was pleased to hear the outcome. I counted the hours, feeling slightly anxious. I wanted to go to and see Debbie, but I was not in a good mood. I even missed a few days of work with Naqvi.

The next afternoon, I nervously approached the passport collection point and whispered my name to the counter staff when she asked for my name. When I received my passport, what joy! I cried, 'La belle France!' Within a couple of months, I had to leave Rome, as I had to get my residence card from the provincial prefecture within three months of the date of the visa. Straight away, I rushed to see Debbie to let her know, and I then went to see Lucille with her. By the time we reached home, it was already six in the evening. We also picked up a bottle of Asti Spumante to uncork in celebration. To my surprise, I was received by Olga, who had returned from her village after some time. She was preparing to cook dinner. As it was a Friday, she wanted to cook fresh cod which she had picked up from the market. Lucille was already home, and she told me that she already knew, as the consul had called her a few hours before. She was pleased to see Debbie with me.

In late July, the summer heat in Rome was unbearable, but fortunately it was not very humid. We had dinner on the balcony during sunset, which was indeed pleasant. It was good to have people around with whom I could share my joy. We uncorked the bubbly and enjoyed the event. Lucille, whom I treated as my Roman mother, seemed sad to see me leave, but she was happy to see my achievements and wished me success. I couldn't have accomplished my Roman dream and dolce

vita without the help of Lucille, Michael, and Barbara. I owe them
greatly. After dinner, I walked Debbie home and stayed there overnight.
Obviously, it was an enjoyable night. However, in the morning, I had to
get back home before going to work at Naqvi's.

On most days in August, I spent time with Debbie, who stayed in
Rome until late August. However, I continued to work for Naqvi, as I
wanted to earn and save some money before I left for Paris in the second
week of September, and I had already booked a seat on an overnight train
to Paris. I started working in the early afternoon and stayed there for
seven hours in the evening. It was interesting and fun to meet people of
diverse characters who flocked to Rome during the summer. While Nino
took care of the garment side of the business, mainly attending to the
street traders, I looked after the tourists who came to browse on handicrafts and artefacts from the Asian subcontinent. Since Olga's return,
Lucille did not have to bother me to prepare dinner, but I occasionally
took it to the kitchen. Cooking had now become part of my dolce vita
lifestyle.

One Saturday near the end of August, Debbie left for Paris, hoping
to return sometime in late September when the college reopened. I had
her mother's phone number, and we decided to meet someday in Paris.
Now I was left alone but had enough time to prepare myself for the
goodbye to dolce vita. I was hopeful that the dolce vita would continue
in France. I had less than two weeks left before I was to leave Rome. My
booking on the night train to Gare de Lyon, in Paris, was confirmed for
tenth of September in the early evening. As I had nothing much to do, I
promised to work for Naqvi until the end of the first week of September.
Meanwhile, Lucille took me out to shop for some items for me, including
good luggage, a suit jacket, and a pair of shoes. By early September, I was
ready and packed, and I managed to call the student support team at
the Grand Ecole about my arrival in Paris. I was promised to be met by
a senior student. First I thought about my friend Zana, who had called
me early that year, but I didn't want to bother him until I got to Paris
and had settled in. He had told me that he had broken up with Julie and
that Fernanda had already left France for good.

On the tenth of September 1983, I had my last meal in Rome. Olga had prepared a simple pasta dish—penne with porcini mushrooms and tomato sauce—to be accompanied by her famous chicken schnitzel. She also prepared a dinner packet for the night train. By the time we finished our lunch, it was four thirty in the afternoon. I had just one large suitcase and a shoulder bag for luggage. Travelling with luggage seemed cumbersome, but mine was better than that of the average folk. At six in the evening, Lucille took me to the Termini station, which I was very familiar with. Lucille managed to park her car on the street corner and accompanied me to the platform, where the Palatino Express was already stationed, but there was plenty of time before it was to depart. Even Olga was with us. And with a sad tone to my voice, I bade farewell to both of them. We shared long and deep hugs, as well as kisses, as I said *arrivederci a Roma* and dolce vita. While I was boarding the train, I saw them waving their hands as they left. This was a memorable day in my life's calendar. I murmured to myself that I would return to Rome to visit them all soon.

As the train started to leave the Termini station and passed through the urban landscape of the historic city, I began to rewind my memories to the past. The day I stepped out of the plane at Fiumicino Airport on that auspicious day of May 1979 was still like yesterday in my mind. The coach rides from the airport with Massimo, a brief pensione stay with new acquaintances, meeting Michael and Barbara at the American College of Rome for the first time, and the overnight train journey to Paris were all indelible memories that wouldn't fade away easily. Memories of my short sojourn in Paris and Deauville during the summer of 1979 and my brief fling with Fernanda were also seemingly written in stone. Most importantly, the life centred around the college and the diverse personalities encountered over the previous three to four years were the story of my dolce vita. The study tours to Sicily, Pompeii, Capri, Tuscany, and the historic sites of Rome, as well as visits to Venice, San Marino, Milano, Lake Garda, and Padua were all part of college life, which still lingered in my mind. My fascination with Italian cuisine and appreciation of renaissance art and architecture were instrumental

in broadening my horizons. Moreover, my experience could have had
no meaning without close friends like Susan, Flavio, Daniel, Debbie,
and Marinela, as well as Lucille, Michael, and Barbara, who cared for
me throughout my sojourn in Rome. Although a brief encounter, I
could not let go of my memories of Sandy, who had shared an intimate
relationship with me.

After a while, as the train traversed the eye-catching Italian landscape of Tuscany, I sat down to have my panini, which Olga had made.
Everyone else in the compartment was already lying flat in their cosy
couchettes, and it was my turn to turn off the lights and say goodnight.
However, before doing that, I had to hand over my passport to the guard
so that the border police could stamp it. As I took a quick walk through
the corridor, I saw the guard collecting travel documents. He took my
passport and handed over a sticker number as a proof of custody.

I woke up at ten in the morning when the train was already in Dijon,
France. Immediately after washing up, with my passport collected from
the guard in my hand, I rushed to get a cup of coffee in the restaurant
car. With a croissant and cup of espresso, I sat on a chair next to a table
facing the window to admire the beauty of the French vineyards as seen
from the fast-moving train. Within a couple of hours, the train arrived
at Gare de Lyon. Voilà! Bon jour France. As I moved off of the platform,
a young woman standing with a placard showing my name approached
me. 'Bon jour Zain, je suis Marie Anne' she said with a smile. This was
the end of my four years of dolce vita. A new chapter in my life had just
begun.

ABOUT THE BOOK

Four Years of Dolce Vita is more than just a memoir; it is a celebration of a defining moment in time when life was marked by both discovery and a sense of boundless possibility. Through the lens of a young South Asian man navigating the nuances of European life in the late 1970s, this narrative captures the essence of personal transformation amidst the vibrancy of Italian and wider European culture. With each turn of the page, readers are invited to join in a journey through art, history, and the lived experiences that shaped an individual's path, interwoven with the grandeur of ancient cities, the taste of authentic cuisine, and the warmth of human connection across borders. This memoir is a testament to the beauty of exploring the unfamiliar, forming deep connections, and embracing the richness of life, no matter how fleeting or unpredictable it may be. As we leave behind the captivating study tours, passionate conversations, and fleeting romances, we carry forward the spirit of *la dolce vita*—a reminder that even the most ephemeral moments leave a lasting impact on the soul.

Printed in the United States
by Baker & Taylor Publisher Services